You did it!
You decorated that beautiful cake.
From the first flourish of fluffy icing to the final rose.
It was your lovely creation. You made it happen.
And oh, how they looked at you!
They made you feel so special.
And you are special!
Because you add that extra touch.

That Means So Much

HERE'S A TASTE OF THE TOUCH

7

All aboard for fun. 24 glorious pages of enchanting birthday cakes for toddlers through teens.

49

Our New Calendar of Cake Celebrations is an exquisite collection of cake ideas for your favorite holidays and some fun-filled new ones, too.

20

Sixteen unique designs to wish family and friends an extra-special Happy Birthday!

73

Santa Claus, jingle-bells and ginger-bread houses too! You'll find lots of festive designs for the merriest, best-decorated Christmas ever.

32

Anniversaries, weddings, showers, First Communion, Bar Mitzvah, too. Milestones and memories you can make even lovelier with a beautiful cake.

80

Learn how to make swirls and shells, borders and beads, beautiful roses and more! 16 pages of clear, concise instructions, delicious recipes and helpful hints.

For photography purposes, many cakes in this book were decorated using royal icing.

THAT MEANS SO MUCH...

Contents

Ideas

Credits

Creative Director **Jack Siegel**
Associate Creative Director **Marc Ross**
Art Directors **Diane Pierson, James Minnick**
Cake Designer **Gretchen McCarthy**
Copywriters **Linda Skender, Marie DeBenedictis,
    Jane Mikis, Marion Doyle Harless**
Senior Decorators **Marie Kason, Amy Rohr**
Cake Decorators **Theresa Anderson, Carolyn Dalpiaz,
    Jeanne Nolan, Nancy Suffolk**
Assistant Decorators **Susan Matusiak, Debbie Kelly**
Production Manager **Ray Romor**
Production/Traffic Coordinator **Peggy Talbot**
Administrative Assistant **Janeen Sellers**
Photography **Tom Zamiar, Robert Ebel**
Illustration **Donald Tate, Roger Harvey**

TO YOU AND YOURS

Compliments

Dear Decorator,

The joys of cake decorating are unparalleled. A beautifully decorated cake affords a great deal of pleasure for family and friends, while providing you with an enormous sense of self-accomplishment.

That's because you are expressing your feelings in a highly personal and creative manner. You are making every birthday, holiday, anniversary even more of an occasion for those people you care about most.

The Wilton Yearbook is filled with imaginative designs, the best in baking and decorating equipment and clear, detailed instructions to show you just how much fun cake decorating can be.

I invite you to try cake decorating. See for yourself how you can add, "that special touch that means so much."

Vince Naccarato

Vincent Naccarato
President, Wilton Enterprises Inc.

decorate your, CHILD'S BIRTHDAY

TIGER-RIFIC!

This perky party pal serves 12.

Decorating Needs
- Circus Clown Pan, p. 179
- Tips 2, 4, 5, 12, 16, p. 112-115
- Decorator's Brush, p. 116
- Uncooked spaghetti

Instructions

1. Ice balloons, background areas and cake sides smooth. With toothpick, mark number 2, hat, tiger's features and bib. (Hint: For easier marking, lightly ice areas smooth.)

2. Outline balloons & strings, tiger, hat and bib with tip 4. Fill in eyes, nose, mouth with tip 4; No. 2 with tip 12; bib trim with tip 5 (smooth with dampened brush). Cover hat, face, paws, bib and shirt with tip 16 stars (overpipe cheeks for dimension).

3. Pipe tip 16 pull-out star pompon on hat. Print tip 2 "nd" on balloon. For whiskers: "Paint" pieces of uncooked spaghetti with brush dipped in icing color. Let dry. Push into cake. Edge cake base with tip 16 shell border.

For more ways to use CIRCUS CLOWN PAN see Pan Index p. 192.

For more ways to use 9"x 13" SHEET PAN, EGG PAN SET & LITTLE LOAFERS see Pan Index p. 192.

BUOY O' BUOY!

Noah's ark cake is bound to serve 21.

Decorating Needs
- 9"x 13" Sheet Pan, p. 165, 169, 176
- Little Loafers, p. 170
- Cookie Maker Gingerbread Set, p. 110
- Pretzel rods, gumdrops, pound or firm textured cake batter (for egg cake)
- Egg Pan Set, p. 186
- Tips 2A, 2, 3, 4, 12, 16, 48, 104, p. 112-115
- Dowel Rods, p. 159
- Cake Circles, p. 154

Instructions

1. Out of cookie dough, cut couple and two 2¾"x 4½" roof panels. Bake and cool. Pipe tip 2 outfits, hair and facial features. Ice roof panel smooth. For giraffes: Attach gumdrop face to pretzel rod with dots of royal icing. Let dry. Ice smooth with royal icing. Trim with tip 4 dots and add tip 2 facial features. For lions and elephants: With royal icing, figure pipe tip 2, 12 and 16 lion heads and tip 12 and 2 elephants (trunks will be piped later on cake). See figure piping, p. 94. For birds: Push gumdrop triangle wings onto gumdrop and add tip 2 faces.

2. Ice sheet cake smooth; top blue, sides white. Pipe tip 104 drape waves. Print tip 3 message on cake top.

3. Ice top of half egg cake and little loafer (cabin) cake smooth on cake circles cut to fit. Position cabin cake. Cover sides, then edge top of ark with tip 48 ribbed stripes. Pipe tip 12 elongated shell bow and stern trim. Edge cabin base and ark top with tip 3 bead borders.

4. Cut and position dowel rods and push into ocean cake where ark will go. Position ark. Mound icing on cabin and position cookie roof. Trim roof with tip 2 scallops and beads. Push giraffes and attach lions, elephants, cookies and birds to ark. Pipe tip 12 elephant trunks on ark.

For more ways to use CROSS PAN see Pan Index p. 192.

LITTLE ONE'S BIG SURPRISE!

This cake of a cake serves 12.

Decorating Needs
- **Cross Pan**, p. 186
- **Tips 4, 16, 18, 225, 349**, p. 112-115
- **Decorator's Brush**, p. 116

Instructions

1. Make 10 tip 225 drop flowers with tip 4 dot centers. Ice cross cake smooth; with spatula, build up beveled area and square off. With toothpick, mark flame, glow lines, candle and plate pedestal.

2. Cover marks with tip 4 strings. Fill in flame center with tip 4 (smooth with dampened brush). Pipe tip 16 zigzag melting wax. Cover candle and cake plate with tip 16 stars.

3. Write tip 4 message on "cake." Pipe tip 16 garlands on "cake." Edge "cake" with tip 16 shell borders. Trim base shells with tip 16 zigzag scallops. Attach flower to "cake" and trim with tip 349 leaves. Edge background on cake top and base with tip 18 shell border.

For more helpful hints, review Decorating Guide, p. 80.

BABY CAKES

Happy tiers serve 45.

Decorating Needs
- **8" & 12" Round Pans**, p. 165, 166, 177
- **Mini Muffin Pan**, p. 171
- **Panda Mold**, p. 116
- **Tips 2B, 3, 4, 16, 18**, p. 112-114
- **ABC Block Separator Set**, p. 135
- **Cake Dividing Set**, p. 116
- **Fancy Foil Wrap**, p. 155
- **Cake Circles**, p. 154
- **Dowel Rods**, p. 159
- Firm-textured or pound cake batter, candles, cupcake papers

Instructions

1. Cover mini cake tops with tip 18 spirals. Push in candles. Position panda cake on cake circle cut to fit. Ice diaper area smooth. Outline nose, mouth, diaper and pin with tip 3. Add dot eyes and fill in inside of ears, nose and pads of feet with tip 3. Cover with tip 16 stars.

2. Position 2-layer 8" cake atop cake circle and separator plate. Cover sides with tip 2B smooth stripes and tip 4 strings (alternate tips and overpipe strings for dimension). With spatula, mound and swirl icing on cake top to resemble a cupcake. Print tip 3 message.

3. Cut and position dowel rods in 2-layer 12" cake top. Ice 12" cake smooth. Using Cake Dividing Set, with toothpick, mark 3½ in. triangles and cover with tip 4 strings. Cover alternating triangles with tip 18 stars. Trim triangle points with tip 18 rosettes and tip 16 stars. Edge cake top with tip 16 rosettes.

4. Assemble cake tiers with separator plates on block pillars. Position panda and mini cupcakes. To make hat: Cut 5" doubled Fancy Foil paper circle. Slit to center and roll in a cone. Tape to secure. Position on panda.

For more ways to use 8" & 12" ROUND, MINI MUFFIN and PANDA MOLD PANS. see Pan Index p. 192.

5

ROUGH 'N READY RUNNING BACK

Serves 12 little All-Stars!

Decorating Needs
- *Holiday Bunny Pan, p. 187*
- *Tips 4, 17, 19, 45, p. 112-113*
- *Decorator's Brush, p. 116*
- *Uncooked spaghetti, licorice stick, pound or firm-textured cake batter*

Instructions

1. Let cake cool in back half of pan. Ice football area smooth (pat with paper towel after icing has dried slightly for leather grain effect). With toothpick, mark helmet, jersey and football details. Outline helmet, face, jersey, paws, leg, foot and football stitching with tip 4.

2. Fill in eyes, nose and teeth with tip 4 (smooth with dampened brush). Cover cheeks with tip 19 stars, the rest with tip 17 stars.

3. Trim helmet with tip 4 dot bolts (flatten with fingertip dipped in cornstarch). Pipe tip 45 smooth stripes and tip 4 laces on football. Push uncooked spaghetti whiskers into face. Bend licorice stick to form face guard and stick into cake. Print tip 4 message.

For more decorating hints, review Decorating Guide, p. 80.

For more ways to use HOLIDAY BUNNY PAN see Pan Index p. 192.

GO-PHER IT... DENNIS

LITTLE DARLIN'

This adorable cake serves 12.

Decorating Needs
- *Frog Pan, p. 187*
- *Tips 1A, 4, 7, 18, 102, 125, p. 112-115*
- *'85 Pattern Book, p. 103 (Girl Pattern)*
- *Decorator's Brush, p. 116*

Instructions

1. Ice cake smooth. With toothpick, mark Girl Pattern on cake top. Cover marks with tip 4 strings.

2. Fill in collar, bodice "V," white of eyes, socks and shoes with tip 4 thinned icing (smooth with dampened brush).
Cover face, dress, arms and legs with tip 18 stars. Pipe in bow with tip 7, dress sleeves with tip 1A (shape with fingertip dipped in cornstarch).

3. Add tip 4 facial features, sleeve gathers and bodice laces.
Pipe tip 18 stripe hair (overpipe several strands for dimension). Trim sleeves and socks with tip 102 and skirt with tip 125 ruffles. Print tip 4 message. Edge cake base with tip 18 star border.

For more ways to use FROG PAN see Pan Index p. 192.

Happy Birthday Little Doll!

"EXPRESS"IVE!
Our birthday train serves 12.

Decorating Needs
- Choo Choo Train Pan, p. 188
- Tips 2, 4, 8, 12, 18, 225, 349, p. 112-115
- Candy Melts™ brand confectionery coating, p. 120
- Cordial Glasses Mold, p. 125
- Easy Melts & Star Molds, p. 122
- Fancy Foil Wrappers, p. 121
- Derby Clown, p. 135
- Decorator's Brush, p. 116
- Gumdrops, ice cream cone

Instructions

1. Make 5 tip 225 drop flowers with tip 2 dot centers. Make Stars and Cordial Cup out of melted candy. Wrap cordial cup in foil. Cut ice cream cone in half for smokestack and attach with icing. Ice cab and engine face. Outline engine details with tip 4 strings.

2. Fill in window frames, bars of cowcatcher, white bands on engine and smokestack with tip 8. Pipe tip 4 dot eyes and string mouth engine face. Trim engine bands with tip 4 dots. Cover engine with tip 18 stars. Pipe tip 8 wheels and brake shaft. Add tip 18 zigzag smoke puffs and rosette trims.

3. Fill in smokestack with tip 12 spiral and edge with tip 18 zigzags. Pipe tip 12 body, arms and hands on cab for clown. Push Derby Clown into body. Cover body with tip 18 stars. Position foil-wrapped candy bell and trim with tip 18 star and gold cord. Make a small hole with knife in star candy and push in toothpicks. Push into cake. Attach gumdrop lights and flowers with icing. Trim flowers with tip 349 leaves. Print tip 4 message.

For more ways to use CHOO CHOO TRAIN PAN see Pan Index p. 192.

BATTER UP!
Square and ball cakes team up to serve 35.

Decorating Needs
- 10" Square Pans, p. 165, 168, 177
- Ball Pan, p. 184
- Egg Mini Cake Pan, p. 186
- Poster board, pretzel rod, pound or firm-textured cake batter, iced marshmallow cookie
- Tips 4, 16, 18, p. 112
- Dowel Rods, p. 159
- Cake Circles, p. 154

Instructions

1. Ice 2-layer square cake smooth. With toothpick, mark bases and base lines (1" from edge). Outline with tip 4 and fill in with tip 16 stars. Cut and position 3 dowel rods where ball cake will go. For shoes: On cake circles cut to fit. ice mini egg cakes smooth. With toothpick, mark shoe details. Outline with tip 4 strings. Cover with tip 16 stars. Pipe tip 4 string laces.

2. With toothpick, mark ball details on cake halves. With knife, slice off round side on one half of ball cake so it sits level and place on a cake circle cut to fit. Outline with tip 4 and cover round side with tip 18 stars. Ice top of this half ball cake smooth. Position other half cake on top to form ball. Push sharpened dowel rod thru ball cake and cake circle to base of square cake.

3. Pipe tip 4 dot eyes (flatten with fingertip dipped in cornstarch), string mouth and ball detail lines. Cover with tip 18 stars. Add tip 4 string stitches. Out of poster board cut crescent-shaped hat brim. Attach to cookie with dots of icing. Push two toothpicks into pretzel. Push bat, position hat and shoes into cake. Overpipe tip 4 string arm extending to bat.

Print tip 4 message. Edge cake base with tip 18 star border.

For more ways to use 10" SQUARE, EGG MINI CAKE & BALL PANS see Pan Index p. 192.

FAIRYTALE PRINCESS

This storybook doll serves 12.

Decorating Needs
- Wonder Mold Pan, p. 183
- Tips 2, 4, 16, 101, 104, 225, p. 112-115
- Freckle-faced Little Girl Pick, p. 183
- Fancy Foil Wrap, p. 155
- Poster board, tulle

Instructions

1. Make 35 tip 225 drop flowers with tip 2 centers. Ice around waist of doll pick and smooth with fingertip dipped in cornstarch. Push doll pick into cake. Ice apron area smooth. Trim with tip 104 ruffles and tip 4 beads. Cover skirt and edge apron at base with tip 16 stars.

2. Pipe tip 4 puffed sleeves (smooth with fingertip dipped in cornstarch). Cover bodice and sleeves with tip 16 stars. Outline corselet and add ties with tip 4. Cover corselet with tip 16 stars.

3. Pipe tip 104 ruffle peplum at waist. Trim neck, sleeves and bodice with tip 101 ruffles. Print tip 4 message. For book: Cut three 2'' squares out of poster board. Fold in half and glue. Write message on cover. For hat: cut two 6'' foil paper circle. Double and slit to center and roll in a cone. Tape secure. Attach tulle veil with dots of icing. Position book and hat on doll pick. Attach flowers.

For more ways to use WONDER MOLD PAN see Pan Index p. 192.

For more ways to use 9'' HEXAGON AND LITTLE LOAFERS PANS see Pan Index p. 192.

DREAM CASTLE

A magical delight that serves 14.

Decorating Needs
- 9'' Hexagon Pans, p. 168
- Little Loafers, p. 170
- Tips 3, 4, 7, 16, 18, 233, p. 112-115
- '85 Pattern Book, p. 103 (Castle Pattern)
- Appaloosa Rocking Horses, p. 134
- Snow White & Dwarfs, p. 134
- Cake Board & Circles, p. 154
- Fancy Foil Paper, p. 155
- Decorator's Brush, p. 116
- Royal Icing Recipe, p. 83
- Wafer cookies, sugar cones and cubes, cone cups, graham cracker, licorice strings, toothpicks, poster board

Instructions

1. Cut and cover cake board to resemble water area. Ice 2-layer hexagon and mini loaf (on cake circle cut to fit) smooth. With art brush, "paint" cones with royal icing.

Position mini loaf on hexagon. With toothpick mark Castle Pattern and bricks on cake sides.

2. Outline walls, door and bricks with tip 4. Cover door arch, window frames and wall bricks with tip 4 zigzags. Cover inside of door and windows with tip 16 stars.

3. Pipe tip 233 grass on cake sides. With knife, cut wafer cookies into 1'' squares.

Attach cookies (¼'' apart) to cake tops with icing. Edge cake tops (between cookies) and base with tip 18 stars.

Position graham cracker. Attach licorice strings. Pipe tip 7 bead fish with tip 3 faces and tail.

Pipe tip 7 dot rocks (shape with fingertip dipped in cornstarch). Make hat and flag. Attach cones, sugar cubes and flag together with icing. Position cones, Snow White and rocking horse.

FIRED UP FOR FUN!

Fast 'n easy to decorate surprise serves 12.

Decorating Needs
- **Mystical Dragon Pan**, p. 188
- **Tips 4, 5, 18**, p. 112
- **Decorator's Brush**, p. 116

Instructions

1. Ice message area on cake top and sides smooth.

Outline dragon with tip 4, message area and fire bursts with tip 5 strings.

2. Fill in mouth, background, ears, nostrils, scales, nails and tail point with tip 4 thinned icing (smooth with dampened brush).

3. Cover face, body and wings with tip 18 stars. Add tip 4 dot eyeballs and pupils. Add tip 18 stripe tongue. Print tip 4 message.

For more ways to use
MYSTICAL DRAGON PAN
see Pan Index p. 192.

NOBLE KNIGHT

This regal guy serves 12.

Decorating Needs
- **Wizard Pan**, p. 188
- **Tips 1A, 4, 8, 18**, p. 112
- **'85 Pattern Book**, p. 103 (Knight Pattern)
- **Decorator's Brush**, p. 116
- **Candy Melts™ brand confectionery coating**, p. 120
- **Coat of Arms Mold**, p. 126

Instructions

1. Mold one Coat of Arms out of melted Candy Melts (see p. 97). Ice cake smooth.

With toothpick, mark Knight Pattern on cake top. With spatula, mound icing where shield will go (smooth with fingertip dipped in cornstarch).

Outline knight and shield with tip 4.

2. Fill in eyes and add tip 4 dot pupils. Pipe tip 1A shield rim and sword handle. Pipe in sword blade and face mask bars with tip 8 (smooth with dampened art brush). Add tip 8 dot face mask hinges (flatten with fingertip dipped in cornstarch).

Cover knight and shield with tip 18 stars.

3. Pipe tip 18 elongated shell hair. Trim vest, shield and cuff with tip 4 dots.

Print tip 4 message. Edge cake base with tip 18 shell border. Position candy.

For more ways to use
WIZARD PAN
see Pan Index p. 192.

9

For more ways to use CIRCUS CLOWN PAN see Pan Index p. 192.

GET UP AND GROW!

Little Johnny Appleseed serves 12.

Decorating Needs
- Circus Clown Pan, p. 179
- Tips 2A, 4, 12, 17, 47, 352, p. 112-115
- '85 Pattern Book, p. 103 (Johnny Pattern)
- Decorator's Brush, p. 116

Instructions

1. Ice cake top and sides smooth (pan "hat" area blue). With toothpick, mark Johnny Pattern on cake top.

Cover marks with tip 4 strings.

2. Pipe in tip 12 pan handle (smooth with dampened brush). Add tip 4 dot handle hole.

Fill in eyes, nose, mouth and apple bite with tip 4. Add tip 4 dot pupils to eyes.

Pipe in apple with tip 2A. Outline bite with tip 4. Pipe tip 47 ribbed stripe patches. Fill bag with tip 4 dot seeds.

Cover face, hands, shirt and bag with tip 17 stars.

3. Pipe tip 17 stripe tree trunk and branches. Add tip 352 pull-out leaf treetop. Pipe tip 4 bead heart apples.

Add tip 4 apple stems and patch stitches. Print tip 4 message.

Edge cake base with tip 17 shell border.

"APPLE"AUSE!
"APPLE"AUSE!

This all-American favorite serves 8.

Decorating Needs
- 9" Heart Pan, p. 175
- '85 Pattern Book, p. 103 (Apple Pattern)
- Decorator's Brush, p. 116
- Paste Icing Colors, p. 131
- Pastry for two double crusts, egg white wash, favorite apple pie recipe

Instructions

1. Prepare pie crust according to directions. Divide dough into three parts.

With two parts of dough, roll out two 9" pie crusts. Place one in heart pan.

2. Prepare your favorite apple pie recipe and place in pie shell. Cover with pie crust. Gently press edges down slightly.

Divide third part of dough into three 8" pieces. Twist pieces together. Brush egg white wash on pie crust. Arrange twisted dough around top and brush with egg white. Bake according to recipe directions.

3. Immediately after removing from oven, with toothpick, mark Apple Pattern.

With art brush dipped in paste icing color (add a few drops of water) "paint" apple and message on crust.

For more ways to use 9" HEART PAN see Pan Index p. 192.

PAUL BUNYAN'S BONANZA!

This legendary fellow serves 12.

Decorating Needs
- Santa With List Pan, p. 180
- Tips 2, 4, 12, 16, p. 112
- '85 Pattern Book, p. 103 (Paul Bunyan Pattern)
- Decorator's Brush, p. 116
- Licorice string

Instructions

1. Ice cake top and sides smooth. With toothpick, mark Paul Bunyan Pattern on cake top. Cover marks with tip 4 strings.

2. Fill in eyes and mouth with tip 4. Add tip 4 dot eyeballs. Pipe in pancakes with tip 12. (Smooth with dampened brush.)

Fill in candles and flames with tip 16 stripes. Cover cap, face, plate and hand with tip 16 stars.

3. Add tip 16 zigzag cuff. Fill in kerchief checks with tip 4 zigzags.

Add tip 16 shell brows, reverse shell beard and stripe mustache. Print tip 2 message.

Edge cake base with tip 16 shell border. Tie cap bow licorice string and attach to cake with icing. Add tip 4 thinned icing to resemble melting butter. With toothpick, mark butter pat. Outline and fill in with tip 4.

For more ways to use SANTA WITH LIST PAN see Pan Index p. 192.

The Adorable Touch That Means So Much

PRETTY POCAHONTAS

She'll serve 12 little indians right!

Decorating Needs
- Easter Bunny Pan, p. 186
- Tips 4, 9, 16, 17, p. 112
- '85 Pattern Book, p. 103 (Pocahontas Pattern)
- Decorator's Brush, p. 116

Instructions

1. Ice cake side and dress area on cake top gold; rest of cake top white. With toothpick, mark Pocahontas Pattern. Cover marks with tip 4 strings.

2. Fill in eyes and mouth with tip 4 (smooth with dampened brush).

Cover feathers, face, neck, headband and pigtail ties with tip 16 stars.

3. Pipe tip 17 stripe hair and pigtails. Print tip 4 message. Add tip 9 ball bead necklace. Edge cake base with tip 17 shell border.

For more decorating hints, see Decorating Guide p. 80.

For more ways to use EASTER BUNNY PAN see Pan Index p. 192.

11

ONE, TWO, TIE MY SHOE

Quick-to-decorate cake serves 12.

Decorating Needs
- Easter Bunny Pan, p. 186
- Tips 3, 17*, p. 112
- '85 Pattern Book, p. 103
  (Ballet Shoes Pattern)

Instructions

1. Ice cake smooth. Use a pencil to transfer Ballet Shoes pattern to sheet of waxed paper. Lightly secure waxed paper on top of cake. With toothpick, mark Ballet Shoes on cake top.

2. Cover marks with tip 3 outlines.

3. Cover ballet shoes and ties with tip 17 stars. Edge cake base with tip 17 shell border. Print tip 3 message.

*Decorate your cakes even faster with our TRIPLE STAR TIP (sold on page 115). All it takes is one squeeze to pipe out three perfectly spaced stars the size of tip 17 stars! Use with any size bag (cut to fit) or with large coupler and bag.

For more helpful hints, review Decorating Guide, p. 80.

For more ways to use
EASTER BUNNY PAN
see Pan Index p. 192.

The Super Touch That Means So Much

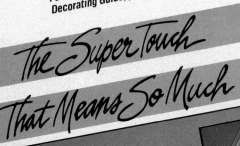

For more ways to use
COOKIE PAN
see Pan Index p. 192.

BANANA BOAT MERINGUES

Recipe makes 4 tropical treats.

Decorating Needs
- Cookie Pan, p. 111 or p. 173
- Tips 2E, 21, p. 112-114
- Meringue Recipe, p. 95
- Stabilized Whipped Cream Recipe, p. 81
- Candy Melts™ brand confectionery coating, p. 120
- Bananas, cherries, lemon juice

Instructions

1. Prepare Wilton Meringue using recipe on p. 95 (each recipe yields 4 boats). Cover bottom of cookie pan with parchment paper. With a pencil, mark outline around each banana, allowing about 1-in. clearance on all sides. Use patterns to outline and fill in meringue bases with tip 2E. Bake at 250° for 10-15 minutes. Turn oven off and leave meringue in oven 3 hours to cool.

2. Prepare stabilized whipped cream. Pipe tip 21 zigzag onto meringue boats.

3. Peel bananas just before serving (or brush with lemon juice to prevent darkening). Place bananas on waxed paper or foil. Drizzle with melted Candy Melts using decorating bag. Position bananas on whipped cream layer. Pipe tip 21 whipped cream rosettes. Place cherries on top of rosettes.

WHEELIN' & SQUEALIN'

Fast-moving cake serves 12.

Decorating Needs
- Up 'N Away Balloon Pan, p. 179
- Tips 4, 17, p. 112
- '85 Pattern Book, p. 103 (Big Wheel Pattern)
- Super Skater Boy, p. 139
- Marshmallows

Instructions

1. Ice cake top and sides smooth. With toothpick, mark Big Wheel Pattern on cake top. Cover marks with tip 4 outlines. Add straight outlines behind wheel.

2. Cover wheel, side wall, whitewall and semi-circles between hubcap with tip 17 stars. Pipe tip 17 zigzag puff of smoke. Outline and fill in triangles and bolts of hubcap with tip 4 (smooth with fingertip dipped in cornstarch). Fill in hubcap areas with tip 4 thinned icing.

3. Add tip 17 shell border at base of cake. Add tip 4 outline smile. Dot marshmallow eyes with tip 4. Attach eyes with dots of icing. Position Super Skater Boy on cake top and enjoy!

For more ways to use UP 'N AWAY BALLOON PAN see Pan Index p. 192.

BIRTHDAY BEAGLE

Man's best friend serves 15.

Decorating Needs
- Little Lamb Pan, p. 187
- Tips 2A, 4, 17, p. 112
- '85 Pattern Book, p. 103 (Bone Pattern)
- Decorator's Brush, p. 116
- Cookie dough, pound or firm-textured cake batter, plastic straws, construction paper, poster board, ribbon.

Instructions

1. Use Bone Pattern to cut cookie dough. Ice baked, cooled cookie with thinned icing. Cut 7-in. paper circle. Slit to center and remove pie-shaped wedge; roll into cone shape and tape edges. Cut cardboard dog tag and print message.

2. With knife, slice off lamb's snout. With toothpick, mark details of dog's body on cake. Use tip 2A to build up cheeks, paws, legs, tail, ears and nose. Smooth and shape features with fingertip dipped in cornstarch.

3. Cover features and remaining toothpick marks with tip 4 outlines. Use tip 4 to fill in eyes and brows (smooth with dampened art brush). Cover body and built-up cheeks, paws, legs, tail and ears with tip 17 stars. Add tip 4 dot pupils (flatten with fingertip dipped in cornstarch) and freckles. Add tip 17 pull-out star tail tip.

4. Just before serving, tie ribbon around dog's bone; string another ribbon through dog's tag. Attach to cake with toothpicks. Place hat on dog's head.

HAPPY 14th BIRTHDAY Love, Mom & Dad

For more ways to use LITTLE LAMB PAN see Pan Index p. 192.

TEEN'S BIRTHDAY

LONG-ON-FLAVOR SHORTCAKES

Fruit-filled desserts serve 1 each.

Decorating Needs
- Shortcakes 'N Treats Pan, p. 171
- Tip 32, p. 112
- Stabilized Whipped Cream Recipe, p. 82
- Assorted fruits: banana slices, mandarin oranges, grapes, pineapple chunks, cherries, peach halves, lemon juice

Instructions

1. Dip banana in lemon juice after cutting to prevent darkening. Arrange assorted fruits in cooled shortcakes.*

2. Pipe tip 32 stars and rosettes. Top rosettes with a whole cherry or grape.

*We've alternated oranges with tapered banana slices (remember to dip bananas after they're cut), pineapple chunks with cherry halves, and topped a peach half with purple grapes. Large green grapes were trimmed and then pressed onto side of peach half. Use a variety of fresh or canned fruits to please your guests. Or fill with pudding or ready-to-eat pie filling!

For more ways to use SHORTCAKES 'N TREATS PAN see Pan Index p. 192.

TURNING SIXTEEN

Birthday turn-on serves 12.

Decorating Needs
- Horseshoe Pan, p. 184
- Tips 1A, 4, 16, p. 112
- Decorator's Brush, p. 116
- Piping Gel, p. 131
- Royal Icing Recipe, p. 83
- Meringue Powder, p. 131

Instructions

1. On waxed paper, figure pipe tip 1A royal icing faucet handle* Set aside to dry about 3 hours.

2. Ice cake top and sides smooth. With toothpick, mark faucet and drip. Cover faucet marks with tip 4 outlines.

Pipe in and build up faucet and drip with tip 1A; shape and smooth with fingertip dipped in cornstarch.

Overpipe faucet with tip 4 outlines.

Use brush to glaze drip with piping gel.

3. Push end of faucet handle into cake. Edge cake top and base with tip 16 shell border. Print tip 4 message and enjoy!

*You could also shape handle using pretzel rods as a base. Connect pretzels by pushing a toothpick through longer piece and into center of shorter pretzel. Cover with royal icing; shape and smooth with dampened brush.

For more ways to use HORSESHOE PAN see Pan Index p. 192.

For more ways to use
8-IN. RING PAN
see Pan Index p. 192.

DONUT WHOLE

Sweet iced ring serves 8.

Decorating Needs
- **8-in. Ring Pan, p. 173**
- **Tip 3, p. 112**
- **Candy Wafer & Fondant Mix, p. 120**
- **Chopped nuts, unsweetened chocolate**

Instructions*

1. Prepare Quick Pour Icing recipe as directed on Candy Wafer & Fondant Mix label. Use 1 oz. melted unsweetened chocolate to flavor and color mixture. Add more water, if necessary, until icing is a pourable consistency.

2. Position cake on serving plate with rounded side up. Pour prepared icing over cake top.

3. Sprinkle with chopped nuts and press lightly. Print tip 3 message and enjoy!

*Cake pan requires only 3-1/2 cups of batter. Boxed mixes yield approximately 4 to 6 cups of batter. Use extra batter to bake a mini-cake or cupcakes.

A MUNCH CUTER CATHY™

Lovely lady serves 12.

Decorating Needs
- **Cathy™ Pan, p. 191**
- **Tips 2, 4, 12, 18, p. 112**
- **Decorator's Brush, p. 116**
- **Candy sprinkles**

Instructions

1. With toothpick, mark donuts on cake top.* Cover marks with tip 4 outlines. Outline face, neck, heart, hands, dress and sleeves with tip 4 strings.

2. Fill in eyes with tip 4; smooth with dampened brush. Add tip 4 dot pupils. Fill in heart with tip 12; smooth with dampened brush. Cover face, neck, dress, donuts and hands with tip 18 stars. Pipe tip 18 side-by-side straight hair. Overpipe donuts with tip 4 strings.

3. Pipe tip 2 message. Top donuts with candy sprinkles and munch away!

*For extra dimension and realism, use a real donut on top of cake. Slice donut through middle and use one half for each of the donuts Cathy™ is holding. Outline and cover with icing stars as stated in directions.

© CATHY™ 1983 Universal Press Syndicate.

For more ways to use
CATHY™ PAN
see Pan Index p. 192.

LIVE EACH DAY TO THE FULLEST
Love Cathy

MAMA MIA IT'S YOUR BIRTHDAY

SLICE OF SPICE

Pretend pizza serves 12.

Decorating Needs
- Treeliteful Pan, p. 181
- Tips 1A, 2A, 4, 10, 47, 101, p. 112-114
- Royal Icing Recipe, p. 83
- Gone Fishin' Signboard, p. 138

Instructions

1. Make about 8 tip 101 ribbon "onions" and about 25 tip 47 "green pepper" pieces with royal icing. Let air dry.

2. Ice "sauce" areas across top edge and along sides of cake smooth in tomato color. Ice top and sides of message area smooth in crust color.

Pipe tip 1A rippled top crust and straight bottom crust. Flatten and push bottom crust to meet "sauce" using fingertip dipped in cornstarch.

Ice "cheese" area smooth. Pipe tip 10 "melting cheese" on sides. Pat with fingertip.

3. Pipe tip 1A "pepperoni"; pat down to flatten with fingertip dipped in cornstarch. Make depressions in pepperoni with tip 4 (no icing). Pipe tip 2A "mushrooms." Scatter onion rings and green pepper pieces (smooth side up). Pipe tip 4 message on Gone Fishin' Signboard and position in message area on cake top.

For more ways to use TREELITEFUL PAN see Pan Index, p. 192.

LIP-SMACKIN' GOOD

Creamy soda serves 13.

Decorating Needs
- Good Cheer Mug Pan, p. 184
- Heart Minicake Pan, p. 182
- Tips 1A, 2A, 4, 17, p. 112
- Piping Gel, p. 131
- Decorator's Brush, p. 116
- Wafer cookies, plastic straw

Instructions

1. Ice cake sides and background areas by mug base and handle smooth. Ice soda on mug smooth.

Outline mug, soda and handle with tip 4. Cover mug with tip 17 stars.

2. Pipe fingers with tip 1A (flatten with fingertip dipped in cornstarch). Use spatula to add soda foam and tip 2A to pipe drips. Use piping gel to add water-like droplets to glass with tip 4.

Pipe tip 17 shell border around base of cake.

3. Ice mini-heart smooth. Pipe lips with tip 1A; flatten and shape with fingertip dipped in cornstarch. Brush lips with piping gel for glossy look. Add tip 17 star border around base of mini-heart.

4. Insert cookies and straw. Position mini-heart lips. Print tip 4 message.

For more ways to use GOOD CHEER MUG and HEART MINICAKE PANS see Pan Index, p. 192.

Sweet Sips For Sweet Lips!

16

SUPER SCOOPER
Cone-clone serves 12.
Decorating Needs
- Up 'n Away Balloon Pan, p. 179
- Tips 1A, 4, 17, p. 112

Instructions
1. Ice cake smooth. With toothpick, mark ice cream and cone on cake top. Outline cone and ice cream swirl with tip 4. Pipe-in and build-up ice cream with tip 1A (smooth with fingertip dipped in cornstarch). Cover with tip 17 stars.

2. Pipe and fill in rims and bottom of cone with tip 1A (smooth with fingertip dipped in cornstarch). Cover remaining cone areas with tip 17 stars. Print tip 4 message.

3. Pipe tip 17 shell border around base of cake.

For more helpful hints, review Decorating Guide, p. 80.

For more ways to use BALLOON PAN see Pan Index, p. 192.

The Super Touch That Means So Much

SOCCER IT TO 'EM
Fast-footed cakes serve 24.
Decorating Needs
- Bunny Pan, p. 187
- Ball Pan, p. 184
- Tips 4, 7, 16, 44, p. 112
- Decorator's Brush, p. 116
- '85 Pattern Book, p. 103 (Soccer Ball Pattern)
- Pound cake or other firm textured cake batter, plastic straws

Instructions
1. With knife, slice off end of baked firm-textured Ball Cake so it stands level. With toothpick, mark Soccer Ball Pattern on ball. Cover marks with tip 4 outlines. Cover ball with tip 16 stars.

2. Allow firm-textured bunny cake to cool completely in back half of pan (at least 4 hours; see pan instructions). With knife, cut off cake at base of ears; cut off bunny's snout. Insert 2 plastic straws down through head and body. Ice top of sock smooth.

3. With toothpick, mark shoe and sock pattern on cake. Cover marks with tip 4 outlines. Fill in tongue and stripes on sides with tip 44 (smooth with dampened art brush).

4. Cover stripes at top of sock with tip 16 zigzag. Cover remaining sock and shoe areas with tip 16 stars.

5. Add tip 7 string shoe laces and bow. Print tip 4 message and start the game!

For more ways to use BUNNY & BALL PANS see Pan Index, p. 192.

17

OVER 40 AND STILL COOKIN'!

SOUP'S ON

The chef's special serves 12.

Decorating Needs
- Easter Bunny Pan, p. 186
- Tips 3, 9, 16, 18, p. 112
- Pretzel stick

Instructions

1. Ice cake sides and top smooth. Lightly ice area where face and bowl will go.

With toothpick, mark hairline, soup bowl, soup, and fingers on cake top. Cover marks with tip 3 strings.

2. Ice hat smooth. Overpipe hat brim with tip 3.

Fill in soup with tip 9. Flatten with finger tip dipped in cornstarch.

Attach pretzel with icing.

Cover face, hands (go over pretzel), and bowl with tip 16 stars.

3. Pipe tip 9 dot eyes, cheeks and nose. Smooth with finger tip dipped in cornstarch. Add tip 3 string eyelashes and mouth.

Pipe tip 18 stripe hair.

Add tip 9 fill-in steam. Smooth with finger tip dipped in cornstarch.

Print tip 3 message. Edge cake base with tip 18 shell border.

For more ways to use EASTER BUNNY PAN see Pan Index p. 192.

For more helpful hints, review Decorating Guide, p. 80.

YOU'RE A KNOCK OUT

AN UNDEFEATED CHAMP!

They'll be pleased as punch! Serves 12.

Decorating Needs
- Mystical Dragon Pan, p. 188
- Tips 3, 12, 16, 18, p. 112
- '85 Pattern Book, p. 103 (Kangaroo Pattern)
- Decorator's Brush, p. 116
- Piping gel, p. 131

Instructions

1. Ice cake smooth. (Lightly ice area where kangaroo will go.)

2. With toothpick, mark Kangaroo Pattern on cake top. Outline with tip 3 strings.

Build up leg and gloves with tip 12.

Pipe tip 3 fill-in eye, nose, ear and gloves. Smooth with dampened brush. Add tip 16 zigzags cuff and tip 4 string laces to gloves.

Cover body with tip 18 stars. Add tip 4 outline eyelashes.

3. Print tip 3 message. Edge cake base with tip 18 shell border.

Glaze gloves with piping gel.

For more ways to use MYSTICAL DRAGON PAN see Pan Index p. 192.

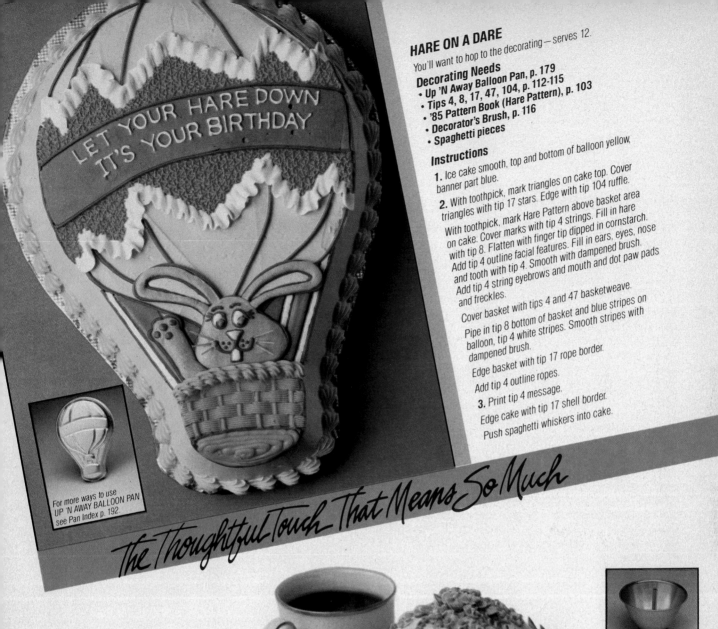

HARE ON A DARE
You'll want to hop to the decorating—serves 12.

Decorating Needs
• Up 'N Away Balloon Pan, p. 179
• Tips 4, 8, 17, 47, 104, p. 112-115
• '85 Pattern Book (Hare Pattern), p. 103
• Decorator's Brush, p. 116
• Spaghetti pieces

Instructions
1. Ice cake smooth, top and bottom of balloon yellow, banner part blue.

2. With toothpick, mark triangles on cake top. Cover triangles with tip 17 stars. Edge with tip 104 ruffle.

With toothpick, mark Hare Pattern above basket area on cake. Cover marks with tip 4 strings. Fill in hare with tip 8. Flatten with finger tip dipped in cornstarch. Add tip 4 outline facial features. Fill in ears, eyes, nose and tooth with tip 4. Smooth with dampened brush. Add tip 4 string eyebrows and mouth and dot paw pads and freckles.

Cover basket with tips 4 and 47 basketweave.

Pipe in tip 8 bottom of basket and blue stripes on balloon, tip 4 white stripes. Smooth stripes with dampened brush.

Edge basket with tip 17 rope border.

Add tip 4 outline ropes.

3. Print tip 4 message.

Edge cake with tip 17 shell border.

Push spaghetti whiskers into cake.

For more ways to use UP 'N AWAY BALLOON PAN see Pan Index p. 192.

The Thoughtful Touch That Means So Much

For more ways to use WONDER MOLD PAN see Pan Index p. 192.

SPRINGTIME WONDER
A delightful design! Serves 12.

Decorating Needs
• Wonder Mold Pan, p. 183
• Tips 3, 20, 224, 225, 352, p. 112-115
• Cake Dividing Set, p. 116
• 15-Piece Pattern Press Set, p. 116

Instructions
1. Make 50 tip 224 and 25 tip 225 drop flowers with tip 3 centers.

Ice cake smooth. Using Cake Dividing Set, with toothpick, dot mark cake sides into eighths.

2. Using Pattern Press Set, imprint design on cake sides. Cover marks with tip 20 scrolls and elongated curved stripes.

3. Encircle cake top and bottom with tip 3 outline vines. Add tip 352 leaves.

Attach flowers to vines and at top of cake with dots of icing.

Trim flowers on cake top with tip 3 "e" motion vines and tip 352 leaves.

Edge cake base with tip 20 shell border.

19

DEVILISHLY DELICIOUS

A "get rich-ness quick" dessert! Serves 12.

Decorating Needs
- **8" Round Pan, p. 165, 166, 177**
- **Tips 21, 104, p. 112-115**
- **Flower Nail No. 7, p. 115**
- **Coconut Pecan Frosting Recipe (below)**
- **Stabilized whipped cream, recipe p. 82**

Instructions

1. Make 4 tip 104 roses and 8 sweet peas.

2. Coconut Pecan Frosting Recipe
   Yield: 3½ cups
   - 1 cup sugar
   - 1 cup evaporated milk
   - 3 eggs, beaten
   - ½ cup butter or margarine
   - 1 teaspoon vanilla
   - 1⅓ cups flaked coconut
   - 1 cup chopped pecans or almonds

   In saucepan, combine sugar, milk and eggs. Add butter. Cook over medium heat until mixture thickens and just begins to boil, stirring constantly. Remove from heat. Stir in remaining ingredients. Cool until of spreading consistency.

   Frost and fill 2-layer cake with Coconut Pecan Frosting.

3. Using stabilized whipped cream, edge cake top with tip 21 double reverse shell border and base with shell border.

   Place flowers on cake top.

For more ways to use 8" ROUND PAN see Pan Index, p. 192.

For more ways to use 9" PIE PAN see Pan Index, p. 192.

CARAMEL 'N CREAM PIE

Luscious combination! Serves 12.

Decorating Needs
- **9" Pie Pan, p. 170**
- **Tip 21, p. 112**
- **One container Candy Maker™ brand Caramel Filling, p. 120**
- **Stabilized whipped cream, recipe p. 82**
- **Vanilla ice cream (½ gal.)**
- **Maraschino cherries, pecan halves, evaporated milk, butter**

Instructions

1. Allow ice cream to soften at room temperature for approximately 30 minutes. Stir with spoon in large bowl until just softened. Pack into baked, cooled pie crust. Smooth with spatula. Cover with foil and freeze until firm (at least 5 hrs.).

   Prepare caramel topping: In small saucepan, combine caramel filling, ¼ cup butter and ¼ cup evaporated milk. Stir over low heat until melted. Cool slightly.

2. Pour caramel topping over ice cream. Using stabilized whipped cream, pipe tip 21 rosettes.

3. Position cherries and pecan halves on cake top.

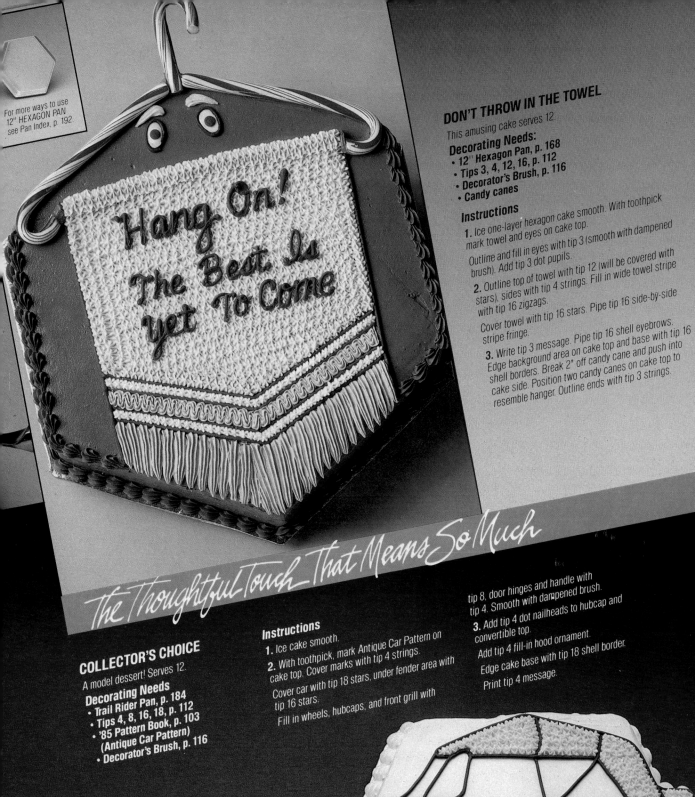

For more ways to use 12" HEXAGON PAN see Pan Index, p. 192.

DON'T THROW IN THE TOWEL

This amusing cake serves 12.

Decorating Needs:
- 12" Hexagon Pan, p. 168
- Tips 3, 4, 12, 16, p. 112
- Decorator's Brush, p. 116
- Candy canes

Instructions

1. Ice one-layer hexagon cake smooth. With toothpick mark towel and eyes on cake top.

Outline and fill in eyes with tip 3 (smooth with dampened brush). Add tip 3 dot pupils.

2. Outline top of towel with tip 12 (will be covered with stars), sides with tip 4 strings. Fill in wide towel stripe with tip 16 zigzags.

Cover towel with tip 16 stars. Pipe tip 16 side-by-side stripe fringe.

3. Write tip 3 message. Pipe tip 16 shell eyebrows. Edge background area on cake top and base with tip 16 shell borders. Break 2" off candy cane and push into cake side. Position two candy canes on cake top to resemble hanger. Outline ends with tip 3 strings.

The Thoughtful Touch That Means So Much

COLLECTOR'S CHOICE

A model dessert! Serves 12.

Decorating Needs
- Trail Rider Pan, p. 184
- Tips 4, 8, 16, 18, p. 112
- '85 Pattern Book, p. 103 (Antique Car Pattern)
- Decorator's Brush, p. 116

Instructions

1. Ice cake smooth.

2. With toothpick, mark Antique Car Pattern on cake top. Cover marks with tip 4 strings.

Cover car with tip 18 stars, under fender area with tip 16 stars.

Fill in wheels, hubcaps, and front grill with tip 8, door hinges and handle with tip 4. Smooth with dampened brush.

3. Add tip 4 dot nailheads to hubcap and convertible top.

Add tip 4 fill-in hood ornament.

Edge cake base with tip 18 shell border.

Print tip 4 message.

For more ways to use TRAIL RIDER PAN see Pan Index, p. 192.

HAPPY BIRTHDAY

THE BIG GAME

An easy scorer! Serves 15.

Decorating Needs
- **9" x 13" Sheet Pan, p. 165, 169, 176**
- **Tips 2B, 4, 8, 17, p. 112**
- **Super Bowl Football Set, p. 139**
- **Decorator's Brush, p. 116**
- **Pretzel cut in two pieces**

Instructions

1. Ice center part of one-layer cake smooth.

With toothpick, mark TV screen and channel selector on cake top. Cover marks with tip 4 strings.

2. Pipe in tip 2B smooth frame. Smooth with dampened brush. Add tip 4 string yardlines.

Cover furniture part of TV and upper channel selector with tip 17 stars.

Pipe in tip 2B ribbed bottom channel selector area. Smooth with dampened brush. Pipe tip 8 dot knobs. Shape with fingers dipped in cornstarch.

3. Print tip 4 brown message and white numbers.

Push toothpicks into pretzel pieces and push into cake for "antennas."

Position The Super Bowl Football Set on cake top.

For more ways to use 9" x 13" SHEET PAN see Pan Index p. 192.

The Thoughtful Touch That Means So Much

A STRIKING PAIR

This will bowl them over! Serves 34.

Decorating Needs
- **11" x 15" Sheet Pan, p. 165, 169, 176**
- **Bowling Pin Pan, p. 185**
- **Ball Pan, p. 184**
- **Tips 4, 17, 789, p. 112-115**
- **Dowel Rods, p. 159**
- **Cake Circle, p. 154**
- **Rectangle Cake Board, p. 154**
- **Decorator's Brush, p. 116**
- **Bowling Pin Set, p. 139**
- **Pound or firm-textured cake for bowling pin and ball, paper party hat**

Instructions

1. Ice sheet cake, sides smooth, top with Cake Icer tip 789, smooth side up. Score with knife to resemble wood planks.

Push dowel rods into sheet cake where ball and bowling pin will go.

Place bowling pin cake on a rectangle cake board cut to fit.

Place ball on cake circle cut to fit.

Position ball and pin cakes atop sheet cake.

2. Outline facial features on ball and pin cakes and details on pin with tip 4 strings. Fill in eyes with tip 4 thinned icing. Smooth with dampened brush.

Cover ball and pin cakes with tip 17 stars.

3. Edge sheet cake top with tip 17 rosettes, cake base border with tip 17 shells.

Place party hat on ball. (If hat is too big, adjust by restapling.)

Print tip 4 message.

SPARE ME ANOTHER YEAR

HOLDING ON THE 50 YEAR LINE

For more ways to use 11" x 15" SHEET PAN, BOWLING PIN PAN and BALL PAN see Pan Index p. 192.

CALM WATERS

You'll sail through the decorating! Serves 12.

Decorating Needs
- Sailboat Pan, p. 185
- Tips 4, 9, 16, p. 112
- Decorator's Brush, p. 116

Instructions

1. Ice sail and sky area smooth, sail white, sky blue.

With toothpick, mark design on spinnaker.

2. Pipe tip 9 mast and boom.

Outline spinnaker, cabin and sailor with tip 4 strings.

Fill in windows with tip 4. Smooth with dampened brush.

Cover spinnaker and cabin with tip 16 stars.

Pipe tip 9 sailor. Smooth with finger tip dipped in cornstarch. Add tip 4 features and hair.

3. Add tip 16 white swirled shell wave caps. Ice water area blue and swirl with spatula to resemble waves.

Print tip 4 message.

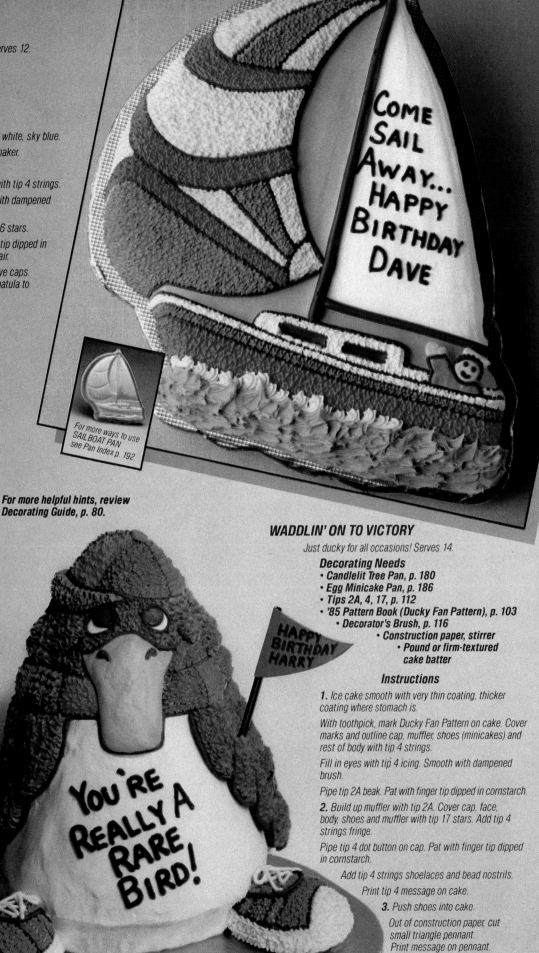

COME SAIL AWAY... HAPPY BIRTHDAY DAVE

For more ways to use SAILBOAT PAN see Pan Index p. 192.

1.

2.

3.

For more helpful hints, review Decorating Guide, p. 80.

For more ways to use CANDLELIT TREE PAN and EGG MINICAKE PAN see Pan Index p. 192.

YOU'RE REALLY A RARE BIRD!

WADDLIN' ON TO VICTORY

Just ducky for all occasions! Serves 14.

Decorating Needs
- Candlelit Tree Pan, p. 180
- Egg Minicake Pan, p. 186
- Tips 2A, 4, 17, p. 112
- '85 Pattern Book (Ducky Fan Pattern), p. 103
- Decorator's Brush, p. 116
- Construction paper, stirrer
- Pound or firm-textured cake batter

Instructions

1. Ice cake smooth with very thin coating, thicker coating where stomach is.

With toothpick, mark Ducky Fan Pattern on cake. Cover marks and outline cap, muffler, shoes (minicakes) and rest of body with tip 4 strings.

Fill in eyes with tip 4 icing. Smooth with dampened brush.

Pipe tip 2A beak. Pat with finger tip dipped in cornstarch.

2. Build up muffler with tip 2A. Cover cap, face, body, shoes and muffler with tip 17 stars. Add tip 4 strings fringe.

Pipe tip 4 dot button on cap. Pat with finger tip dipped in cornstarch.

Add tip 4 strings shoelaces and bead nostrils.

Print tip 4 message on cake.

3. Push shoes into cake.

Out of construction paper, cut small triangle pennant. Print message on pennant. Secure pennant to stirrer with icing. Push into cake.

HAPPY BIRTHDAY HARRY

23

MUCHO-MACHO HEART

A double delectable delight! Serves 12.

Decorating Needs
- **Double Tier Heart Pan, p. 182**
- **Tips 3, 16, 19, p. 112**
- **Candy Melts™ brand confectionery coating, p. 120**
- **Hearts I Mold, p. 124**
- **Chopped nuts**

Instructions

1. Mold 20 Candy Melts™ hearts. See p. 96.

2. Slowly pour melted Candy Melts™ over tiered heart. Ice rest of cake smooth.

Press chopped nuts and shaved Candy Melts™ around sides of cake.

Edge tiered heart cake base border with tip 16 shells.

3. Attach hearts to cake top with dots of icing.

Edge cake top and cake base border with tip 19 shells.

Write tip 3 message.

For more ways to use
DOUBLE TIER HEART PAN
see Pan Index p. 192.

For more ways to use
TART PAN
see Pan Index p. 192.

AMBROSIA TART

A divine way to please all! Serves 12.

Decorating Needs
- **10" Tart Pan, p. 172**
- **Tip 21, p. 112**
- **Stabilized whipped cream, recipe p. 82**
- **1 stick pie crust (or recipe for single pie crust)**
- **Instant vanilla pudding**
- **Orange sections, kiwi fruit slices, maraschino cherries**

Instructions

1. Prepare pie crust. Bake and cool.

Prepare instant pudding, using only 2/3 of the amount of milk recommended on the package.

Pour pudding into pie shell.

2. Arrange fruit on top.

3. Pipe tip 21 elongated shells between orange slices and tip 21 rosettes down the middle. Top rosettes with cherries.

For more helpful hints, review Decorating Guide, p. 80.

FAITHFUL FRIEND

This will get you out of the doghouse! Serves 12.

Decorating Needs
- **Holiday House Kit, p. 181**
- **Tips 1D, 2B, 3, 4, 8, 12, p. 112**
- **'85 Pattern Book (Dog in House Pattern), p. 103**
- **Royal Icing, Recipe p. 83**
- **Rectangle Cake Board, p. 154**
- **Fancy Foil Wrap, p. 155**
- **Decorator's Brush, p. 116**
- **Firm-textured or pound cake**

Instructions

1. On waxed paper, pipe tip 12 royal icing dog face and ears, tip 8 nose and feet, using pattern. Outline facial features with tip 3 strings. Fill in eyes with tip 4. Flatten with dampened brush. Add tip 3 dot eyeballs and whiskers.

2. Position cake on 7½" x 8" foil-covered cake board.

With toothpick, mark 4½" high doorway on house. Cover marks with tip 4 strings. Fill in doorway with tip 12. Flatten with finger tip dipped in cornstarch.

Cover doghouse with tip 1D smooth stripe wood slats. Pat down with finger tip dipped in cornstarch. Add tip 4 outline boards and dot nailheads.

Working from back to front, pipe tip 2B roof tiles. Pat with finger tip dipped in cornstarch.

3. Attach dog to doghouse with dabs of icing.

Print tip 4 message on roof top and above door.

For more ways to use
HOLIDAY HOUSE KIT
see Pan Index p. 192

The Thoughtful Touch That Means So Much

ABSENTMINDED FOOL

A surprise to remember! Serves 12.

Decorating Needs
- **Wizard Pan, p. 188**
- **Tips 2, 4, 6, 12, 16, 18, 103, p. 112-115**
- **'85 Pattern Book (Jester Pattern), p. 103**
- **Decorator's Brush, p. 116**

Instructions

1. Ice cake smooth.

With toothpick, mark Jester Pattern on cake top. Outline facial features, hands, wand, ball, bells, hat and costume with tip 4 strings.

2. Cover hat, back of collar, sleeves, hands, face and wand with tip 16 stars.

Fill in eyes with tip 4. Smooth with dampened brush.

Pipe tip 18 eyebrows. Add tip 4 "e" motion hair.

Cover collar ruffle with tip 18 zigzag; pipe in tip 18 ruffle border.

Pipe tip 12 wand ball and large bells. Shape with fingers dipped in cornstarch. Pipe tip 6 small bells. Shape with fingers dipped in cornstarch. Add tip 2 details on bells.

Trim wand with tip 103 ruffle and tip 6 piped-in top.

3. Print tip 4 message. Edge cake base with tip 18 shell border.

For more ways to use
WIZARD PAN
see Pan Index p. 192

25

GRAND TRIBUTE

This impressive masterpiece will serve 285 guests.

Decorating Needs

- 6," 8," 10," 12," 16" Round Pans, p. 166
- Tips 3, 17, 18, 21, 32, 103, 224, 225, 349, 352, p. 112-115
- Flower Nail No. 7, p. 115
- 4½" Arched Pillars, p. 160
- 13" Arched Pillars, p. 158
- Four 9," two each 7" & 14," Round Separator Plates, p. 159
- 15-Pc. Decorator Pattern Press, p. 116
- Cake Dividing Set, p. 116
- Tuk-N-Ruffle, Cake Circles, Boards, p. 154
- Filigree Bridge & Stairway, p. 158
- Filigree Fountain Frame, p. 157
- Kolor-Flo Fountain, p. 157
- Dowel Rods, p. 159
- Wedding Couples, p. 153
    - Piping Gel, p. 131
    - Decorator's Brush, p. 116
        - Reflection, p. 143
        - Flowers

Instructions

1. Make 50 tip 103 roses, 120 tip 103 sweet peas, 60 tip 224 and 90 tip 225 drop flowers with tip 3 dot centers. With art brush dipped in paste color mixed with small amount of piping gel, paint four bridesmaids dresses.

Read Tiered Cake Assembly, p. 86. Ice one 6," 12," 16" and two 8" and 10" 2-layer cakes smooth on cake circles, separator plates and Tuk-N-Ruffle trimmed, foil-covered cake boards.

2. Using Cake Dividing Set, with toothpick dot mark 6" cake sides into 3rds, 8" cakes into 4ths, one 10" cake into 5ths, 12" cake into 6ths, 16" cake into 8ths.

Make 3" garlands on 6," one 10" and 16" cake sides. Using Pattern Press, imprint single scroll designs between garlands and pairs of scrolls on 8," one 10" and 12" cake sides.

Pipe tip 17 (on 6" and 8") and tip 18 (10," 12" and 16") double drop string garlands and scroll designs on cake sides.

3. Edge 6" top and base with tip 17; 8" tops and bases with tip 18; 10" tops and bases with tip 21; 12" top with tip 18, base with 21; 16" top with tip 21, base with tip 32 shell borders. Attach flowers to cake tops (except 10" cakes where stairway will go), sides, bases, separator plates and stair railing with dots of icing. Trim flowers with tips 349 and 352 leaves. Assemble tiers with separator plates on pillars at reception. Position Kolor Flo Fountain on 16" cake top with Filigree Fountain Frame. Assemble tiers with plates on pillars. Position Filigree Stairway with Wedding Couples. Attach flowers to 10" cake tops around stairway. Trim with tip 352 leaves. Position Reflection on 6" cake.

Wedding Joy

26

CAPTIVATING CLASSIC

These lovely hexagon tiers will serve 144.

Decorating Needs

- 4-Pc. Hexagon Pan Set, p. 174
- Tips 3, 10, 18, 21, 103, 104, 129, 224, 225, 349, p. 112-115
- Flower Nail No. 7, p. 115
- 5" Square Filigree Pillars, p. 160
- 10" Hexagon Separator Plates, p. 159
- 15-Pc. Decorator Pattern Press Set, p. 116
- Cake Circles & Boards, p. 154
- Dowel Rods, p. 159
- Fancy Foil Wrap, p. 155
- Happy Hearts, p. 150

A show of taste... Wilton Wedding Cake Ornaments.

Each is a beautiful statement of true love. Exquisitely detailed couples in enchanting settings will enhance your wedding masterpiece and be a lasting keepsake. See the complete collection on pages 142-151.

Instructions

1. Make 20 tip 103 and 60 tip 104 sweet peas, 10 tip 103 and 25 tip 104 roses; 20 tip 129, 30 tip 224 and 80 tip 225 drop flowers with tip 3 dot centers.

Read Tiered Cake Assembly, p. 86. Ice one-layer 6" and two-layer cakes smooth atop cake circles, separator plates and foil-covered cake board.

2. Edge 6" and 9" cake bases with tip 18; 12" and 15" bases with tip 21 shell borders. Using Pattern Press pieces, imprint small "C" scrolls on 6" and 12"; "fleur de lis" design on 9" and 15" cake sides.

Pipe tip 18 shells between scrolls on 12" and 15" cake sides. Cover scroll marks on 6" and 9" sides with tip 18; 12" and 15" sides with tip 21.

3. Edge separator plate with tip 18 scallop border. Edge cake tops with reverse shell borders (tip 18 on 6" and 9", tip 21 on 12" and 15").

Pipe tip 10 icing mound on separator plate. Attach flowers to mound and cake sides with dots of icing. Pipe tip 349 leaves.

Assemble cake with separator plates on pillars at reception. Position Happy Hearts atop cake.

For more helpful hints, review Decorating Guide, p. 80.

Wedding Romance

PETAL PERFECTION

This delicate delight will serve 100 guests.

Decorating Needs
- 9," 12," 15" Petal Pans, p. 169, 174
- Tips 3, 16, 17, 18, 103, 104, 129, 352, p. 112-115
- '85 Pattern Book, p. 103 (Oval Patterns)
- 13" Round Separator Plates, p. 159
- 7½" Corinthian Pillars, p. 160
- Dowel Rods, p. 159
- Cake Circles, Boards, p. 154
- Fancy Foil Wrap, p. 155
- Florist Wire, p. 130
- Swirls, p. 152
- Heart Bowl Vase, p. 153
- Cherish, p. 142
- Tulle

Instructions

1. Make 30 tip 103 and 40 tip 104 spatula striped apple blossoms with tip 3 dot centers; 100 tip 129 drop flowers with tip 3 dot centers. Pipe tip 3 calyxes on ten florist wires (6" long). Let dry. Attach 10 large apple blossoms to calyxes with dot of icing.

Read Tiered Cake Assembly, p. 86. Ice 2-layer cakes smooth (9" and 12" atop cake circles and separator plate, 16" atop foil-covered cake board).

Edge cake bases with shell borders (9" with tip 17, 12" and 15" with tip 18).

2. With toothpick, mark Oval Patterns on petal curves. Cover marks on 9" and 12" cake sides with tip 16, 15" with tip 17 elongated swirled shells (alternate colors). Trim ovals with swirled shell trios (tip 16 on 9," 12," tip 17 on 15").

Edge separator plate on 15" cake with tip 16 "e" motion shells. Outline 12" and 16" cake tops with pairs of tip 17 elongated swirled shells.

Trim centers with tip 16 "C" scrolls (alternate colors).

3. Pipe tip 17 fleur de lis on 12" and 15" cake sides. On 12" and 15" cakes trim "C" scrolls and shell border (at fleur de lis) with tip 17 stars.

Place tulle in Heart Bowl Vase. Add wired flowers. Attach flowers to cake sides, tulle and separator plate with dots of icing. Trim flowers on cake sides and plate with tip 352 leaves. Assemble tiers with separator plates on pillars at reception. Attach Swirls to cakes and pillars with dots of icing. Position Cherish with plate atop cake.

Wedding Glory

BEVELED BEAUTY

This charming eye-catcher will serve 100 guests.

Decorating Needs
- **8", 10", 12" Round Pans, p. 165, 166, 175, 177**
- **Beveled Pan Set, p. 175**
- **Tips 2A, 3, 4, 6, 7, 9, 224, 225, 349, p. 112-115**
- **5" Grecian Pillars, p. 160**
- **8" Round Separator Plates, p. 159**
- **Tuk-N-Ruffle, Cake Circles, Boards, p. 154**
- **Cake Dividing Set, p. 116**
- **Fancy Foil Wrap, p. 155**
- **Dowel Rods, p. 159**
- **Musical Trio, p. 153**
- **Captivation, p. 143**
- **Fresh flowers**

Instructions

1. Make 100 tip 224 and 80 tip 225 drop flowers with tip 3 dot centers. Read Tiered Cake Assembly, p. 86. Ice 2-layer cakes with beveled tops and bases smooth (8", 10 on cake circles; 12" on Tuk-N-Ruffle trimmed, foil-covered cake board).

Using Cake Dividing Set, with toothpick dot mark diamonds and triangles. For diamonds, divide 8" and 12" beveled tops into 16ths (mark alternate 1/8ths in center to form diamond).

For triangles, divide 10" top and 16" base into 8ths. Also dot mark 1½" garlands on 8", 2" garlands on 10" and 2½" garlands on 12" cake sides.

2. Outline diamonds and triangles with tip 6 strings. Pipe tip 4 drop string garlands.

Edge 8" and 10" tops and bases with tip 7 bead borders. Trim 8" and 10" outer beveled edges with tip 5 bead borders.

Edge base of 12" cake with tip 9 and 16" base with tip 2A bead borders. Trim cake sides with tip 5 elongated beads and dot trios.

3. Attach flowers to cake sides and Captivation with dots of icing. Pipe tip 349 leaves. Assemble cake with separator plates on pillars at reception. Position Captivation atop cake. Arrange flowers and musical trio on 8" separator plate.

Wedding Serenade

CHOCOLATE LOVERS DREAM COME TRUE

This unique sight will delight 156 guests.

Decorating Needs
- 8," 12," 16" Round Pans, p. 166
- Tips 12, 17, 18, 21, 103, 104, 352, p. 112-115
- Flower Nail No. 7, p. 115
- Crystal-Look Tier Set, p. 158
- 9" Crystal-Look Separator Plates, p. 159
- 5" Crystal-Look Pillars, p. 160
- Kolor-Flo Fountain, p. 157
- Cake Dividing Set, p. 116
- Cake Circles, p. 154
- Dowel Rods, p. 159
- Chocolate Buttercream Icing Recipe, p. 82
- Rhapsody, p. 143
- Flowers

Instructions

1. Make 20 tip 104 and 15 tip 103 roses. Read Tiered Cake Assembly, p. 86. Ice 2-layer cakes smooth on cake circles and separator plates. To mark cream scrolls, using Cake Dividing Set, with toothpick, dot mark 8" cake sides into 8ths, 12" and 16" cakes into 12ths. Connect dots to form scrolls. Using these marks as a guide, mark top row (brown) scrolls. Pipe tip 12 (cream) scrolls and tip 18 (brown) scrolls.

2. Edge 8" cake top with tip 17, base with tip 18, 12" and 16" cake tops with tip 18 and bases with tip 21 shell borders.

3. Attach roses to cake sides and 9" separator plate with dots of icing. Trim roses with tip 352 leaves. At reception, assemble tiers with separator plates on pillars. Position Kolor-Flo Fountain on Crystal-Clear Separator Plate. Arrange fresh flowers on separator plates. Position Rhapsody atop 8" cake.

* Serving size is 2 square inches. By tradition, the top tier is saved for the couple's first wedding anniversary. We do not figure it in with the number of servings.

Wedding Drama

ELEGANT SIMPLICITY

This fresh-as-spring enchanter serves 200.

Decorating Needs

- **6" Square Pan, p. 120**
- **12", 16" Square Pans, p. 168, 174**
- **Tips 3, 8, 16, 18, 103, 104, 349, 352, p. 112-115**
- **Flower Nail No. 7, p. 115**
- **7," 9" Square Separator Plates, p. 159**
- **Expandable Pillars, p. 160**
- **15-Pc. Decorator Pattern Press, p. 116**
- **Edible Glitter, p. 130**
- **Flower Formers, p. 130**
- **Dowel Rods, p. 159**
- **Cake Circle, Boards, Tuk'N Ruffle, p. 154**
- **Promise, p. 142**
- **Fresh flowers**

Instructions

1. Make 100 tip 104 sweet peas, 45 tip 103 daisies (see p. 93) with tip 8 dot centers (pat center with edible glitter). Let daisies dry on flower formers.

Read Tiered Cake Assembly p. 86. Ice 2-layer square cakes smooth (6" and 12" atop cake circles and separator plate, 16" atop Tuk-N-Ruffle trimmed, foil-covered cake board).

2. Using Pattern Press, imprint small back-to-back "C" scrolls on 6" cake, larger "C" scrolls on 12" and 16" cake sides.

Outline small scrolls with tip 16, larger scrolls with tip 18. With toothpick, mark "V" scrolls on 12" cakes sides. Cover marks with tip 18. Pipe tip 18 elongated upright shells between "V" scrolls.

3. Edge cake tops (allow space for flowers) and bases with tip 18 shell borders. With toothpick, dot mark center of 6" and 16" cake sides. On 12" cake sides, mark two 4" and one 3" (center) garlands.

Pipe tip 18 elongated upright shells in corners and in between (at marks) on 6," 12" and 16" cake sides. Pipe tip 104 ruffle garlands on cake sides. Trim ruffles with tip 3 bead borders.

Edge separator plates with tip 16 scallops. Pipe tip 3 vines on cake sides. Attach flowers with dots of icing. Trim daisies with tip 352 leaves, sweet peas and vines with tip 349 leaves. Assemble tiers with separator plates on pillars at reception. Position Promise and arrange flowers.

Wedding Grace

HAPPY HEARTED

This true love cake serves 12.

Decorating Needs
- Double Tier Heart Pan, p. 182
- Tips 3, 16, 21, 104, 352, p. 112-115
- Flower Nail No. 7, p. 115

Instructions

1. Make 3 tip 104 roses and 10 tip 104 sweet peas. Ice cake smooth; top "tier" pink, bottom "tier" white. With toothpick, dot mark 2½" intervals on cake sides. Pipe tip 21 upright shells on cake sides at marks.
Edge base with tip 21 tail-to-tail pairs of shells. Trim centers with tip 16 rosettes.

2. Pipe tip 16 zigzag scallops on cake sides. Pipe tip 21 shells on cake top. Edge "tiered" heart top and base with tip 16 shell borders.

3. Trim top border with tip 3 dots. Print tip 3 message on cake top. Attach flowers to cake top and trim with tip 352 leaves.

For more ways to use DOUBLE TIER HEART PAN see Pan Index p. 192.

MARBELOUS MARBLE CHEESECAKE

Delectable! Serves 24.

Decorating Needs
- 9" Springform Pan, p. 170
- Tip 16, p. 112
- Candy Melts™ Brand Confectionery Coating, p. 120
- Cake Dividing Set, p. 116
- Marble Cheesecake Recipe, p. 95

Instructions

1. Make 24 cut-out Candy Melts™ 2½" high triangles 1½" wide. See p. 95 for how to make.

2. Prepare Marble Cheesecake Recipe on page 95. After adding chocolate mixture, use knife to swirl chocolate through cheese-cake in zigzag motion. Refrigerate several hours until firm.

3. When cake is firm, release from springform pan. Using Cake Dividing Set, with toothpick, dot mark cake top into 12ths. Position six triangles in center. With sweetened, whipped cream cheese, pipe tip 16 rows of shells and scrolls on cake top. Edge cake base with tip 16 shell border. Push candy triangles into cake top and sides.

Birds Of A Feather Still Happy Together

POULTRY IN MOTION
This loving pair serves 39.

Decorating Needs
- 12" x 18" Sheet Pan, p. 165, 169, 176
- Bowling Pin Pan Set, p. 185
- Tips 4, 8, 12, 17, 18, p. 112
- Dowel Rods, p. 159
- Cake Boards, p. 154
- Pound or firm-textured cake batter for Bowling Pin Pan

Instructions
1. Ice sheet cake smooth. Place half bowling pin pound cakes on cake boards cut to fit. Cut and position dowel rods in sheet cake where birds will go. Position cakes on sheet cake.

2. With toothpick, mark facial features, wings and feet on cakes. Outline heads, bodies, wings and smiles with tip 4 strings. Pipe in tip 12 beaks and feet (smooth and shape with fingertip dipped in cornstarch).

3. Cover birds with tip 17 stars. Pipe tip 8 dot eyes and cheeks (flatten with fingertip dipped in cornstarch). Pipe tip 8 string brows and feather plumes. Add tip 4 dot pupils, string lashes and bow. Print tip 4 message. Edge cake top and base with tip 18 shell border.

For more ways to use 12" x 18" SHEET PAN & BOWLING PIN PAN SET see Pan Index p. 192

The Tender Touch—That Means So Much

LOVE TRIANGLES
Pretty petal tiers will serve 38.

Decorating Needs
- 9", 12" Petal Pans, p. 169, 174
- Tips 3, 16, 17, 47, 102, 224, 225, 347, p. 112-115
- Flower Nail No. 7, p. 115
- Cake Circles, p. 154
- Dowel Rods, p. 159
- Petite Anniversary, p. 149

Instructions
1. Make 35 tip 225, 80 tip 224 drop flowers with tip 3 dot centers and 5 tip 102 roses. Ice 2-layer petal cakes smooth (9" on cake circle cut to fit). Position dowel rods in 12" cake where 9" cake will go. Position 9" cake.

2. With toothpick, mark 3" triangles on cake sides. Pipe tip 3 latticework on cake sides. Outline latticework with tip 47 smooth stripes.

3. Edge cake tops with tip 16, bases with tip 17 shell borders. Position Petite Anniversary atop 9" cake. Attach flowers to cake top, Petite Anniversary and sides with dots of icing. Trim flowers with tip 347 leaves.

For more helpful hints, review Decorating Guide p. 80.

For more ways to use 9" SPRINGFORM PAN see Pan Index p. 192.

For more ways to use 9", 12" PETAL PANS see Pan Index p. 192

33

RUFFLED GO-ROUND

This pretty attention-getter serves 24.

Decorating Needs
- 10" Round Pans, p. 165, 166, 177
- Tips 2B, 3, 9, 18, 22, 127, 131, 352, p. 112-115
- Cake Dividing Set, p. 116
- Petite Dainty Charm, p. 151

Instructions

1. Make 35 tip 131 drop flowers with tip 3 dot centers. Ice 2-layer round cake smooth. Using Cake Dividing Set, with toothpick, dot mark cake sides into 8ths. Pipe tip 2B ribbed stripes on cake sides.

2. Edge cake top with tip 22, base with tip 18 shell borders. Pipe tip 127 ruffle border on cake top (rests slightly on shell border). Trim sides with tip 104 ruffle swags.

3. Edge top ruffle with tip 9 and side ruffles with tip 3 beadwork borders. Write tip 3 message on cake top. Attach flowers to cake top and sides with dots of icing and trim with tip 352 leaves. Position Petite Dainty Charm.

For more ways to use 10" ROUND PANS see Pan Index p. 192

GLORIFIED SANDWICH LOAF

This layered lovely will serve 12.

Decorating Needs
- Loaf Pan, p. 165, 171
- Tips 21, 789, p. 112-115
- Cake Board, p. 154
- Fancy Foil Wrap, p. 155
- Yeast dough recipe (optional), three 8 oz. cream cheese, 2 cups each ham, chicken, and egg salad, 2 Tablespoons unflavored gelatin, sliced carrots, green onions, black olives and pimento drained.

Instructions

1. Bake bread according to recipe directions. Let cool. With serrated knife, remove crusts. Slice bread lengthwise into four equal parts (push toothpicks into sides as cutting guide). Butter each slice, both sides.

2. Place slice of bread on foil-covered cake board or serving plate. Spread with egg salad. Top with bread slice and spread with ham. Add bread and spread with chicken. Top with bread.

3. With softened cream cheese ice top and sides with tip 789. Smooth with spatula. With soft cream cheese, edge top with tip 21 reverse shell cream cheese border, base with tip 21 cream cheese shell borders. (Note: Small amount of milk may need to be added to achieve decorating consistency.) With knife, cut out carrot flowers and onion leaves. Slice olive and pimento petals. Mix 2 packages plain gelatin with ½ cup water. Let set. Heat over very low heat until gelatin is dissolved.

Cool until consistency of heavy cream. Dip vegetable garnishes into glaze and arrange flowers on top and sides. Place on cake rack over cookie sheet and pour on glaze. Remove from rack and refrigerate.

For more ways to use LOAF PAN see Pan Index p. 192

34

For more ways to use
ROUND MINI-TIER SET
see Pan Index p. 192.

ROMANTIC WELL WISHER

Lovely and so impressive. Serves 12.

Decorating Needs
- **Round Mini-Tier Set, p. 175**
- **Tips 16, 18, 104, 352, p. 112-115**
- **Flower Nail No. 7, p. 115**
- **Wishing Well, p. 152**

Instructions

1. Make 20 tip 104 roses and 55 tip 104 sweet peas. Ice one-layer cakes smooth (5" and 6½" on cake circles atop separator plates).

2. Edge 5" and 6½" cake tops and bases with tip 16 and 8" cake top and base with tip 18 shell borders. Pipe tip 104 rows of ruffles on 5" and 8" cake sides.

3. Assemble cake tiers with separator plates on pillars. Attach flowers to cake tops, sides and Wishing Well with dots of icing.

Trim flowers with tip 352 leaves. Position Wishing Well on cake top.

For more helpful hints, review Decorating Guide p. 80.

DAINTY DELIGHTS

Make dozens of these bite-size beauties.

Decorating Needs
- **Madeleine Pan, p. 170**
- **Tip 1, 3, 225, 352, p. 112-115**
- **CookieMaker Cookie Dips Candy Wafers, Icing Mix, p. 108**
- **Candy Wafer and Fondant Mix, p. 120**
- **Chopped nuts**

Instructions

1. Follow madeleine recipe on pan label. Bake and cool. Make mint patties following recipe on container. Make desired amount of tip 225 drop flowers with tip 3 dot centers.

2. Dip half or whole madeleines into melted Cookie Dips. Garnish with chopped nuts or tip 1 melted Cookie Dips drizzle. Fill two madeleines with icing or melted Cookie Dips and sandwich together.

3. With melted Cookie Dips, pipe tip 1 strings, dots, scallop designs or mint patties. Attach flowers to patties with dots of icing. Trim with tip 352 leaves.

For more ways to use
MADELEINE PAN
see Pan Index p. 192.

The Loving Touch That Means So Much

THE STORK ARRIVES! *Home sweet home serves 12.*

Decorating Needs

- *Holiday House Kit, p. 181*
- *Tips 1, 2B, 3, 4, 16, 47, 104, 224, 233, 349, p. 112-115*
- *Cookie Maker Gingerbread Cookie Cutters, p. 110*
- *Rectangle Cake Board, p. 154*
- *Fancy Foil Wrap, p. 155*
- *Decorator's Brush, p. 116*
- *Mama Stork, p. 132*
- *Dainty Bassinette, p. 132*
- *Royal Icing Recipe, p. 83*
- *Wafer cookies, roll candies*

Instructions

1. Make 25 tip 224 drop flowers with tip 4 dot centers. Out of cookie dough, cut baby with small cutter. Bake and cool. With art brush, "paint" face and dress. Add tip 1 facial features, hair and dress details. Ice 7" x 9" foil-covered cake board; pat area smooth and pat grass with spatula for grassy effect.

Outline windows and door with tip 4 strings. Pipe tip 47 smooth stripe "Tudor" trim and side-by-side smooth stripe door with tip 4 dot doorknob.

2. Position cake on cake board atop serving tray for support. Cover sides of house and windows with tip 16 stars.

Pipe tip 104 rows of ruffle roof shingles (work up from bottom). Add tip 2B smooth stripe eaves.

3. Pipe tip 233 blades of grass at base of house. Attach flowers, candies and cookie shutters with icing. Trim flowers with tip 349 leaves. Print tip 4 message.

For chimney: cut two cookie ends at 45° angles. Attach four cookies together with royal icing. Let dry. Attach to roof with royal icing. Position Mama Stork on chimney. Position Dainty Bassinette and cookie baby beside cake.

For more ways to use HOLIDAY HOUSE KIT see Pan Index p. 192.

IN FOR LOTS OF CHANGES *Serves 24.*

Decorating Needs

- *10" Round Pans, p. 165, 166, 177*
- *Petite Doll Pan, p. 183*
- *Tips 3, 6, 9, 17, 104, 125, p. 112-115*
- *Tuk-N-Ruffle, p. 154*
- *Cake Dividing Set, p. 116*
- *Cake Circle, p. 154*
- *Baby Rattles, p. 132*
- *Ice cream cone*

Instructions

1. Ice petite doll cake smooth on cake circle cut to fit. With toothpick, mark numbers and oz. measure lines. Cover marks with tip 3 strings. Ice 2-layer round cake smooth atop Tuk-N-Ruffle trimmed cake board. Using Cake Dividing Set, with toothpick, dot mark cake sides into eighths.

2. Edge cake base with tip 6 zigzag border. Trim zigzags with tip 6 dots. Edge cake top with tip 17 shell border. Add tip 125 ruffle border on cake top. Trim ruffle with tip 6 beads.

3. Pipe tip 9 stripe posts on cake sides. Add tip 9 dot tops. Pipe tip 3 string clothesline and bows. Pipe tip 104 ruffle diapers on cake sides. Add tip 3 dot clothespins. Print tip 3 message on cake top. Position "bottle" cake with ice cream cone cap and Baby Rattles on cake top. Edge bottle cake with tip 6 bead border.

For more ways to use 10" ROUND PANS see Pan Index p. 192.

THE BIG SHAKE UP!

Super rattle cake serves 12.

Decorating Needs
- *Guitar Pan, p. 185*
- *Tips 4, 10, 32, 126, p. 112-115*

Instructions

1. Ice cake smooth. Mound icing on cake top to resemble rattle (smooth and pat with spatula dipped in cornstarch). With toothpick, mark rattle handle and scallop design. Cover scallop marks with tip 4 string. Add tip 4 dots.

2. Edge rattle with tip 32 rope border. Pipe tip 32 rope handle. Print tip 4 message.

3. Pipe tip 126 ribbon bow. Add tip 10 dot knot (flatten with fingertip dipped in cornstarch). Edge cake base with tip 32 shell border.

For more helpful hints, review Decorating Guide p. 80.

IT'S BABY TIME...
DON'T GET RATTLED

For more ways to use
GUITAR PAN
see Pan Index p. 192

The Adorable Touch That Means So Much

JOYS MULTIPLY!

This bouncing baby bunny will serve 12.

Decorating Needs
- *Holiday Bunny Pan, p. 187*
- *Tips 2, 4, 12, 18, 125, p. 112-115*
- *Candy jelly rings*

Instructions

1. Ice message area on egg smooth. With toothpick, mark diaper and egg design (hint: for easier marking, lightly ice areas smooth).

Outline eyes, paws, diaper, leg, foot and egg design with tip 4 strings.

2. Fill in tip 4 eyes (flatten with fingertip dipped in cornstarch). Add tip 4 dot pupils and nose. Cover bunny with tip 18 stars. Add tip 2 string diaper pin.

3. Print tip 4 message on egg. Pipe tip 18 pull-out star tail. Pipe tip 125 bonnet ruffle. Add tip 125 ribbon bow and tip 12 ball knot (smooth knot with fingertip dipped in cornstarch).

For pacifier: Attach jelly rings together with icing and position on cake. (If toothpicks are used to secure, be sure to remove before serving.)

WELCOME LITTLE SKIPPER

For more ways to use
HOLIDAY BUNNY PAN
See Pan Index p. 192

decorate a
BLESSED DAY

BAT MITZVAH

GLOWING AND GROWING
This shining salute to her achievements serves 60.

Decorating Needs
- **15" Hexagon Pan**, p. 168
- **16" Square Pan**, p. 168
- **Petite Doll Pan Set**, p. 183
- **Tips 3, 4, 16, 18, 101, 104, 225, 349, 352**, p. 112-115
- **'85 Pattern Book**, p. 103 (Star Pattern)
- **Candle Tapers**

Instructions
1. Make 5 tip 16 and 150 tip 225 drop flowers with tip 3 dot centers. Push doll pick into petite doll cake and ice smooth on cake circle. Cover sleeves with tip 16 stars. Edge skirt hem (to make ruffle stand out) with tip 16 shell border. Pipe tip 101 sleeve ruffles and tip 104 skirt ruffles. Trim neck and skirt ruffles with tip 4 beads. Add tip 4 string belt, bows and flower stems. Attach small flowers to hand with dots of icing. Trim with tip 352 leaves.

2. Ice one-layer hexagon (on cake board cut to fit) and square cake smooth. Position hexagon cake atop square.

With toothpick, mark Star Pattern on hexagon cake top and 1" wide "v" stripes on cake sides. Outline star and "v" stripes with tip 4 strings. Cover with tip 18 stars.

3. Edge hexagon cake top and base with tip 18 and square cake top and base with tip 21 shell borders. Pipe tip 21 outline circles (encircle tapers) in square cake corners. Attach flowers to cake tops and sides and trim with tip 349 leaves. Push tapers into square cake and position girl on hexagon.

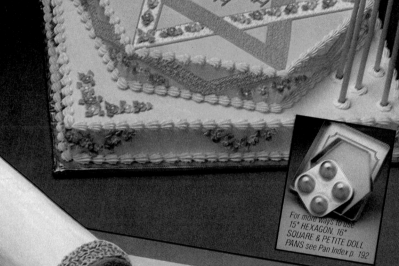

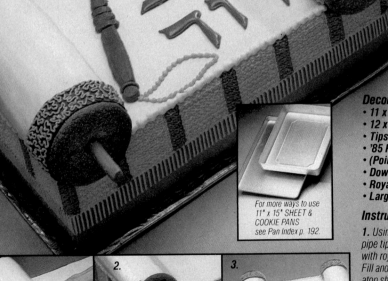

For more ways to use 15" HEXAGON, 16" SQUARE & PETITE DOLL PANS see Pan Index p. 192.

For more ways to use 11" x 15" SHEET & COOKIE PANS see Pan Index p. 192.

BAR MITZVAH
TRIBUTE TO MANHOOD
Ideal for a large celebration. Serves 68.

Decorating Needs
- **11 x 15" Sheet Pan**, p. 165, 169, 176
- **12 x 18" Cookie Pan**, p. 111, 173
- **Tips, 1D, 2, 4, 8, 12, 16, 18**, p. 112-115
- **'85 Pattern Book**, p. 103
- **(Pointer & Letter Patterns)**
- **Dowel Rods**, p. 159
- **Royal Icing Recipe**, p. 83
- **Large round molasses cookies, pretzel rods**

Instructions
1. Using Pointer and Letter Patterns, on waxed paper, using royal icing, pipe tip 8 pointer. Outline and fill in letters with tip 4. Ice four pretzel rods with royal icing. Ice 2-layer sheet cake smooth; top yellow, sides brown. Fill and ice two jelly roll cakes on cake boards to fit. Position "scroll" cakes atop sheet cake. Push sharpened dowel rods into jelly roll and sheet cakes.

2. With toothpick, mark 2" band on sheet cake sides. Outline with tip 4 strings. Cover with tip 16 stars. Add tip 4 string fringe. Cut holes in center of cookies. Attach cookies to ends of scroll cakes with icing. Push iced pretzel rods through center of cookies into scroll cakes.

3. Pipe tip 1D smooth stripe bands around scrolls. Trim with tip 2 cornelli lace. Edge cake base with tip 18 shell border; cake top with tip 8 bead border. Position Pointer and Letters. Pipe tip 4 bead chain.

For more ways to use
CROSS PAN
see Pan Index p. 192.

For more ways to use
ROCKIN' JUKE BOX PAN
see Pan Index p. 192.

COMMUNION
HEAVENLY GRACE

Symbolic cross cake will serve 12.

Decorating Needs
- Cross Pan, p. 186
- Cookie Sheet, p. 111, 173
- Tips 1, 3, 10, 16, 21, p. 112
- '85 Pattern Book, p. 103 (Chalice & Host Pattern)
- Decorator's Brush, p. 116
- Cookie Dough Recipe, p. 95
- Royal Icing Recipe, p. 83
- Uncooked spaghetti

Instructions

1. Using Chalice Pattern, out of cookie dough cut and shape Chalice and Host. (Hint: Roll dough out on cookie sheet, lay pattern on dough and cut out with knife.) Bake and cool. Outline and fill in cookie with tip 3 (smooth with dampened brush). Alternate way to make: On waxed paper, using royal icing, outline pattern with tip 3. Pipe in with tip 10 (smooth with dampened brush).

2. Ice cake smooth; top blue, sides white. Cover beveled sides with tip 1 cornelli lace. Edge top and sides with tip 16, base with tip 21 shell borders.

3. Position chalice cookie atop cake. Edge top with tip 3 bead and dot border. For rays: With art brush, paint seven pieces of uncooked spaghetti. Let dry. Push into cake. Print tip 3 message on chalice.

CONFIRMATION
HOLY BOOK

A special way to mark a memorable day! Serves 12.

Decorating Needs
- Rockin' Juke Box Pan, p. 185
- Tips 2, 4, 16, 18, 46, 48, p. 112-114
- '85 Pattern Book, p. 103 (Stained Glass & Book Pattern)
- Piping Gel, p. 131
- Ribbon

Instructions

1. Ice cake smooth: top white, sides brown. With toothpick, mark Stained Glass and Book Pattern on cake top.

With spatula mound icing on book area (smooth and pat with spatula dipped in cornstarch to resemble open book).

2. Outline window and book with tip 4 strings. Fill in window with tip 4 tinted piping gel (smooth with spatula). Pipe tip 46 smooth stripe book cover and tip 48 ribbed stripe book pages.

3. Trim page corners with tip 2 cornelli lace. Cover background area on cake top with tip 16 stars. Edge cake base with 18 shell border. Print tip 2 message. Position ribbon bookmark.

39

New Year.
New beginnings. New resolutions.
To make it better.
To turn a new leaf.
To try something special
for those you care about.
For bowl games…gettogethers…
cozy moments in front of a fire.
January.
It's the perfect month
to bake and decorate!

For more ways to use
10" TART PAN
see Pan Index p. 192.

For more ways to use
EGG PAN SET
see Pan Index p. 192.

A.

B.

C.

A. PARTY PIGSKIN

The crowd will cheer this dessert! Serves 12.

Decorating Needs
- Egg Pan Set, p. 186
- Tips 4, 17, 47, p. 112-115
- Cake Circle, p. 154
- Pound or firm-textured cake batter

Instructions

1. Slice bottom of cake so cake is level. Place cake on cake circle, cut to fit. With toothpick, mark rings and laces on cake. Cover marks with tip 4 strings.

2. Cover cake with tip 17 stars. Pipe tip 47 smooth stripe laces. Add tip 4 outline around laces.

**For more helpful hints, review
Decorating Guide, p.80.**

B. CHEERFUL QUICHE

Real men and women will love this! Serves 12.

Decorating Needs
- 10" Tart Pan, p. 172
- Tip 16, p. 112
- Pastry for single pie crust, quiche recipe, sliced egg, cherry tomatoes, green pepper, cheese spread

Instructions

1. Prepare pastry for single crust. Place in pan. Pour in quiche. Bake and cool according to recipe directions.

2. Place slice of egg in center of quiche. Using cheese spread, pipe tip 16 "rays" around "sun."

3. Place sliced cherry tomatoes around edge of quiche to represent flowers. Trim with green pepper stems and leaves.

C. HELMET HUDDLE

An exciting treat for each guest!

Decorating Needs
- Mini Football Helmet Pan, p. 178
- Tips 3, 9, 13, 16, p. 112
- Cake Circles, p. 154
- Decorator's Brush, p. 116

Instructions

1. Cut cake circles to fit cakes, so you can serve individually with ease. With toothpick, mark individual designs on cakes. (Hint: For easier marking, lightly ice cakes.) Outline designs with tip 3 strings.

2. Cover large areas on helmets with tip 16 stars, small areas with tip 13 stars.

Pipe tip 16 stripe helmet trims on A & B.

Pipe tip 9 chin guards and circles. Smooth with dampened brush.

Happy New Year

1986

RING IN THE NEW

A sweet way to greet the New Year! Serves 12.

Decorating Needs
- **Treeliteful Pan, p. 181**
- **Tips 3, 17, 21, 131, 224, 352, p. 112-115**
- **Tiny Toddler, p. 132**

Instructions

1. Make 10 tip 224 and 2 tip 131 flowers with tip 3 centers.

2. Ice cake smooth.

With toothpick, mark bell and clapper on cake top. Outline bell with tip 17. Cover clapper with tip 17 white stars, underpart of bell with tip 17 brown stars. Add tip 17 scrolls and tip 21 star rim with tip 3 dot centers. Print tip 3 message on clapper.

3. Attach flowers to bell and clapper with dots of icing. Trim with tip 352 leaves. Edge cake base with tip 21 shell border. Cut out a 2" x 4" paper "banner." Print ink message. Attach "banner" to Tiny Toddler with dots of icing. Position Tiny Toddler on cake top.

For more ways to use TREELITEFUL PAN, see Pan Index p. 192.

The Adorable Touch That Means So Much

BEVELED BEAUTY

Something out of the ordinary for 30 guests.

Decorating Needs
- **10" & 14" Bevel Pans, p. 175**
- **10" x 3" Round Pan, p. 167, 176**
- **Tips 3, 16, 18, 21, 104, 131, 352, p. 112-115**
- **Flower Nail #7, p. 115**
- **Cake Dividing Set, p. 116**
- **Swirls, p. 152**

Instructions

1. Make 60 tip 131 drop flowers with tip 3 centers and 12 tip 104 sweet peas and 4 roses.

2. Ice cake smooth.

Using cake dividing set, with toothpick, mark bevel cakes into 16ths. Pipe tip 21 upright shells where marks are. Edge 10" bevel cake top and bottom and 10" round cake bottom with tip 16 shell border. Pipe tip 3 string garlands between upright shells on 10" round cake, double garlands on 14" bevel cake. With toothpick, mark second row of garlands between garlands on first row on 10" round cake. Cover marks with tip 3 strings.

3. Position Swirls on cake top. Attach flowers to cake top and sides with dots of icing. Trim with tip 352 leaves. Edge cake base with tip 18 shell border.

For more ways to use BEVEL PAN SET and 10" x 3" ROUND PAN, see Pan Index p. 192.

Whistling winds.
Shadowed sunlight.
Crackling ice
on a frozen pond.
Winter's place soon to fade.
Valentines sent to a distant shore.
A loving thought to share.
A special treat to show you care.
February.
It's the perfect month
to bake and decorate!

For more ways to use
COOKIE SHEET
see Pan Index p. 192.

LOVE NOTES

Each serves 1.

Decorating Needs
- Sweetheart Cookie Greeting Card Kit, p. 164
- 12½ x 16½ Cookie Sheet, p. 111, 173
- Tips 4, 16, 224, 343. p. 112-115
- Candy Melts™ brand confectionery coating, p. 120
- Sprinkle Tops, p. 108
- Disposable Decorating Bags, p. 117

Instructions

1. Make 12 tip 224 drop flowers. Out of cookie dough, cut 4 heart-shaped cookies. Bake and cool. Ice 3 cookies smooth. Sprinkle sugar crystals.

2. Pipe tip 4 outlines, strings, dots and bead hearts and tip 16 reverse shells. Cut decorating bag and drizzle melted confectionery coating over cookies.

3. Attach flowers and trim with tip 349 leaves. Write tip 4 message. Place cookies in boxes.

The Loving Touch That Means So Much

HEARTS GO ROUND

A luscious carousel for 24.

Decorating Needs
- 10" Round Pans, p. 165, 166, 177
- Tips 16, 18, 21, p. 112-115
- '85 Pattern Book, p. 103 (Mini Heart Pattern)
- Candy Melts™ Brand Confectionery Coating, p. 120
- Hearts I Candy Mold, p. 124
- Cake Dividing Set, p. 116
- Maraschino cherries, candy hearts

Instructions

1. Using Mini Heart Pattern, cut out 10 Candy Melts™ hearts. Cut them in half. Mold 8 hearts out of Candy Melts.™ See p. 95 for techniques.

2. With serrated knife, torte one chocolate cake and one cherry cake into two layers each. When filling and stacking layers, alternate colors.

Ice cake smooth. Using Cake Dividing Set, with toothpick, dot mark cake top and sides into eighths.

Pipe tip 18 elongated shells and zigzags and tip 21 rosettes on cake top. Pipe tip 18 elongated shells and stars on cake side. Edge cake top with tip 16 shell border.

3. Edge cake base with tip 32 shell border. Position cut-out hearts at cake base. Position cherries and cherry "leaves" on cake top center and cake base, and candy hearts atop rosettes.

For more ways to use
10" ROUND PAN
see Pan Index p. 192.

42

TWO HEARTS AS ONE

A cake they'll truly love! Serves 12.

Decorating Needs
- **Double Heart Pan, p. 182**
- **Tips 3, 9, 16, 17, 104, 352, p. 112-115**
- **Flower Nail No. 7, p. 115**
- **Candy Wafer and Fondant Mix, p. 120**

Instructions

1. Make 3 tip 104 roses and 3 sweet peas.

2. Make poured fondant, using recipe on package. Cover small heart with fondant. Ice cake sides smooth. Edge large cake top border with tip 16 shell border. Add 3 rows of tip 104 ruffles. Edge small heart with tip 17 shell border.

3. Edge cake base with tip 9 heart bead border.

Position flowers on cake top. Trim with tip 352 leaves.

Write tip 3 message.

For more ways to use
DOUBLE HEART PAN
see Pan Index p. 192

VICTORIAN HEART

An old-fashioned valentine for 16.

Decorating Needs
- **12" Heart Pan, p. 175**
- **Tips 4, 5, 10, 104, 352, p. 112-115**
- **'85 Pattern Book, p. 103 (Sweetheart Pattern)**

Instructions

1. Make 5 tip 104 roses and 10 sweet peas. Ice one-layer cake smooth. With toothpick, mark Sweetheart Pattern on cake top. Ice inner heart.

2. Cover outlines around heart with tip 5 beads, scallops with tip 5 strings; pipe tip 5 elongated beads and dots.

3. Print tip 4 message.

Edge cake top with tip 10 bead border, bottom with tip 10 dot and bead border

Trim with tip 352 leaves.

For more ways to use
12" HEART PAN
see Pan Index p. 192

RUFFLES AND ROSES

Perfect duo to show affection!
Serves 12.

Decorating Needs
- **Be Mine Heart Pan, p. 182**
- Tips 2, 3, 17, 21, 104, 127, 224, 352, p. 112-115
- **Flower Nail No. 7, p. 115**
- **Heart Charm, p. 140**

Instructions

1. Make 6 tip 104 roses, 12 sweet peas, and 6 tip 224 drop flowers with tip 2 centers.

Ice cake smooth.

2. Edge cake top with tip 17 shell border under ruffle. Add tip 127 ruffles.

Position Heart Charm on cake top. Write tip 3 message on Heart Charm.

Attach flowers to cake top with dots of icing. Trim with tip 352 leaves.

3. Trim cake top and cake base with tip 21 shell border. Add tip 21 rosettes at points.

For more ways to use
BE MINE HEART PAN
see Pan Index p. 192.

The Loving Touch That Means So Much

ENCHANTING CONFECTION

A lovely show of affection! Serves 20.

Decorating Needs
- **Heart Mini-Tier Set, p. 182**
- 10" Square Pan, 165, 168, 177
- Tips 16, 17, 103, 104, 352 p. 112-115
- **Flower Nail #9, p. 115**
- '85 Pattern Book, p. 103 (Heart Pattern)
- **Candy Melts™ brand** confectionery coating, p. 120
- **Cake Circles, p. 154**
- **Disposable Decorating Bags,** p. 117
- **Valentine Hearts, p. 140**

Instructions

1. Make 8 tip 104 roses and 8 tip 103 roses and 12 sweet peas.
Using Heart Pattern, make one cut-out Candy Melts™ heart. See p. 95. Cut it in half. Half-fill disposable decorating bag with melted Candy Melts™ (approx. ⅛") and drizzle Candy Melts™ heart halves with melted coating.

Ice two-layer 7½" heart and one-layer 10" square cakes smooth (7½" heart on cake circle cut to fit.)

2. With toothpick, mark Heart Pattern on 10-in. cake top. Cover with tip 16 stars. Edge heart with tip 17 shell and tip 103 ribbon border.

With toothpick, lightly mark 1½-in. "C" scrolls on 10-in cake top. Cover marks with tip 17. Add tip 17 elongated shells between scrolls.

Attach separator plate to pillars and position 7½ in. heart cake on top.

3. Edge each cake top with tip 17 shells. Add tip 16 shell and tip 103 ribbon border to 10" cake base.

With toothpick, dot mark 2 in. garlands on sides of each cake. Cover marks with tip 103 ribbon drapes (double drapes on 10" cake).

Attach roses and sweet peas to cakes with dots of icing. Pipe tip 352 leaves. Push Valentine Hearts picks into center of top tier cake. Position candy heart halves on cake top.

For more ways to use
HEART MINI-TIER SET and
10" SQUARE PAN
see Pan Index p. 192.

PRESIDENTS' DAY
PRESIDENT'S PASTRY

In February we honor our two great presidents, Washington and Lincoln with a special holiday. Mark the day with this big favorite! Serves 12.

Decorating Needs
- 12" x 18" Cookie Pan, p. 111, 173
- Tips 18, 352, p. 112-115
- Maraschino cherries, jelly roll cake recipe and cherry filling, chopped nuts

Instructions

1. Follow jelly roll cake recipe on cookie pan label or use your favorite recipe for a 12" x 18" pan. Cool according to directions. Spread cherry filling over cake, leaving a 1" edge, and roll up.

2. Pipe tip 18 elongated zigzag bark on cake.

Pipe tip 18 stripe and rosettes on cake top.

3. Trim rosettes with tip 352 leaves. Place Maraschino cherries on rosettes. Sprinkle cake top with chopped nuts.

For more ways to use COOKIE PAN see Pan Index p. 192.

MARDI GRAS
KING OF THE MARDI GRAS

A royal treat for your Mardi gras festivities. Serves 17.

Decorating Needs
- Panda Pan, p. 187
- Egg Minicake Pan, p. 186
- Tips 1A, 2, 4, 4B, 16, 17, 18, p. 112-115
- '85 Pattern Book, p. 103 (Mask/Mustache Pattern)
- Decorator's Brush, p. 116
- Royal Crown, p. 140
- Straw, large jelly drop, pound or firm-textured cake batter

Instructions

1. Allow cake to cool completely in back half of pan (at least 4 hours). With toothpick, mark Mask and Mustache Pattern on face. Cover marks with tip 4 strings. Add tip 4 lips, nose, and detail outlines to body. Fill in eyes and mouth with tip 4. (Smooth with dampened brush.)

2. Cover face, hands, pants, stockings, shoe and buckles with tip 16 stars, robe with tip 17. Pipe tip 18 zigzag collar. Pipe again. Pipe tip 1A ermine; add tip 4 outline ermine trim and tip 4 dots buttons on pants.

Pipe tip 4B elongated shells hair and curls, top curls with tip 17.

3. Push feet into place. Push jelly drop into straw to assemble scepter. Add tip 2 outline and dot "jewels" to jelly drop. Push straw through hand.

For more ways to use PANDA and EGG MINICAKE PANS see Pan Index p. 192.

45

Collars turned
against the icy blast.
Melting snow swells
a silver-cold stream.
Naked branches reach for the sun.
The earth awaits
the promise of spring.
The boistrous sounds
of a Green Parade.
March.
It's the perfect month
to bake and decorate.

For more ways to use
WONDER MOLD PAN
see Pan Index p. 192.

St. Joseph's Day

LILIES AND THE STAFF

A symbolic tribute to a revered saint. Serves 12.

Decorating Needs
- **Wonder Mold Pan p. 183**
- **Tips 4, 12, 14, 18, 65, 349, 352, p. 112-115**
- **'85 Pattern Book, p. 103 (Staff pattern)**
- **Cake Dividing Set p. 116**
- **Lily Nail Set, p. 115**
- **Shining Cross, p. 134**
- **Stamens, p. 130**

Instructions

1. Make 18 tip 68 & 14 lilies (p. 93). Ice cake smooth. Using Cake Dividing Set, divide cake in six sections. With toothpick mark Staff Pattern and vines design.

2. Outline staff design with tip 12 (smooth with fingertip dipped in cornstarch). Outline vines with tip 4. Add tip 349 leaves to vines. Add Shining Cross.

3. Edge base with tip 18 shell border. Push Shining Cross in cake top. Attach lilies with dots of icing and trim with tip 352 leaves.

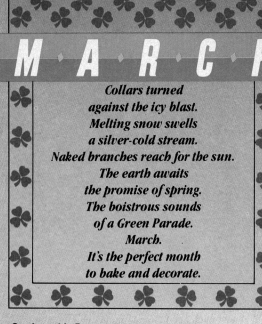

For more ways to use
GARFIELD STAND-UP
PAN SET
see Pan Index p. 192.

Teenager's Day

A MESSAGE TO TEENAGERS FROM GARFIELD:

"Teens and Garfield — they're exasperating...and wonderful!" Celebrate Teenager's Day, March 21, with their own decorated cake. Serves 12.

Decorating Needs
- **Garfield Stand-Up Cake Pan Set, p. 193**
- **Tips 4, 16, 18, p. 112**
- **Plastic straws, construction paper, firm-textured cake batter**

Instructions

1. Make construction paper pennant (3½" triangle, and tape it to straw. Allow pound cake or firm-textured cake to cool completely in back of pan (at least 4 hours). Insert two plastic straws down through head and body (see pan instructions). Ice face area smooth. Position face mask. Outline face mask, ears, hands, paws, stripes and tail with tip 4 strings.

2. Cover body with tip 18 stars. Fill in inside ears, stripes and cover paws with tip 16 zigzag. Pipe tip 16 elongated zigzag tail.

3. Push pennant into cake at paw.

Garfield © 1978 United Features Syndicate, Inc.

SHAMROCK SENSATION!
This beautiful cake is wearin' the green. Serves 23.

Decorating Needs
- 12" Square Pan p. 165, 168, 177
- Heart Minicake Pan p. 182
- Tips 2A, 4, 16, 21 p. 112
- '85 Pattern Book p. 103 (Horseshoe Pattern)
- Cake Circles p. 154

Instructions
1. Ice one-layer cake and heart mini cakes (on cake circles cut to fit) smooth. For square cake: With toothpick mark Horseshoe Pattern on cake top. Outline horseshoe with tip 4 strings. Cover horseshoe with tip 16 stars. Print tip 4 message. Add tip 4 outline horseshoe indentations.

2. Pipe in stem with tip 2A (smooth with fingertip dipped in cornstarch).

3. For shamrock: Position heart cakes on square cake to form shamrock. Edge heart tops and bases with tip 16 shell borders. Edge square cake top and base with tip 21 shell borders.

The Personal Touch That Means So Much

TOP 'O THE MORNIN' TOPPER
Sure, and it's darlin' enough for a leprechaun! Serves 24.

Decorating Needs
- 6'', 8'' Round Pans p. 165, 166, 177
- '85 Pattern Book p. 103 (Shamrock Pattern)
- Mini Shamrock Pan p. 184
- Tips 1A, 4, 8, 16, 17, 789 p. 112, 114
- Lucky Leprechaun p. 140
- Shamrock Picks p. 140
- Leprechaun Picks p. 140
- Dowel Rods p. 159
- Cake Circles p. 154
- 1¼'' thick ribbon, 18'' long

Instructions
1. For minicakes: Ice shamrock cake sides smooth (on cake circles cut to fit and covered with foil). Cover pan indentations with tip 4 strings. Fill in with tip 16 stars. Pipe tip 4 bead heart shamrocks and outline stems. Edge cake base with 16 star borders.

2. For Hat: Make brim by doubling 2 cake circles to build up thickness and taping together. Ice cake circles smooth. Cover edge with ribbon. Position one layer 6'' cake atop 2-layer 8'' cake. Push 2 dowel rods through both cakes (see page 86). With tip 789 ice cakes smooth. Build up icing with tip 1A. Smooth and shape between layers with fingertips dipped in cornstarch. Pipe tip 789 smooth stripe hatband. With toothpick, mark Shamrock Pattern on cake side. Fill in with tip 16 stars. Pipe tip 4 bead heart shamrocks with tip 4 outline stems, randomly, on cake sides.

3. Edge top of hat with tip 17 shell border, base with tip 8 bead border. Print tip 4 message on cake and brim. Position Lucky Leprechaun. Push picks in shamrock minicakes.

47

A·P·R·I·L

Rainy days.
Thunderclaps and bumbershoots,
rainbow colored puddles.
Painted eggs hidden 'midst
awakening fields.
Children looking, laughing.
Families gathering,
rejoicing and renewing.
April.
It's the glorious month
to bake and decorate.

GREAT EGGS™! SUGAR FANTASY

A charming centerpiece.

Decorating Needs
• *Great Eggs Kit, p. 186*
• *Tips 3, 4, 6, 224, 349, p. 112-115*
• *Royal Icing recipe, p. 83*
• *1½ yds. ½" ribbon*

Instructions

1. Make ribbon bow. With royal icing make 28 tip 224 flowers with tip 3 centers. Following Great Eggs Kit instructions, hollow out large tinted sugar egg; use ½ of small egg for base. Secure large egg to base with royal icing. Mark scallop pattern with pencil on each side beginning 1" from open edge and 2" from closed edge, allowing 1" through center of scallop. Mark horizontal pattern allowing 1" between each line.

2. Cover all marks with tip 4 outlines beginning with scallops. Edge opening with double row tip 6 bead.

3. Attach flowers in center of scallops and on base with dots of icing. Trim with tip 349 leaves. Wrap ribbon down each side of large egg and around base; secure with royal icing. Position bow on top with royal icing.

Candy Egg instructions inside Great Eggs Kit.

LATTICE "EGG"ERTAIN YOU!

An Easter Egg Garden celebrates spring! Serves 12.

Decorating Needs
• *Happy Easter Egg Pan, p. 186*
• *Tips 3, 9, 16, 18, 224, 349, p. 112-115*

Instructions

1. Make 15 tip 224 drop flowers with tip 3 dot centers. Ice cake smooth; sides lavender, top green and lavender. With toothpick mark scallops and lattice designs. Outline message with tip 3. Fill in letters with tip 9 (smooth with fingertips dipped in cornstarch).

2. Pipe tip 3 lattice work design. Add tip 16 scallops. Pipe tip 16 zigzags. Edge cake top with tip 16, cake base with tip 18 shell borders.

3. Attach drop flowers with dots of icing and trim with tip 349 leaves.

For more helpful hints, review Decorating Guide p. 80.

For more ways to use HAPPY EASTER EGG PAN see Pan Index p. 192.

For more ways to use EGG PAN SET AND PETITE DOLL PAN see Pan Index p. 192.

'EARS A FUNNY BUNNY

He's bound to keep the party hoppin'.
Serves 14.

Decorating Needs
- **Egg Pan Set, p. 186**
- **Petite Doll Pan, p. 183**
- **Tips 2, 2B, 4, 6, 224, 349, p. 112-115**
- **Cake Circles, p. 154**
- **Plastic drinking straws, poster board, jelly bean, firm textured cake batter.**

Instructions

1. Make 30 tip 224 flowers with tip 3 centers. With poster board make 2 ears; tape toothpick at rear of each one. Allow pound cake or firm textured cake to cool completely (at least 4 hours). Position straws in egg cake where bunny will be placed.

For bunny: Ice bunny smooth on cake circle cut to fit. With toothpick, mark facial features. Outline with tip 2. Fill in eyes with tip 4, teeth with tip 2 (smooth with fingertips dipped in cornstarch).

2. For egg: Ice smooth and mark with toothpick, 1½" from edge, two circles and large scallop design allowing 1" through center of scallop. Mark ribbon design around each side and down center of egg. Outline circles and large scallops with tip 4. Cover side ribbon design with tip 2B ribbed stripes. Edge ribbon design and inside of circles with tip 2 scallops.

3. Position bunny cake on top of egg. Attach flowers with dots of icing. Trim with tip 349 leaves. Pipe 2B ribbon down front of egg and around bunny neck. Attach jelly bean with dot of icing. Push ears into cake just before serving.

The Jubilant Touch That Means So Much

SIR RABBIT

The rabbit who came to dinner. Serves 12.

Decorating Needs
- **Bunny Pan p. 187**
- **Tips 4, 6, 17, p. 112**
- **Plastic straws, brown poster board, uncooked spaghetti**

Instructions

1. For hat brim: Cut out 6" poster board circle; cut out center leaving 1½" to edge. Allow pound cake or firm textured cake to cool completely in back of pan (at least 4 hours). Trim ears at top and at sides. Insert 2 plastic straws down through ears, head and body. Ice cake smooth (shape hat with fingertip dipped in cornstarch). Cut poster board circle at one point and wrap around head pushing into cake to form brim. Tape at rear. With toothpick mark hat, shirt, jacket and tie. With tip 4 outline hat, facial features, outfit and paws.

2. Fill in eyes, nose, teeth and button on jacket with tip 6 icing (smooth with fingertip dipped in cornstarch). Cover hat, face and body with tip 17 stars; tail with tip 17 pull-out stars. Add tip 4 string monacle.

3. Push uncooked spaghetti into cake to make whiskers.

For more ways to use BUNNY PAN see Pan Index p. 192.

It's Spring! Alive with the promise of the new and the wonderful. Tulips, hyacinths and sunny-yellow jonquils. Nature is wearing her springtime frocks.

CROSS OF FLOWERS

Springtime flowers commemorate the Resurrection. Serves 16

Decorating Needs
• Cross Pan p. 186
• Tips 4, 16, 18, 131, 352 p. 112-115
• '85 Pattern Book, p. 103 (Diamond Pattern)

Instructions

1. Make 34 tip 131 drop flowers with tip 4 centers. Ice cake smooth. With toothpick, mark diamond pattern on cake top. Cover marks with tip 4 strings.

2. Edge cake top and sides with tip 16, base with tip 18 shell borders.

3. Pipe tip 4 outline stems on cake sides. Attach drop flowers with dots of icing. Add tip 352 leaves.

For more helpful hints, review Decorating Guide p. 80.

For more ways to use CROSS PAN see Pan Index p. 192.

For more ways to use EGG PAN SET see Pan Index p. 192.

ALMOND-BERRY EASTER EGG

A festive treat for family and friends. Serves 12

Decorating Needs
• Egg Pan Set p. 186
• Tip 16, 352 p. 112-115
• Dowel Rods p. 159
• Strawberries, almonds, pound cake or firm-textured cake batter.

Instructions

1. Cut and position dowel rods in bottom sides of cake.

2. With dots of icing arrange sliced almonds, slightly overlapping, in three tiers. Fill in at top with sliced strawberries, slightly overlapping, in two tiers.

3. Pipe tip 16 double shell around seam of cake. Add tip 352 leaves to strawberries.

CHERRY LOCKET
Meringue cake serves 12

Decorating Needs
- **9" Happiness Heart Pans, p. 182**
- **Tip 21 p. 114**
- **Chocolate Cherry Cake Recipe (see below)**
- **Meringue Recipe, p. 95**
- **1-16 oz. can Cherry Pie Filling**

Instructions
Cherry Cake Recipe
  2-layer packaged chocolate cake mix
  (pudding in the mix)
  ½ cup cherry juice
  8 oz. jar maraschino cherries, chopped
  ½ tsp. almond flavoring

1. Preheat oven to 350°. Grease and flour 2 Happiness Heart Pans. Prepare cake mix according to package directions substituting cherry juice for ½ cup of the water. Stir in cherries and flavoring. Pour batter into prepared pans. Bake at 350° for 25-30 minutes or until cake tests done with toothpick. Cool ten minutes in pan and release. Cool at least one hour before decorating. Fill 2-layer cake with thin layer of cherry pie filling. (Place on ovenproof plate.)

2. Ice cake smooth with meringue. With toothpick outline heart on top of cake. Outside edge of heart should be 2 inches from the edge. Fill in heart with cherry pie filling.

3. Pipe tip 21 shell border around cherry heart. Pipe tip 21 zigzags on cake sides. Bake at 500° on an ovenproof plate for 2-3 minutes or until lightly browned. Serve at room temperature, can be made up to 4 hours in advance.

For more ways to use 9"HAPPINESS HEART PAN see Pan Index p. 192

For more ways to use HOLIDAY BUNNY PAN see Pan Index p. 192

IT'S THE EASTER BUNNY!
Invite him to dinner for an Easter Fun-Day!
Serves 12

Decorating Needs
- **Holiday Bunny Pan p. 187**
- **Tips 4, 9, 17, 224, 352 p. 112-115**
- **Cake Circle p. 154**
- **Decorator Brush p. 116**
- **2 Plastic drinking straws, uncooked spaghetti, pound or firm-textured cake batter.**

Instructions
1. For whiskers: With brush dipped in paste icing color, paint six 6" pieces of uncooked spaghetti. Let dry. Make 10 tip 224 drop flowers with tip 4 dot centers. Allow pound or firm textured cake to cool completely in back of pan (at least 4 hours). Insert 2 plastic drinking straws down through head and body (see pan instructions). Ice egg area smooth. With toothpick mark egg design. Outline chick, facial features, ears, tie and body design with tip 4.

2. Pipe in chick and zigzag on egg with tip 9 (smooth with fingertip dipped in cornstarch). Pipe tip 4 dot eyes; outline and fill in beak with tip 4 (smooth with fingertip dipped in cornstarch). Cover egg shell with tip 4 zigzag, tip 17 stars. Fill in bunny eyes, nose, teeth with tip 9 (smooth with fingertip dipped in cornstarch). Cover bunny and tie with tip 17 stars; tail with tip 17 pull-out stars. Pipe tip 4 eyelashes. Trim tie with tip 4 dots.

3. Attach drop flowers with dots of icing; trim with tip 352 leaves.

51

*Bursting blossoms
trumpet the spring.
The warming days
coaxing the earth to splendor.
Fluttering birds
building their nests.
Mothers loved, cherished and honored.
Tiny hands clasping
a dandelion bouquet.
May.
It's the perfect month
to bake and decorate.*

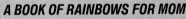

WE
LOVE YOU
SEW MUCH

SWEET TOMATO!

Especially for Mom! Serves 12.

Decorating Needs
• *Ball Pan p. 184*
• *Tips 3, 4, 12, 16 p. 112*
• *Cake Dividing Set p. 116*
• *Dowel Rod p. 159*
• *Cake Circles p. 154*
• *Royal Icing Recipe p. 83*
• *Pound or firm textured cake batter*

Instructions

1. Pipe 12 tip 12 royal icing pins on waxed paper and let dry. Allow pound cake or firm textured cake to cool completely. With knife slice off end so cake rests level (on foil covered cake circles cut to fit). Insert dowel rod through center of cake. Ice cake smooth. Using Cake Dividing Set, with toothpick mark ball into eighths. Mark rope design with toothpick. Coming down 3" from the top, mark leaf design with toothpick. (Mark tip of leaves to meet each rope design and then mark another leaf in between).

2. Cover rope design with tip 4 rope. With tip 4 outline leaves and fill in with tip 16 stars.

3. With royal icing pipe tip 12 stem. Print tip 3 message. Position pins randomly on cake.

*For more ways to use
BALL PAN
see Pan Index p. 192.*

WE LOVE YOU

*For more ways to use
BOOK PAN
see Pan Index p. 192.*

A BOOK OF RAINBOWS FOR MOM

She's the gold in your rainbow! Serves 12.

Decorating Needs
• *Book Pan p. 179*
• *Tips 4, 17, p. 112*
• *Decorating Comb p. 116*
• *'85 Pattern Book p. 103 (Rainbow Pattern)*

Instructions

1. Ice cake smooth; top white, sides orange. With decorating comb mark sides to resemble book pages. Position Rainbow Pattern and mark with toothpick. Outline pattern with tip 4.

2. Fill in rainbow, butterflies, letters and face with tip 17 stars. Cover hair with tip 17 side-by-side stripes. Outline tip 4 facial features and fill in eyes (smooth eyes with fingertips dipped in cornstarch).

3. Print tip 4 message. Edge cake top and base with tip 17 shell border.

MUMS FOR MOM

A beautiful bouquet. Serves 8.

Decorating Needs
- **6" Round Pans p. 166, 177.**
- **Tips 4, 6, 17, 45, 81, 352, 789 p. 112-115**
- **Flower Nail 7 p. 115**
- **Lollipop Sticks p. 121**
- **Royal Icing Recipe p. 83**
- **Gone Fishin' Signboard p. 138**
- **Brown sugar**

Instructions

1. With royal icing make 9 tip 6 and 81 chrysanthemums (see page 93). Let dry completely. Attach to lollipop sticks with dots of icing. Pipe tip 352 leaves on lollipop sticks. Print tip 4 message on Gone Fishin' Signboard.

2. Ice 2-layer cake smooth with tip 789. Edge cake top with tip 17 zigzag; base with tip 17 shell border. Wrap cake with tip 45 ribbon and bow.

3. Sprinkle cake top with granulated brown sugar. Push mums then Gone Fishin' Signboard well into cake.

**For more helpful hints,
review Decorating Guide , p. 80.**

For more ways to use
6" ROUND PAN
see Pan Index p. 192.

The Gentle Touch That Means So Much

Kentucky Derby Day

KENTUCKY DERBY PIE

It's a winner! Serves 8.

Decorating Needs
- **9" Pie Pan p. 170**
- **Tip 21, p. 112**
- **Unbaked pie shell**
- **Recipe for Kentucky Derby Dessert**

Instructions

Recipe:
4 eggs, 1 cup sugar, 1 cup light corn syrup
¼ cup butter or margarine, melted
2 tablespoons bourbon
¾ cup chopped pecans or walnuts
½ cup chocolate chips
1 (9 in) pie shell, unbaked
Stabilized whipped cream recipe, p. 82

1. Beat eggs and sugar together until well blended. Add corn syrup, butter and bourbon. Beat only to blend. Stir in chocolate chips and pecans. Pour into unbaked pie shell and bake at 425° for 10 minutes; reduce heat to 350° and continue baking about 30 minutes or until set in the middle. Allow to cool at room temperature before decorating.

2. With stabilized whipped cream pipe eight tip 21 elongated C motion shells; center with tip 21 rosette. Pipe tip 21 "C" motion shell border.

3. Place pecan on top of rosette.

For more ways to use
9" PIE PAN
see Pan Index p. 192.

J U N E

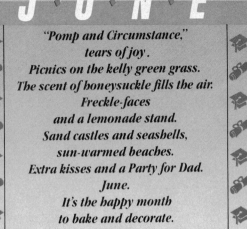

"Pomp and Circumstance,"
tears of joy.
Picnics on the kelly green grass.
The scent of honeysuckle fills the air.
Freckle-faces
and a lemonade stand.
Sand castles and seashells,
sun-warmed beaches.
Extra kisses and a Party for Dad.
June.
It's the happy month
to bake and decorate.

SMOOTH SAILING, DAD!

A delicious treat for the captain from his mate. Serves 12.

Decorating Needs
- Sailboat Pan p. 185
- Tips 3, 6, 9, 16, p. 112
- Decorator Brush p. 116

Instructions

1. Ice cake sides and background smooth. With toothpick, mark sun and clouds. Outline sun, clouds, birds and sailboat design with tip 3; dot birds with tip 3.

2. Fill in sails, cabin, boat sides and sun with tip 16 stars. Cover stripe on side of boat, and sail boom with tip 6 (smooth with dampened decorator brush). Cover mast and fill in cloud with tip 9; fill in windows with tip 3 (smooth with dampened decorator brush). Fluff waves with spatula.

3. Edge cake base with tip 16 shell border. Print tip 3 message.

For more ways to use
SAILBOAT PAN
see Pan Index p. 192.

The Caring Touch That Means So Much

DAD'S "CHEESE CAKE"

Treat him royally! Serves 24.

Decorating Needs
Treeliteful Pan p. 181
- Tips 4, 12, 16, p. 112
- Royal Crown p. 140

Instructions

1. Ice 2-layer cake smooth (place 2nd Treeliteful cake top side down). With toothpick mark facial features and randomly mark hole design.

2. Outline top edge, holes and facial features with tip 4. Fill in cheese holes with tip 12 and eyes with tip 4 (smooth with fingertip dipped in cornstarch).

3. Edge base with tip 16 star border. Position Royal Crown. Print tip 4 message.

For more ways to use
TREELITEFUL PAN
see Pan Index p. 192.

54

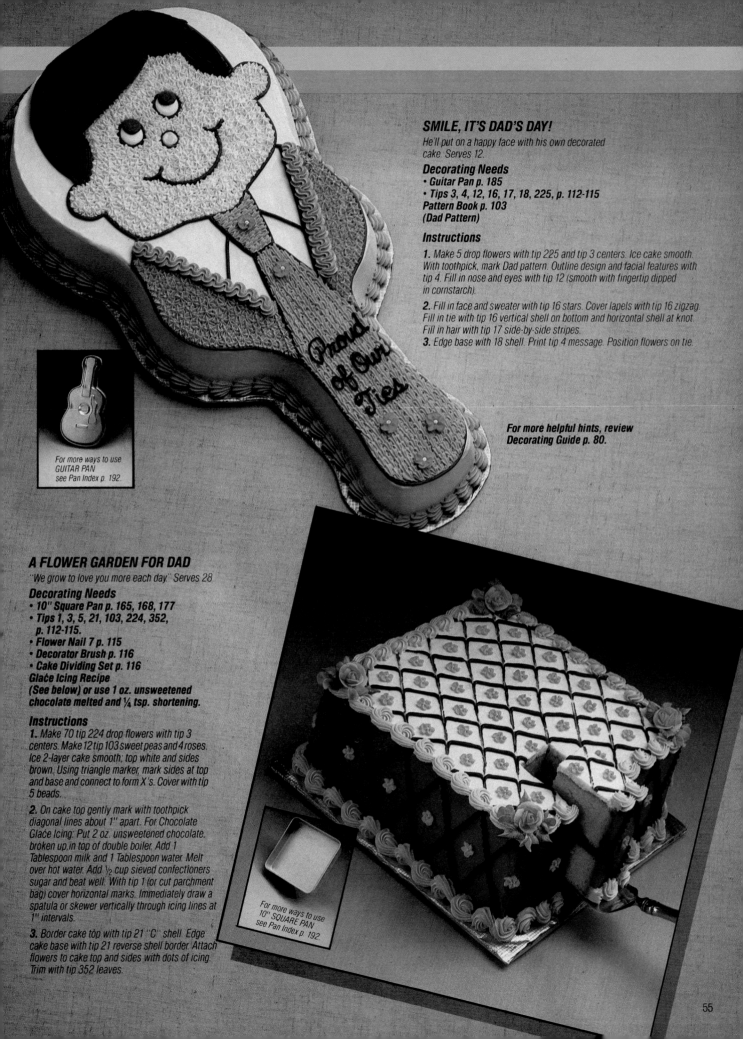

SMILE, IT'S DAD'S DAY!

He'll put on a happy face with his own decorated cake. Serves 12.

Decorating Needs
• Guitar Pan p. 185
• Tips 3, 4, 12, 16, 17, 18, 225, p. 112-115
Pattern Book p. 103
(Dad Pattern)

Instructions

1. Make 5 drop flowers with tip 225 and tip 3 centers. Ice cake smooth. With toothpick, mark Dad pattern. Outline design and facial features with tip 4. Fill in nose and eyes with tip 12 (smooth with fingertip dipped in cornstarch).

2. Fill in face and sweater with tip 16 stars. Cover lapels with tip 16 zigzag. Fill in tie with tip 16 vertical shell on bottom and horizontal shell at knot. Fill in hair with tip 17 side-by-side stripes.

3. Edge base with 18 shell. Print tip 4 message. Position flowers on tie.

For more ways to use
GUITAR PAN
see Pan Index p. 192.

**For more helpful hints, review
Decorating Guide p. 80.**

A FLOWER GARDEN FOR DAD

"We grow to love you more each day." Serves 28.

Decorating Needs
• 10" Square Pan p. 165, 168, 177
• Tips 1, 3, 5, 21, 103, 224, 352,
  p. 112-115.
• Flower Nail 7 p. 115
• Decorator Brush p. 116
• Cake Dividing Set p. 116
Glacé Icing Recipe
(See below) or use 1 oz. unsweetened
chocolate melted and ¼ tsp. shortening.

Instructions

1. Make 70 tip 224 drop flowers with tip 3 centers. Make 12 tip 103 sweet peas and 4 roses. Ice 2-layer cake smooth, top white and sides brown. Using triangle marker, mark sides at top and base and connect to form X's. Cover with tip 5 beads.

2. On cake top gently mark with toothpick diagonal lines about 1" apart. For Chocolate Glacé Icing: Put 2 oz. unsweetened chocolate, broken up, in top of double boiler. Add 1 Tablespoon milk and 1 Tablespoon water. Melt over hot water. Add ½ cup sieved confectioners sugar and beat well. With tip 1 (or cut parchment bag) cover horizontal marks. Immediately draw a spatula or skewer vertically through icing lines at 1" intervals.

3. Border cake top with tip 21 "C" shell. Edge cake base with tip 21 reverse shell border. Attach flowers to cake top and sides with dots of icing. Trim with tip 352 leaves.

For more ways to use
10" SQUARE PAN
see Pan Index p. 192.

55

*See, the fledgling bird
Leaves its nest to soar away
Upon out-stretched wings.*

THE KEY TO YOUR FUTURE
Serves 12.

Decorating Needs
- Trail Rider Pan p. 184
- Tips 3, 9, 16, 17, p. 112
- Pattern Book p. 103 (Key Pattern)
- 15-Pc. Pattern Press Set p. 116

Instructions

1. Ice cake smooth. With toothpick mark Key Pattern on cake top.

2. Outline design with tip 3. Fill in key indentations and hole with tip 9 (smooth with fingertip dipped in cornstarch). Cover with tip 16 star and outline hole with tip 16. Position pattern press at top of key and cover with tip 17 scroll.

3. Pipe 5 tip 17 stars to top of key. Print tip 3 message. Edge cake base with tip 16 star.

For more ways to use TRAIL RIDER PAN see Pan Index p. 192.

A LOVING CUP FILLED WITH LOVE!
Serves 12.

Decorating Needs
- **Number One Pan p. 188**
- **Tips 3, 4, 18, 21, 352 p. 112-115**
- **Pattern Book p. 103**
- **(Graduation Pattern)**
- **Glad Grad p. 133**

Instructions

1. Ice cake smooth. With toothpick mark pattern and then draw circle for laurel wreath. Outline loving cup with tip 4.

2. Fill in cup with tip 18 stars. Pipe tip 21 rope border at top of cup. Cover laurel wreath with tip 352 leaves building up from the bottom and tapering to one leaf at the top of each side.

3. Edge top border and base with 18 stars. Write tip 3 message. Position Glad Grad.

For more ways to use NUMBER ONE PAN see Pan Index p. 192

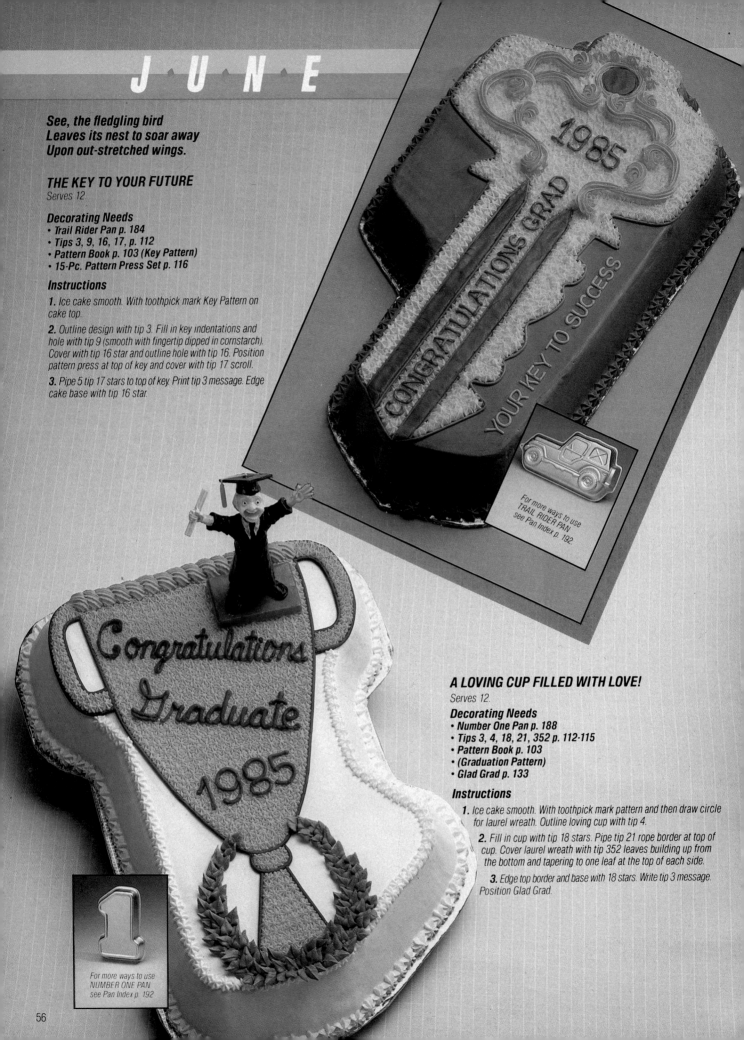

CONGRATULATIONS GRADUATE, YOU'RE FLYING HIGH!

Serves 12.

Decorating Needs
- **Up 'N Away Balloon Pan p. 179**
- **Tips 2, 4, 6, 7, 8, 12, 17, 18, p. 112**
- **Cathy™ Says p. 136**
- **Cookie Maker Heart Cookie Cutters p. 110**
- **Poster board**

Instructions

1. Ice cake smooth; sides white, top pink. Double outline each rope of balloon with tip 4; outline basket with tip 4. Cover outside line on balloon and message area with tip 7 rope border; inside lines with tip 6 rope border.

2. Cover balloon area with tip 17 stars. Mark large hearts on balloon (use 2" heart cutter as guide). Pipe tip 12 bead hearts: (flatten and smooth with fingertip dipped in cornstarch) trim with tip 4 bead hearts. Add tip 8 bead hearts to balloon. Position Cathy topper on cake and build up basket over lower portion of topper with tip 17 stars. Cover bottom of basket with tip 17 stars. Add tip 4 bead hearts to basket.

3. Make poster board hat and attach to Cathy with dots of icing. Edge cake base with tip 17 star border.

* © 1983 Universal Press Syndicate

For more ways to use UP 'N AWAY BALLOON PAN see Pan Index p. 192.

The Caring Touch That Means So Much

WE'RE "OWL" SO PROUD OF YOU!

For the wise hostess. Serves 12.

Decorating Needs
- **Frog Pan p. 187**
- **Tips 3, 4, 6, 13, 17 p. 112**
- **Pattern Book p. 103 (Owl Pattern)**

Instructions

1. Ice cake smooth. Position Owl Pattern and mark with toothpick.

2. Outline design with tip 4. Build up beak with tip 6 (smooth with fingertip dipped in cornstarch). Cover face, gown with tip 17 stars; build up wings, cap with tip 17 double star.

3. Pipe 13 string tassel with tip 4 dot. Print tip 3 message. Edge cake base with tip 17 shell border.

For more ways to use FROG PAN see Pan Index p. 192.

J·U·L·Y

Flags a'flying.
Bugles a'blaring.
Drums a'beating.
Fireworks boom in a burst of color.
It's the grandest gala of them all!
The day
when freedom came to stay.
When a great nation came into creation.
July.
It's the perfect month
to bake and decorate.

For more ways to use
10" ROUND PANS
see Pan Index p. 192.

*indicates trademark of
Warner Bros., Inc. © 1979.

HATS OFF FOR FREEDOM!
Serve 24 celebrating patriots with this chapeau.

Decorating Needs
- 10" Round Pans, p. 165, 166, 177
- Tips 3, 18, 789, p. 112-115
- Cake Circles, p. 154
- Star Cookie Cutters, p. 110
- Cookie dough recipe, p. 95
- Cookie icing recipe, p. 95
- Looney Tunes* Topper Set, p. 136
- Stars 'N Stripes, p. 141
- Ribbon; long, wide-diameter straws

Instructions
1. Out of cookie dough, cut 6 star cookies. Place the cookies on a rack over a drip pan. Pour the cookie icing over the cookies: Starting in the center of the cookie, work towards the edge with the spatula until the entire cookie is covered. Cover both sides. Let dry. Hold two 14" Cake Circles together and bind with ribbon. Position 2-layer cake on Cake Circles.

2. Pipe tip 789 hat band. Cover hat and rim (Cake Circles) with tip 18 stars.

3. Attach cookie stars to straws with dabs of icing. Push stars and Stars 'N Stripes into cake top. Position Looney Tunes Topper Set around rim. Print tip 3 message.

The Patriotic Touch That Means So Much

Frontier Day
FRONTIER EXPRESS Remember America's brave settlers this month with this adventure express that serves 12 modern pioneers!

Decorating Needs
- Little Locomotive Pan, p. 188
- Tips 1, 2, 3, 5, 11, 17, p. 112-115
- '85 Pattern Book (Cowboy Engineer Pattern), p. 103
- Royal Icing Recipe, p. 83
- Decorator's Brush, p. 116

Instructions
1. Outline and fill in Cowboy Engineer Pattern with Royal Icing (see p. 83). Let dry. Outline hat, face, kerchief, hand and arm with tip 2 strings. Add tip 1 eyes and mouth. Ice cake smooth, top background area blue, smoke area white, sides and bottom background area brown.

2. Outline engine, cab, wheels and smoke with tip 4 strings. Fill in cab windows and name plate with tip 4. Smooth with dampened brush. Add tip 4 string outline trim to smoke stack. Cover engine and cab with tip 17 stars. Fill in spokes with tip 4. Pipe in wheels and axles with tip 4 string outline. Smooth with dampened brush. Trim engine and cab with tip 4 dot nails and fill-in headlight. Smooth with dampened brush. Add tip 5 scrolls bell trim and tip 11 scrolls smoke puffs. Trim nameplate with tip 5 elongated beads.

3. Attach Cowboy Engineer with dabs of royal icing. Edge cake base with tip 17 shell base border. Print tip 3 name on plate and message.

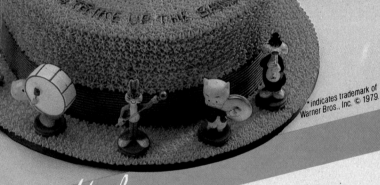

For more ways to use
LITTLE LOCOMOTIVE PAN
see Pan Index p. 192.

Pioneer Day
COZY HOME
A modest home for a courageous family. Celebrate Frontier Day with this welcome sight for our pioneers. Serves 12.

Decorating Needs
• Holiday House Kit, p. 181
• Tips 2A, 2B, 4, 47, 74, 101s, p. 112-115
• Rectangle Cake Boards, p. 154
• Gingerbread Cookie Cutters, p. 110
• Tree Formers, p. 130
• Decorator's Brush, p. 116
• Fancy Foil Paper, p. 155
• Pound or firm-textured cake batter
• Ice cream cones

Instructions
1. Out of cookie dough, cut boy and girl. Outline clothes with tip 4. Fill in with tip 4 thinned icing. Smooth with dampened brush. Add tip 101s ruffles to bonnet. Add tip 4 facial features.

Place ice cream cones on tree formers. Cover cones with tip 74 leaves. Remove cones from tree formers.

Cover cake board with Fancy Foil Paper. Position cake on cake board.

2. Pipe tip 47 doors and window. (Use flat side up for window.)

Pipe tip 2A logs. Alternate with tip 4 outlines between logs. Flatten log ends with fingertip dipped in cornstarch.

Cover roof with tip 2B stripes. For shingle effect, score with knife dipped in cornstarch.

3. Position cookie people with dabs of icing. Position trees on cake board.

For more ways to use HOLIDAY HOUSE KIT See Pan Index, p. 192

For more ways to use CHARACTER PANS see Pan Index p. 192

STAR-SPANGLED BUGS BUNNY™
He'll beat up some fun on the 4th! Serves 12

Decorating Needs
• Bugs Bunny Pan, p. 191
• Tips 3, 4, 9, 11, 17, 18, p. 112-115
• Decorator's Brush, p. 116

Instructions
1. Ice cake sides, drum skin and ears area of cake top smooth. With toothpick, mark hat on Bugs' head. Cover marks and outline drum and Bugs with tip 4 strings.

2. Fill in eyes, inner ears, mouth, teeth, tongue and nose with tip 4. Smooth with dampened brush. Fill in drumstick handle, edge of drum and hat peak with tip 9, drumstick ball with tip 11 dot. Smooth with finger tip dipped in cornstarch.

3. Cover ears, hat, face, coat, legs, hands and feet with tip 17 stars. Cover tail with tip 17 stripes. Add tip 4 fill-in front paw pads. Smooth with dampened brush.

Trim drum and hat with tip 18 stars. Add tip 4 outline whiskers.

Print tip 3 message. Edge cake base with tip 18 star border.

* indicates trademark of Warner Bros., Inc. © 1983.

Drifting clouds.
Humming crickets.
A swaying hammock on a
hot afternoon.
Paddling on a mountain lake.
The perfect picnic in a peaceful place.
Sights and sounds of a
summer to remember.
August.
It's the perfect month
to bake and decorate.

For more ways to use
LITTLE LAMB Pan
see Pan Index p. 192.

Lefthander's Day

WON'T BE LEFT OUT

Lefties have rights, too! They won't be left out anymore. Celebrate Lefthanders' Day and help promote the rights of lefties. Make your own special leftie feel right in with this "Hooray for Lefties" cake. Serves 12.

Decorating Needs
- **Little Lamb Pan, p. 187**
- **Tips 1A, 1D, 3, 4, 17, p. 112**
- **Stars 'N Stripes, p. 141**
- **Decorator's Brush, p. 116**
- **Pound or firm-textured cake batter**

Instructions

1. Allow firm-textured or pound cake to cool completely in back half of pan. With knife, cut off cake at base of ears. Ice hand part of cake smooth. With toothpick, mark hand and fingernail on cake. Cover marks with tip 4 strings. Build up fingers with tip 1A.

2. Cover cuff with tip 1D stripe. Cover hand, fingers and coat with tip 17 stars. Make tip 4 fill-in fingernail. Smooth with dampened brush.

3. Print tip 3 message. Position Stars 'N Stripes in hand.

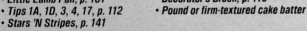

For more ways to use
TREELITEFUL PAN
see Pan Index p. 192.

American Indian Day

WELCOME TO THE POW WOW

Join in the celebration of American Indian Day — a tribute to the heritage and contributions of our truly native Americans. This cake is just perfect for the party on American Indian Day or any other occasion. Serves 12.

Decorating Needs
- **Treeliteful Pan, p. 181**
- **Tips 3, 4, 6, 17, p. 112**
- **'85 Pattern Book (Indian and Tepee Pattern) p. 103**
- **Decorator's Brush, p. 116**
- **Long macaroni**

Instructions

1. Ice bottom half of cake top and all cake sides smooth. With toothpick, mark Indian and Tepee Pattern on cake top. Cover marks with tip 4 strings.

2. Fill in sun; V and wavy designs on tepee; door, and Indian with tip 6. Smooth with dampened brush. Outline facial features, costume, headband, feathers, shoes and fringe with tip 4. Fill in with tip 4. Smooth with dampened brush. Add tip 4 string hair. Cover tepee with tip 17 stars. Add tip 4 middle seam, arrow and sun rays.

3. Edge cake base with tip 17 shell border. Print tip 3 message. Position macaroni at top of tepee.

FACE FULL OF SUMMER

A super cool cake for 12 smiling summer faces.

Decorating Needs
• 10" Round Pan, p. 165, 166, 177
• Tips 4, 9, 16, 18, p. 112
• '85 Pattern Book (Sunglasses & Watermelon Pattern) p. 103
• Decorator's Brush, p. 116

Instructions
1. Ice 1-layer cake smooth. With toothpick, mark Sunglasses and Watermelon Pattern on cake. Cover marks with tip 4 strings.

Outline mouth and cheeks with tip 4.

2. Cover watermelon with tip 16 stars.

Fill in sunglasses with tip 9; add tip 4 bead seeds.

Smooth with dampened brush.

Pipe tip 18 scrolls for hair.

3. Edge cake base with tip 18 shell border.

Print tip 4 message.

For more ways to use 10" ROUND PAN see Pan Index p. 192.

The Carefree Touch That Means So Much

ON THE GRAND TOUR

A sweet bon voyage surprise! Serves 28.

Decorating Needs
• 9" x 13" Sheet Pan, p. 165, 169, 176
• Tips 3, 4, 12, 17, p. 112
• Decorator's Brush, p. 116

Instructions
1. Ice 2-layer cake smooth. With toothpick, mark center opening, locks, handle, corners and stickers. Cover marks with tip 4 strings.

2. Cover corners with tip 17 stars.

Fill in handle, stickers and lock with tip 12. Smooth with dampened brush.

3. Edge cake base with tip 17 shell border. Write and print tip 3 message and sticker names.

For more ways to use 9" x 13" SHEET PAN see Pan Index p. 192.

STRAWBERRY DELIGHTS

The more the merrier! Each serves 1.

Decorating Needs
- Shortcake 'N Treats Pan, p. 171
- Mini Muffin Pan, p. 171
- Tips 16, 18, 22, p. 112
- **Berry Nice Strawberry Shortcake,**™★ p. 136
- *Apricot Glaze, p. 95*
- *Shortcake Recipe (below)*
- Fresh Strawberries

Instructions

1. Shortcake Recipe

2 cups all-purpose flour	½ cup butter or margarine
½ cup sugar	¾ cup milk
1 Tablespoon baking powder	2 eggs
½ teaspoon salt	

Generously grease Shortcake 'N Treats or Mini Muffin Pans. Combine flour, sugar, baking powder and salt. Cut in shortening until consistency resembles coarse meal. Mix milk and eggs together; add to dry ingredients, stir until dry ingredients are just moistened. Place batter in each cavity (¹/₃ cup in Shortcake 'N Treats pan, 1 Tablespoon in Mini Muffin). Bake at 375° for approximately 15 minutes or until cakes spring back when touched. Cool 5 minutes in pan; release. Let cool. Makes about 12 shortcakes or 5 dozen muffins.

2. Cover with Apricot Glaze (see p. 95).

3. Pipe tip 22 swirls on mini cake tops. Fill shortcakes with sliced strawberries. With stabilized whipped cream, pipe tip 16 zigzags, tip 18 rosettes and pull-out stars, tip 22 scrolls and swirls on shortcake tops. Highlight with perky Strawberry Shortcake.

™★MCMLXXXIII
American Greetings Corp.

For more ways to use SHORTCAKE 'N TREATS & MINI MUFFIN PANS see Pan Index p. 192.

"BERRY" SPECIAL

The pick of the crop will serve 12.

Decorating Needs
- **Happiness Heart Pan Set, p. 182**
- **Tips 3, 4, 5, 12, 17, 113, p. 112-115**
- **Flower Formers, p. 130**
- **Candy Melts™ brand confectionery coating, p. 120**
- **Royal Icing Recipe, p. 83**

Instructions

1. Pipe tip 113 royal icing leaves and tip 12 string stem. Let dry on flower formers. Ice 2-layer heart cake smooth on cake circle cut to fit. With toothpick, mark off "dipped chocolate" area. Cover mark with tip 5 string. Let set.

2. Pour melted Candy Melts over "dipped chocolate" area. (Hint: Position cake atop cake rack over cookie sheet to catch excess Candy Melts.) Let set completely. Carefully place on serving plate.

3. Edge cake base with tip 17 shell borders. Add tip 4 bead strawberry seeds. Attach leaves and stem to cake with dots of icing. Print tip 3 message on cake top. When serving, cut with a warm knife.

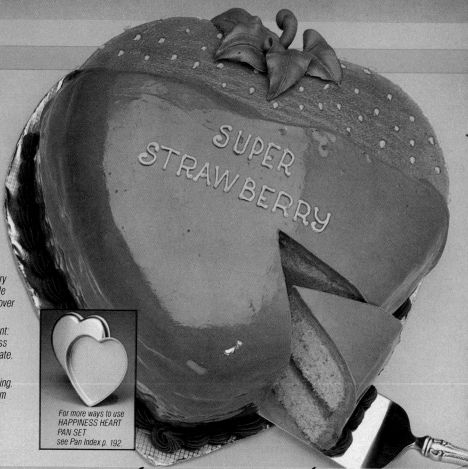

For more ways to use HAPPINESS HEART PAN SET see Pan Index p. 192.

The Successful Touch That Means So Much

STRAWBERRY SURPRISE

Pretty, torted layers serves 12.

Decorating Needs
- **9" Petal Pan, p. 169**
- **Tips 5, 16, 18, p. 112**
- **Candy Wafer & Fondant Mix, p. 120**

Instructions

1. Ice 2-layer petal cake smooth. Edge cake top with tip 5 outline to confine fondant. Pour fondant icing on cake top (begin in center). Score top into 16ths with spatula.

2. Edge cake top with tip 16 shells. Add tip 18 "C" scrolls. Pipe tip 16 rows of shells on cake top.

3. Edge cake base with tip 16 shell border. Pipe tip 16 rows of shells between curved sides, tip 18 upright shells and stars on curved sides. Add tip 16 pairs of "C" scrolls at cake base. Position strawberry on cake top.

For more ways to use 9" PETAL PAN see Pan Index p. 192.

Golden leaves stirring
in a cool breeze.
School kids clowning.
Teachers frowning.
Memories of an idyllic summer.
Autumn waits to take her place.
Books to explore.
Friends to greet. Teams to beat.
September.
It's the perfect month
to bake and decorate.

For more ways to use
6" x 2" ROUND PAN
see Pan Index p. 192.

Grandparent's Day
FILLED WITH LOVE

A honeyed gift she'll remember always. Serves 12.

Decorating Needs
- *6" x 2" Round Pan, p. 166*
- *Tips 3, 4, 10, 16, 47, 102, 125, 224, p. 112-115*
- *Decorator's Brush, p. 116*

Instructions

1. Make 30 tip 224 drop flowers with tip 3 centers.

Bake 3 layers; level the tops off the two bottom layers and keep the round top on the top layer. Ice the 3-layer cake, the 2 bottom layers brown, the top one pink.

With toothpick, mark label on the cake. Cover marks with tip 4 strings. Fill in label with tip 10. Smooth with dampened brush.

2. Edge cake top with tip 125 ruffle. Pipe tip 47 ribbon around cake; add tip 102 bow. Add tip 16 star cake base border.

3. Print tip 3 message. Attach flowers to cake top and sides with dabs of icing.

The Cherished Touch That Means So Much

LOVING RECOGNITION

A caring thought for someone who cares. Serves 12.

Decorating Needs
- *Be Mine Heart Pan, p. 182*
- *Tips 3, 5, 16, p. 112*
- *15-pc. Decorator Pattern Press Set, p. 116*

Instructions

1. Ice cake smooth, top pink, sides brown. Using pattern press, lightly mark scrolls on cake top, about ½" apart. Cover marks with tip 5 strings.

2. Cover outer heart edge with tip 16 white stars. Pipe tip 5 pink beads and brown bead Fleur-de-Lis between scrolls. Pipe tip 5 pink bead border.

3. Edge cake top with tip 16 reverse shell border, cake base with tip 16 shell border.

Write tip 3 message.

For more ways to use
BE MINE HEART PAN
see Pan Index p. 192.

Rosh Hashanah

MESSAGE OF HOPE FOR ROSH HASHANAH

The first day of the Jewish New Year is celebrated in September. The message on this lovely centerpiece cake expresses the prayers of those who observe this joyful holiday! Serves 12.

Decorating needs
- Good News Stork Pan, p. 183
- Tips 4, 17, 131, 352, p. 112-115
- '85 Pattern Book (Dove Pattern), p. 103
- Decorator's Brush, p. 116

Instructions

1. Make 6 tip 131 flowers with tip 4 centers.

Ice cake smooth. With toothpick, mark Dove Pattern on cake top. Cover marks with tip 4 strings.

2. Cover dove with tip 17 stars. Add tip 4 fill-in beak (smooth with dampened brush) and tip 4 bead eye.

Make tip 4 outline vines. Trim with tip 352 leaves.

3. Attach flowers with dots of icing. Edge cake base with tip 17 shell border.

Print tip 4 message.

For more ways to use
GOOD NEWS STORK PAN
see Pan Index p. 192

Back To School

AN APPLE FOR THE SCHOLAR

A great opening day treat for 20 back-to-schoolers!

Decorating Needs
- Ball Pan, p. 184
- 8" Square Pan, p. 165, 168, 177
- Tips 3, 4, 12, p. 112
- Dowel rod, p. 159
- Decorating Comb, p. 116
- Cake Circles, p. 154
- Rolled chocolate-flavored caramel, gumdrop leaves
- Pound or firm-textured cake

Note: Use Wilton Watermelon Paste Icing Color for apple.

Instructions

1. Ice one-layer square cake smooth. top and one side gold. other three sides white.

With decorating comb, make "pages" on the book. Pipe tip 12 book edges and binding around top and bottom edge of cake. Print tip 3 message on cake top.

Cut and position dowel rod where ball cake will go.

2. With knife, slice off round part of one half of ball cake so it sits level on square cake.

Ice ball cake smooth (on cake circle cut to fit). Position ball cake atop square cake on dowel rod.

With toothpick, mark eyes, eyebrows and mouth on ball cake. Cover marks with tip 4 strings. Fill in eyes with tip 4. Smooth with dampened brush.

3. Stick rolled caramel "stem" on ball cake. Pipe with tip 12. Stick gumdrop leaves on toothpicks. Push into ball cake top.

Pipe tip 12 worm. Add tip 4 features and eyeglasses.

For more ways to use
BALL PAN and 8"
SQUARE PAN see
Pan Index p. 192

O·C·T·O·B·E·R

Sweet sentiments to send.
Raucous toasts to hold high.
Spirits and witches float
across the clear Autumn sky.
Lovers and others dance well into
the night, while little ones delight
in the night full of fright,
hoping to see a visiting ghost!
October.
It's the perfect month
to bake and decorate.

Sweetest Day

BON BON LOOK-ALIKES

Make something sweet for your Sugar this Sweetest Day (October 20)! Pretend-candy cakes serve one each.

Decorating Needs
- Petite Doll Pan, p. 183
- Tips 2, 6, 127D, p. 112-113
- Cherry stem, nuts, cocoa powder

Instructions

1. Ice three cakes smooth in light brown.* Ice top of one cake red; ice remainder smooth in dark brown. Dust one iced cake with cocoa powder.

2. Pipe ruffle around base of each cake with tip 127D.

3. Decorate tops of pretend candies with tip 6 scroll and tip 2 drizzle. Add nuts; set cherry stem in center of red-iced cake.

*For an extra smooth, glossy icing, cover cakes with our Quick Pour Icing—see recipe on canister of Candy Wafer & Fondant Mix (page 120).

For more ways to use
PETITE DOLL PAN
see Pan Index p. 192.

OctoberFest

OCTOBERFEST MUG

Spirited cake serves 12. What a fitting way to celebrate the German harvest festival. You can almost hear the oom-pa-pa of the polka band leading the singing and dancing! Wunderbar!

Decorating Needs
- Good Cheer Mug Pan, p. 184
- Tips 4, 10, 12, 16, p. 112
- Dutch-style pretzel

Instructions

1. Ice cake top and sides smooth; use gold for mug area, white for foam and sides by handle.

With toothpick, mark sleeves, hat and facial features; cover marks and outline mug, foam, hands and fingers with tip 4 strings.

Cover hat, sleeves and background by arm with tip 16 stars.

2. Use tip 12 to pipe in foam swirls. Position pretzel on cake top. Use tip 10 to pipe in hands, fingers and whites of eyes (smooth with fingertip dipped in cornstarch).

3. Use tip 4 to add dot pupils to eyes, to print message and to overpipe hands and fingers. Add tip 16 star border at base of cake and let the party begin!

For more ways to use
GOOD CHEER MUG PAN
see Pan Index p. 192.

66

For more ways to use
JACK-O-LANTERN PAN
see Pan Index p. 192

THE UNKNOWN PUMPKIN

Masked Marvel serves 12.

Decorating Needs
- **Jack-O-Lantern Pan, p. 178**
- **Tips 4, 8, 12, 17, p. 112**
- **'85 Pattern Book, p. 103
  (Mask Pattern)**
- **Decorator's Brush, p. 116**

Instructions

1. Ice cake smooth where mask will go. With toothpick, mark mask pattern on cake top. Use tip 4 to outline mask, eyes and pumpkin ridges and to pipe parallel outlines around nose and mouth.

2. Fill in centers of eyes, nose and mouth with tip 4 (smooth with dampened art brush).

Overpipe outlines on mask, eyes, nose and mouth with tip 4. Build up and fill in mask with tip 12 (smooth with fingertip dipped in cornstarch). Fill in mouth and nose outlines with tip 8 (smooth with fingertip dipped in cornstarch).

3. Cover pumpkin with tip 17 stars. Pipe tip 17 zigzag and rosette for stem. Add tip 4 strings to mask and your surprise guest is ready!

The Spooky Touch That Means So Much

FRIGHTENING FIELD OF FIENDS

Gruesome garden serves 24.

Decorating Needs
- **10-in. Square Pan, p. 165, 168 or 177**
- **Tips 4, 18, 68, 199, 352, p. 112-115**
- **Tree Formers, p. 130**
- **Scary Ghost, p. 141**
- **Little Trickers, p. 141**
- **Jack-O-Lanterns, p. 141**
- **Royal Icing Recipe, p. 83**

Instructions

1. Cover Tree Formers with waxed paper. Use royal icing and tip 68 to pipe side by side stripes and floppy leaves for corn stalks. Set aside to air dry about 5 hours.

2. Ice cake top green and sides brown. Pipe tip 18 shell borders.

Pipe tip 4 vines over cake top and sides. Trim with tip 352 leaves.

3. Pipe tip 199 pumpkins. Add tip 4 pull-out dot stems. Attach Jack-O-Lanterns to cake sides with icing. Position Little Trickers, Scary Ghosts and corn stalks on cake top. Invite your trick or treaters in for a scary slice!

**For more helpful hints, review
Decorating Guide p. 80.**

For more ways to use
10-IN. SQUARE PAN
see Pan Index p. 192

PUMPKIN BREADS & WITCHES HEADS

Frightening faces serve one each.

Decorating Needs
- Mini Pumpkin Pan, p. 178
- Tips 3, 6, 46, p. 112-114
- Jelly beans, cookies, ice cream cones

Instructions

1. Prepare one pumpkin minicake per person. You can bake pumpkin bread recipe that follows or mold sherbet or ice cream.

PUMPKIN BREAD — Yield: about 12 minicakes. Beat together 2 eggs and 1½ cups sugar until thick. Add 1 cup canned pumpkin, ⅓ cup water, ½ cup oil, 1¼ cups flour, 1 tsp. baking soda, ½ tsp. salt, ¼ tsp. baking powder and ½ tsp. each: cinnamon, nutmeg and ground cloves. Beat together until well blended. Grease and flour minicake pan. Bake at 325°F for 13 to 15 minutes. Cool 5 minutes in pan; release. Cool before decorating. (Cream cheese frosting is particularly tasty!)

2. For pumpkins — Use tip 3 to outline facial features, fill in with tip 3 and different color for contrast (smooth with fingertip dipped in cornstarch). Or, cover features with tip 3 zigzag (smooth eyes and nose with fingertip dipped in cornstarch).

3. For Witches — Ice cake smooth (or use sherbet). Mark facial features with a toothpick; cover marks with tip 3 strings. Pipe tip 6 side-by-side strings for hair. Add jelly bean nose.

To make hat, attach ice cream cone to cookie with dabs of icing. Pipe tip 46 smooth ribbon around hat, pipe outline and fill in buckle with tip 3. Attach hat to Witch with additional icing.

For more ways to use MINI PUMPKIN PAN see Pan Index p. 192

The Spooky Touch That Means So Much

HALLOWEEN COOKIE TREATS

Tricksters can eat more than one!

Decorating Needs
- Cookie Sheet, p. 111 or 173
- Cookie Maker Round Cutters, p. 110
- Tip 3, p. 112
- Cookie dough, jellied candies, nuts, raisins, coconut, candy corn, mint wafer, ice cream cone

Instructions

1. Use ready-to-bake refrigerated cookie dough or prepare your favorite recipe or box mix.

2. For "BOO" Cookies...Roll cookie dough into a long rope. If dough is too soft to handle, refrigerate until firm. Place on cookie sheet and bend to form message, flatten slightly before baking. Pipe tip 3 dot eyes and pupils onto cooled cookie. Attach jellied candy tongues with dots of icing.

3. For FACES...Roll out dough (plain or tinted) and cut large circles using second largest size from Round Cutter Set. Bake and cool cookies.

For Ghost — Ice cookie smooth. Mark features with a toothpick; cover marks with tip 3 strings. Press on chopped nuts for hair, slivered almonds for teeth. For Witch — Use dots of icing to attach chocolate chip eyes, candy corn nose and raisin smile. Ice hair area lightly and sprinkle with tinted coconut. To make hat, cut off tip of sugar ice cream cone. Dip in melted Candy Melts™ Dark Cocoa coating (or ice smooth). Attach cone to chocolate mint patty with melted coating (or icing). Attach hat to Witch. For Cat — Use cookie made from dough tinted green. With sharp knife, carefully mark facial features; cover marks with tip 3 strings. Use tip 3 to pipe "e" motion hair, zigzag mouth and dot eyes. Attach candy corn ears, gum drop nose and slivered almond teeth with dots of icing.

For more ways to use COOKIE SHEET see Pan Index p. 192

For more ways to use
HOLIDAY HOUSE KIT
see Pan Index p. 192.

CREEPY COTTAGE

Halloween homestead serves 12.

Decorating Needs

- **Holiday House Kit, p. 181**
- **Tips 1, 2, 5, 17, 45, p. 112-114**
- **Wacky Witch, p. 141**
- **Happy Ghost, p. 141**
- **Black Pot, p. 141**
- **Rectangle Cake Board, p. 154**
- **Brown sugar, pretzels, assorted candies**

Instructions

1. Ice cake front and sides smooth with thinned icing. Outline broken windows with tip 2 and fill in using two icing colors and tip 5 (smooth with fingertip dipped in cornstarch). Outline door and top window with tip 2.

2. Pipe tip 45 smooth ribbons for boards on front and sides. Add tip 1 dot nails.

Pipe tip 45 smooth ribbons for shutters. Add tip 2 outlines and string details.

Attach cake upright on cake board or serving plate with small amount of icing. Use tip 5 to build up chimney (smooth and shape with fingertip dipped in cornstarch). Cover roof and back of cake with tip 17 stars. Decorate chimney and roof with candy pieces.

3. Use spatula to add fluffy icing grass. Sprinkle granulated brown sugar path. Build fences with pretzels; use tip 2 icing dots to join pieces.

Position Wacky Witch, Black Pot and Happy Ghost and your Halloween centerpiece is ready!

MONSTER RING

Crazy character cake serves 10.

Decorating Needs

- **8-in. Ring Pan, p. 173**
- **Tips 1A, 3, 7, p. 112**
- **Marshmallows, jellied candies, cookie, coconut, almonds.**

Instructions

1. Ice cake smooth (we used orange for inside, green for top and brown for outside).

2. Tint coconut "hair;" press onto cake. Add jellied candy ears and nose, marshmallow eyes, almond teeth and cookie.

3. Pipe tip 1A hands; smooth with fingertip dipped in cornstarch. Add slivered almond "nails."

Add tip 7 dot pupils on eyes and bead borders on top and bottom of cake. Print tip 3 message and scary cake is complete.

**For more helpful hints, review
Decorating Guide, p. 80.**

For more ways to use
8-IN. RING PAN
see Pan Index p. 192

It's time to be grateful,
thankful and together.
Freedom of choice.
Pilgrim's pride and bountiful harvest.
Jack Frost is on the doorstep.
Tom Turkey is in the oven.
Cranberries, stuffing, pumpkin pie…
so much to taste and tempt the eye!
November.
It's the perfect month
to bake and decorate.

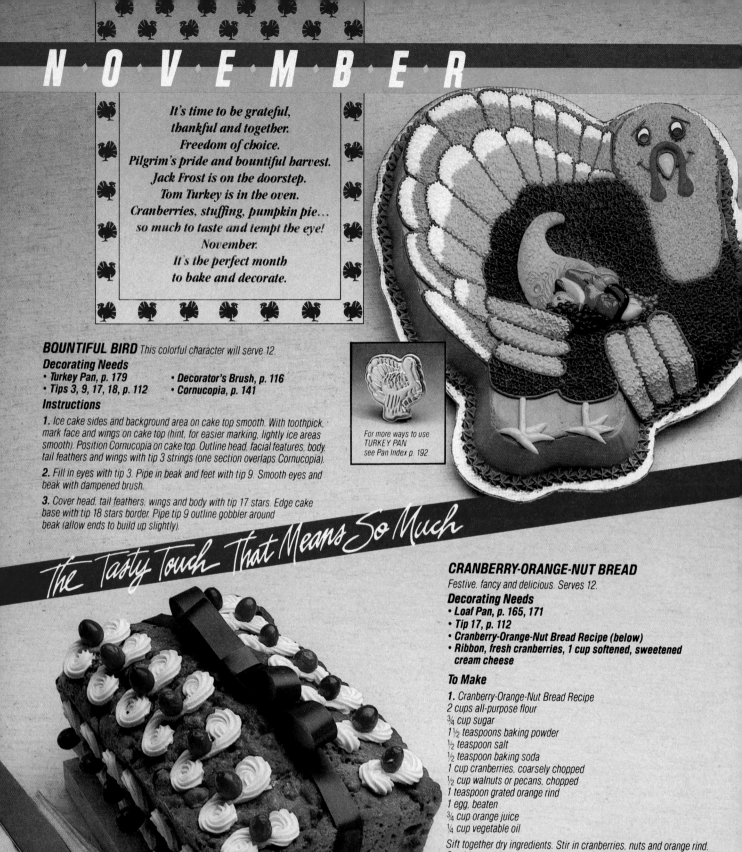

BOUNTIFUL BIRD This colorful character will serve 12.

Decorating Needs
• **Turkey Pan, p. 179**
• **Tips 3, 9, 17, 18, p. 112**
• **Decorator's Brush, p. 116**
• **Cornucopia, p. 141**

Instructions

1. Ice cake sides and background area on cake top smooth. With toothpick, mark face and wings on cake top (hint, for easier marking, lightly ice areas smooth). Position Cornucopia on cake top. Outline head, facial features, body, tail feathers and wings with tip 3 strings (one section overlaps Cornucopia).

2. Fill in eyes with tip 3. Pipe in beak and feet with tip 9. Smooth eyes and beak with dampened brush.

3. Cover head, tail feathers, wings and body with tip 17 stars. Edge cake base with tip 18 stars border. Pipe tip 9 outline gobbler around beak (allow ends to build up slightly).

For more ways to use
TURKEY PAN
see Pan Index p. 192.

The Tasty Touch That Means So Much

CRANBERRY-ORANGE-NUT BREAD

Festive, fancy and delicious. Serves 12.

Decorating Needs
• **Loaf Pan, p. 165, 171**
• **Tip 17, p. 112**
• **Cranberry-Orange-Nut Bread Recipe (below)**
• **Ribbon, fresh cranberries, 1 cup softened, sweetened cream cheese**

To Make

1. Cranberry-Orange-Nut Bread Recipe
2 cups all-purpose flour
¾ cup sugar
1½ teaspoons baking powder
½ teaspoon salt
½ teaspoon baking soda
1 cup cranberries, coarsely chopped
½ cup walnuts or pecans, chopped
1 teaspoon grated orange rind
1 egg, beaten
¾ cup orange juice
¼ cup vegetable oil

Sift together dry ingredients. Stir in cranberries, nuts and orange rind. Combine eggs, orange juice and vegetable oil. Add to dry ingredients, stirring until just moistened. Pour batter into greased and floured loaf pan. Bake in preheated 375° oven for 45-50 minutes or until done. Let bread cool 10 minutes in pan; release. Yields 1 loaf.

2. For cream cheese: Add confectioners sugar to softened cream cheese to desired sweetness and beat well. Pipe tip 17 scrolls (about 2" apart). Make ribbon bow. Attach ribbon and cranberries with dots of cream cheese.

For more ways to use
LOAF PAN
see Pan Index p. 192.

POSIED PINWHEEL

All will gather 'round and enjoy. Serves 12.

Decorating Needs
- 8" Round Pans, p. 165, 166, 177
- Cake Dividing Set, p. 116
- Tips, 3, 16, 17, 224, 225, 349, p. 112-115

Instructions

1. Make 60 tip 225 and 25 tip 224 drop flowers with tip 3 dot centers. Ice 2-layer cake smooth.

2. With toothpick, mark a 5" circle on cake top. Using Cake Dividing Set, with a toothpick, mark cake top into 8ths, center of cake sides into 16ths. Pipe tip 16 curved stripes on cake top (work out from center to circle mark, stop and alternate color). Pipe tip 16 white "V" garlands, then brown garlands on cake sides.

3. Edge cake top and base with tip 17 shell borders. Attach flowers to cake top and sides. Trim flowers with tip 349 leaves.

For more ways to use
8" ROUND PANS
see Pan Index p. 192.

**For more helpful hints, review
Decorating Guide, p. 80.**

Election Day

MANY HAPPY RETURNS

Whatever the outcome on Election Day, this whimsical cake will win their votes. Serves 12.

Decorating Needs
- Up 'n Away Balloon Pan, p. 179
- Tips 2A, 3, 4, 6, 12, 17, 104, p. 112-115
- '85 Pattern Book, p. 103
  (? Mark Pattern)
- Stars 'N Stripes, p. 141
- Royal Icing Recipe, p. 83

Instructions

1. See figure piping directions p. 94. On waxed paper, figure pipe tips 2A, 12, 104 and 3 pink elephants and tips 2A, 12, 6 and 3 donkeys with royal icing.

2. Ice cake smooth. With toothpick, mark ? Mark Pattern on cake top. Cover marks with tip 4 strings. Fill in ? mark with tip 17 stars.

3. Edge cake base with tip 17 star border. Print tip 4 message on cake top. Position elephants, donkeys, and Stars 'n Stripes on cake top.

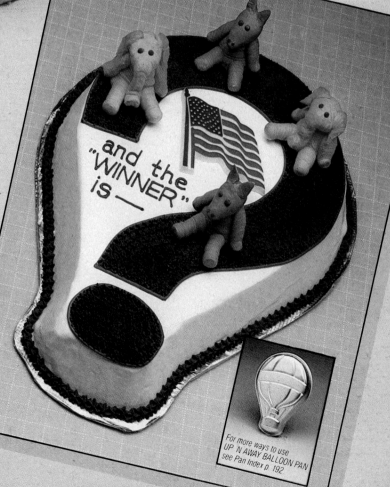

For more ways to use
UP 'N AWAY BALLOON PAN
see Pan Index p. 192.

Wonderment!
Enchantment!
Joy!
Shimmering snowflakes and
twinkling lights.
Hustle, bustle, wondrous sights.
Little faces all aglow with
hopes that Santa soon will show.
December.
It's the perfect month
to bake and decorate!

SANTA'S FLIGHT

Decorating Needs
• Santa's Cookie Sleigh Kit, p. 164, 181
• Tips 3, 11, 14, 46, 101, p. 112-115
• Silver dots, confetti

Instructions

1. Outline reindeer, Santa and sleigh with tip 3 strings. Add tip 3 dot eyes. Pipe tip 46 stripe harness and edge with tip 101 zigzags. Trim Santa's suit with tip 14 zigzag fur and cover with tip 14 stars. Cover scarf with tip 3 beads. Add tip 14 rosette to hat. Pipe tip 14 shell beard and mustache.

2. Pipe in edge and runner of sleigh with tip 11. Add silver dots. Add tip 3 scrolls. Attach confetti to form flowers with icing. Trim with tip 3 dot centers and leaves.

3. Assemble sleigh with Santa and reindeer according to Santa's Cookie Sleigh Kit instructions.

ENCHANTING GINGERBREAD HOUSE ➡

What a masterpiece! It even has electricity!

Decorating Needs
• Gingerbread House Kit, p. 164
• Cookie Sheets, p. 111, 173
• Tips 2B, 2, 3, 16, 46, 74, 349, p. 112-115
• '85 Pattern Book, p. 103
  (Tower, Windows, Chimney and Arch Patterns)
• Piping Gel, p. 131
• Tree Formers, p. 130
• Edible Glitter, p. 130
• Rectangle Cake Board, p. 154
• Christmas Carollers, p. 141
• Royal Icing Recipe, p. 83
• Easy Melts,™ p. 122
• Candy canes, electric night light socket, 15 watt bulb, aluminum foil, 11 x 13 x 2" styrofoam block

For more helpful hints, review Decorating Guide p. 80

JOYFUL RING

You'll have this gala great cake decorated in a flash. Serves 12.

Decorating Needs
• Fancy Ring Mold Pan, p. 173
• Tips 4, 16, p. 112
• Red & green candied cherries

Instructions

1. Outline flutes with tip 4 strings. Cover alternating top and each side flutes with tip 16 stars.

2. Add tip 16 rows of stars on cake sides; tip 16 rosettes around center.

3. Cut leaves out of green cherries. Attach red and green cherries to base with dots of icing.

For more ways to use
RING MOLD PAN
see Pan Index p. 192.

PRESENT-PERFECT PUP!

This adorable surprise will serve 12

Decorating Needs
- Bunny Pan, p. 187
- Tips 3, 4, 12, 16, p. 112
- Lollipops, hard candy ball, firm-textured cake batter, plastic straws

Instructions

1. Bake cake according to pan instructions. With knife, slice off snout. Lightly ice cake smooth. With toothpick, mark cap, face and stocking design. Cover marks with tip 4 strings. Fill in eyes with tip 4.

2. Pipe tip 16 shell stocking cuff (pipe shells in horizontal rows to resemble stocking knit). With toothpick, mark paws and tongue on cuff. Outline with tip 4. Pipe in tip 4 tongue and tip 12 scalloped design on stocking (shape and flatten with fingertip dipped in cornstarch). Pipe tip 16 zigzag cap cuff.

3. Cover face, cap, paws and stocking with tip 16 stars. Add tip 3 dot pupils and freckles. Push lollipops in cake. Attach candy ball to cap with dot of icing.

For more ways to use BUNNY PAN see Pan Index p. 192

Instructions

1. Cut an opening in 7" x 11" cake board to fit night light base. Cover board with foil. Position atop styrofoam (hollow out to fit light and board). Using patterns for Cozy Cottage in Gingerbread House Kit, Tower, Windows and Chimney Patterns, cut pieces out of dough. Bake. With toothpick, immediately mark doors.

2. Make 35 lacework arches: On waxed paper, outline Arch pattern with tip 2 royal icing strings.

For "stained glass" windows: Melt Easy Melts™ according to directions on p. 96. Lightly oil large sheet of aluminum foil. Pour melted candy onto foil (approx about 1/8" thick). Pour colors next to each other for multi-color effect. Let set. Attach windows to wall panels with royal icing. Let dry.

3. **To decorate house panels:** NOTE: For all decorating on house done with tip 2 or 3, add 1½ teaspoon piping gel to each cup royal icing. Pipe tip 3 reverse scrolls on dormer, roof and tower wall. Pipe tip 2 scallop garlands and dots on eaves and front of dormer. Trim doors and windows with tip 2 strings beads, scallops, ''C'' scrolls and dots. Assemble chimney and tower roof. When dry, pipe tip 2 string bricks and scallop garlands on roof. Edge chimney with tip 2B smooth stripe.

4. Ice styrofoam & cake board with spatula to resemble drifting snow. Assemble house with tower walls. Let dry. Cover roof with tip 3 scallop garlands. Attach tower roof and chimney with icing. Edge roof and walls with tip 16 shell borders. Pipe tip 349 leaf wreaths on door and side. Trim with tip 3 dots and bow. Attach lacework arches to roofs with icing. Position candy canes. For Trees: Pipe tip 16 stripe around base of tree former. Cover with tip 74 rows of leaves (work up from base). Sprinkle with Edible Glitter. Position trees and Christmas Carollers.

1.   2.   3.   4.

FONDANT GEMS
Bite-size beauties that look so inviting!

Decorating Needs
- Mini Muffin Pan, p. 171
- Cookie Sheet, p.111, 173
- Candy Wafer & Fondant Mix, p. 120
- Hard candy balls, crushed

Instructions
Bake and cool mini cakes. Place on wire rack over cookie sheet. Pour fondant icing over cakes. Add crushed hard candy. Let set.

For more ways to use MINI MUFFIN PAN see Pan Index p. 192

Wilton Cookie Maker

Holiday cookie making the Wilton way...now you can make cookies look as good as they taste! *Discover how easy it is to create festive, fancy cookies to serve or give. Wilton New CookieMaker molds, cutters, pans and decorating products will help you make dozens of tasteful, elegant cookies that are bound to impress.*
For the complete scoop, see pages 104 through 111.

The Merry Touch That Means So Much

HOLLY BERRY TARTS
These fruit-filled pleasures will be treasured!

Decorating Needs
- Tartlet Mold Set, p. 162
- Tip 21, p. 112
- Cookie Dough Recipe, p. 95
- Fruit filling, strawberries

Instructions
Line pan wells with cookie dough. Prick bottom with fork. Bake at 400° for 7-10 minutes or until golden brown. When cool remove from pan and fill with fruit or tip 21 whipped or pastry cream zigzags. Top with strawberries.

NOEL NIBBLES
It's easy to pipe these traditional favorites!

Decorating Needs
- Cookie Sheet, p. 111, 173
- Tips 1C, 2D, 4, 6B, 16, 112-115, 109
- CookieMaker Cookie Dips, p. 108
- CookieMaker Cookie Sprinkle Tops, p. 108
- Chopped nuts, candied cherries

Instructions
1. Use Butter Cookie recipe, p. 95. On cookie sheet, pipe tip 1C drop flowers, tip 2D stripe candy canes and 6B shells. Bake and cool.

2. Trim flowers with candied cherries or tip 16 stars. Pipe tip 4 string bows on candy canes. Dip one end of shell into melted Cookie Dips and sprinkle with Sprinkle Tops. Let set.

For more ways to use COOKIE SHEET see Pan Index p. 192

HOLIDAY ELEGANTS

Luscious melt-in-your-mouth confections dipped and drizzled with melted Cookie Dips.

Decorating Needs
- Marseilles Classic Cookie Mold, p. 106
- Tips 2, 16, p. 112
- CookieMaker Cookie Dips, Icing Mix, Sprinkle Tops, p. 108
- Butter Cookie Recipe, p. 95
- Chopped nuts

Instructions

1. Bake and cool cookies according to Butter Cookie recipe on p. 95. Cool.

2. Follow directions for dipping and decorating on Cookie Dips package. Sprinkle with Cookie Sprinkle Tops or chopped nuts. Let set.

3. For sandwich cookies: Pipe tip 16 icing zigzags on flat surface of cookie. Position another cookie atop icing.

JOLLY SNOWMEN & RADIANT ROUNDS

Decorating Needs
- Cookie Sheet, p. 111, 173
- Tips 4, 16, p. 112
- CookieMaker Cookie Dips, p. 108
- CookieMaker Round Cutters, p. 111
- Favorite Russian tea cakes, pecan crescent or sandy recipe, Chocolate roll candy, confectioners sugar, apricot jam, nuts

Instructions

1. For snowmen: Roll chilled cookie dough into 1" balls. Bake on cookie sheet. While warm, roll in confectioners sugar. Attach two balls together with icing. Pipe tip 4 dot facial features and tip 16 stripe scarf with tip 4 string fringe. Flatten a section of chocolate roll candy. Attach another section with icing. Secure to head.

2. For radiant round butter cookie sandwiches: Cut rounds out of chilled dough. Use small round cutter to make center holes in top cookies (in half of batch). Sandwich cookies together with apricot jam. Dip ⅛ into melted Cookie Dips. Sprinkle part with chopped nuts.

FESTIVE FLUTES

Sweet surprises trimmed with Cookie Dips or icing decorations.

Decorating Needs
- Tartlet Mold Set, p. 162
- Tip 21, p. 112
- CookieMaker Cookie Dips, Icing Mix, p. 108
- Brown Butter Cookie Recipe, p. 95

Instructions

Line pan with cookie dough. Prick bottom with fork. Bake at 400° for 7-10 minutes. When cool, fill with tip 21 icing zigzags. Let set; then dip in melted Cookie Dips. Sprinkle with nuts.

For more ways to use CLASSIC HOUSE PAN see Pan Index p. 192

INVITING OPEN HOUSE

This welcomed sight will serve 12.

Decorating Needs
- **Classic House Pan, p. 178**
- **Tips 2, 4, 5, 16, 349, p. 112-115**
- **Santa Claus 'N Tree, p. 141**
- **Decorator's Brush, p. 116**
- **Chocolate roll candy**

Instructions

1. Ice cake sides smooth. Outline roof, chimney, windows, shutters, porch and door with tip 4. Fill in windows and door; pipe in chimney bricks and small rectangles on eaves with tip 5 (smooth with dampened brush).

2. Cover roof, walls, eaves, window frames and porch with tip 16 stars. Pipe tip 16 zigzag shutters. Position Santa 'N Tree.

3. Pipe tip 349 wreaths and porch garland. Add tip 2 dot berries, string bows and candles. Trim windows with tip 4 string arch and panes. Edge chimney with tip 16 stripe. Trim attic eaves with tip 4 elongated bead "V"s. Push chocolate roll candy smokestack into cake side. Edge cake base with tip 16 shell border.

ROLY-POLY SNOWMAN

This merry gent will warm every heart. Serves 24.

Decorating Needs
- **Stand-up Snowman Cake Pan Kit, p. 180**
- **Tips 3, 16, 18, 352, p. 112-115**
- **Firm-textured or pound cake batter**

Instructions

1. Bake cake and assemble halves together according to pan instructions. Outline eyes, nose, mouth, hat, scarf, buttons, arms and waist with tip 3.

2. Fill in eyes, nose and buttons with tip 3 (smooth with fingertip dipped in cornstarch). Pipe tip 16 zigzag scarf (alternate colors).

3. Cover hat, band and head with tip 16 stars. Cover body with tip 18 stars. Print tip 3 message. Pipe tip 352 leaves with tip 3 dot berries on hat.

For more ways to use STAND-UP SNOWMAN CAKE PAN KIT see Pan Index p. 192

For more ways to use
LONG LOAF PAN
see Pan Index p. 192.

"TREE" MENDOUS!

It won't take long to decorate this festive eye-catcher.
Serves 18.

Decorating Needs
- Long Loaf Pan, p. 171
- Tips 4, 17, p. 112
- Cake Dividing Set, p. 116
- Candy-coated chocolates

Instructions

1. Ice cake smooth. Using triangle marker, dot mark cake top and sides in half. Now mark half sections at 2" intervals. On ends, mark two 2" (wrapping around sides) and one large triangle below. Connect dots to form triangle trees.

2. Outline triangles with tip 4 strings. Cover end and alternate triangles on top and sides with tip 17 elongated zigzags.

3. Attach candy-coated chocolates to triangle trees with dots of icing. Pipe tip 4 dot ornaments on trees.

**For more helpful hints,
review Decorating Guide p. 80.**

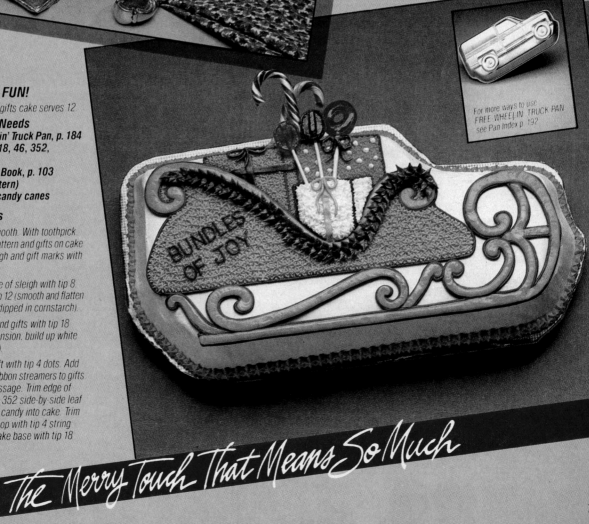

For more ways to use
FREE-WHEELIN' TRUCK PAN
see Pan Index p. 192.

LOADS OF FUN!

Sleigh bearing gifts cake serves 12.

Decorating Needs
- Free-Wheelin' Truck Pan, p. 184
- Tips 4, 12, 18, 46, 352, p. 112-115
- '85 Pattern Book, p. 103 (Sleigh Pattern)
- Lollipops, candy canes

Instructions

1. Ice cake smooth. With toothpick, mark Sleigh Pattern and gifts on cake top. Cover sleigh and gift marks with tip 4 strings.

2. Pipe in edge of sleigh with tip 8, runners with tip 12 (smooth and flatten with fingertip dipped in cornstarch).

Cover sleigh and gifts with tip 18 stars (for dimension, build up white gift with stars).

3. Trim one gift with tip 4 dots. Add tip 46 stripe ribbon streamers to gifts. Print tip 4 message. Trim edge of sleigh with tip 352 side-by-side leaf garland. Push candy into cake. Trim gifts and lollipop with tip 4 string bows. Edge cake base with tip 18 star border.

The Merry Touch That Means So Much

SANTA'S JOY RIDE

Everyone will smile when he arrives. Serves 12.

Decorating Needs
- Santa 'N Sleigh Pan, p. 181
- Tips 2, 3, 4, 12, 17, p. 112
- Decorator's Brush, p. 116

Instructions

1. Ice cake sides and background area on cake top smooth. Outline Santa, bag and sleigh with tip 4 strings. Fill in face and mouth with tip 3 (smooth with dampened brush). Add tip 4 dot nose, cheeks, string eyes and lip.

2. Write tip 2 message on cake top. Pipe in edge of sleigh and runner with tip 12 (smooth with fingertip dipped in cornstarch). Cover hat, mitten, suit, belt, bag, scarf and sleigh with tip 16 stars.

3. Edge cap and cuffs with tip 17 zigzags. Add tip 17 rosette pompon to cap. Pipe tip 17 shell mustache, hair and reverse shell beard. Edge cake base with tip 17 shell border.

For more ways to use
SANTA 'N SLEIGH PAN
see Pan Index p. 192

Merry Christmas

The Merry Touch That Means So Much

For more ways to use
TREELITEFUL PAN
see Pan Index p. 192

SANTA'S TREE TRIMMING PARTY

Fast, easy and delightful. Serves 12.

Decorating Needs
- Treeliteful Pan, p. 181
- Tips 3, 4, 18, p. 112
- '85 Pattern Book, p. 103 (Ladder & Stars Pattern)
- Santa 'N Tree, p. 141
- Decorator's Brush, p. 116
- Royal Icing Recipe, p. 83
- Poster board, candy-coated chocolates, candy canes, gumdrops

Instructions

1. On waxed paper, with royal icing, outline Ladder and Star Patterns with tip 3. Let outlines dry. Fill in with tip 4 royal icing (smooth with dampened brush). Let dry.

2. Cover cake with tip 18 stars. Cut pastry chef's hat out of poster board and attach to Santa with dots of icing. Pipe tip 3 pastry bag over Santa's hand.

3. Position Santa on cake top. Trim cake with tip 18 stripe garlands. Attach star, ladder and candy to cake with dots of icing.

LITTLE TOY DREIDEL

Decorating this won't put you in a spin. It's fast and easy. Serves 12.

Decorating Needs
- 12" Hexagon Pan, p. 168
- Tips 2, 4, 16, 18, p. 112
- '85 Pattern Book, p. 103 (Dreidel Pattern)
- Decorator's Brush, p. 116
- Pretzel rod

Instructions

1. Ice one-layer hexagon cake smooth. With toothpick, mark Dreidel Pattern on cake top. Cover marks with tip 4 strings.

Ice 4" pretzel rod smooth and position on cake top.

2. Fill in Hebrew letters with tip 2 (smooth with dampened brush). Cover dreidel with tip 16 stars.

3. Print tip 4 message. Edge cake top with tip 16 shells; cake base with tip 18 shells.

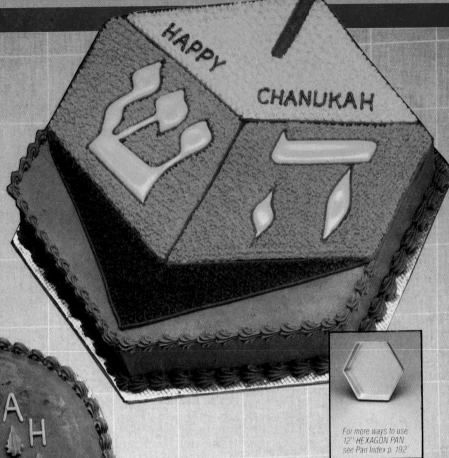

For more ways to use 12" HEXAGON PAN see Pan Index p. 192

Happy Chanukah

FESTIVAL OF LIFE

A glowing way to celebrate the joyful holiday. Serves 12.

Decorating Needs
- Guitar Pan, p. 185
- Tips 4, 12, 17, 21, p. 112
- '85 Pattern Book, p. 103 (Menorah Pattern)

Instructions

1. Ice cake smooth. With toothpick, mark Menorah Pattern on cake top. Cover marks with tip 4 strings.

2. Pipe in menorah with tip 12 (smooth and shape with fingertips dipped in cornstarch).

3. Pipe tip 21 stripe candles. Add tip 17 spatula-stripe shell flames. Print tip 4 message. Edge cake base with tip 17 shell border.

For more helpful hints, see Decorating Guide p. 80.

For more ways to use GUITAR PAN see Pan Index p. 192

DECORATING GUIDE

Cake Decorating Makes Everyone Feel Special!

There's fun in the doing! It's satisfying to show off your cake decorating talents to the delight of everyone. The ohhhs, ahhhs and super smiles are your rewards for going out of your way to make it such a special day! This Decorating Guide will show you the basics of cake decorating as well as more advanced techniques, such as making a beautiful icing rose. Practice the techniques described in this section, and soon you'll be able to execute any '85 Yearbook cake design. If after you've tried your hand at the following decorating techniques, you're ready to learn more, the Wilton Home Study

Courses (page 97-129) and our library of decorating books (pages 98-103) have a wealth of decorating expertise to share. Also watch for Wilton Method Classes in a store near your home. This Yearbook's product section is bigger and better than ever! Many exciting, new specialty and character pans, decorating tools, baking utensils, cake accents, and cookie and candy making products have been added to make your decorating easier and more enjoyable. See them all on pages 104-191. All set? Let's learn how to decorate.

BAKING YOUR CAKE

The First Step To Success

A properly baked cake makes the best foundation for your icing and the decorations that follow, so it's important to carefully follow these step-by-step instructions. Remember, you may bake your cake up to 3 months ahead of decorating day and freeze in heavy-duty foil. Always thaw cake completely before icing. Your cake will still be fresh and easy to ice because it will be firm. NOTE: If you're using one of the Wilton shaped pans, follow the specific instructions included with the pan. For 3-dimensional, stand-up cakes, use batters that bake a firm-textured cake such as pound or pudding-added cake.

Now Let's Begin

1. Preheat oven to temperature specified in recipe or on packaged mix.

2. Generously grease the inside of the cake pan, or pans, with solid vegetable shortening. Use a pastry brush to spread the shortening evenly. Make sure that all inside surfaces (sides, corners and any indentations) are well covered. (Fast and easy method: Use the latest grease/flour pan spray available at supermarkets. You

just spray the inside of pan evenly.) TIP: Simple geometric shaped pans such as round, hexagon, square, etc. (not character or novelty shapes) pan bottoms may be lined with waxed paper after greasing. There's no need to flour pans. This will ensure easy unmolding.

3. Sprinkle flour inside of pan and shake the pan back and forth so the flour covers all the greased surfaces. Tap out excess flour, and if any shiny spots remain, touch up with more shortening and flour. This important step will help prevent the cake from sticking to the pan.

4. Bake the cake according to temperature and time specifications in recipe or on package instructions. Remove cake from oven and let cool 10 minutes in pan on a cake rack. Larger cakes over 14" diameter may need to cool 15 minutes.

5. To remove cake from pan, place cake rack against top of cake and turn both cake pan and rack over. Lift off pan carefully. If cake will not release from pan, return it to a warm oven, 250°, for a few minutes, and repeat procedure. Cool cake completely, at least 1 hour. Then brush loose crumbs off cake and it's ready to ice.

GREASE

FLOUR

SHAKE

PLACE RACK

REMOVE

HOW TO COVER A CAKE BOARD

Many of your shaped cakes will look best on a foil-covered cake board that follows the contours of the pan. **To make:**

1. Trace the shaped pan onto a Wilton cake board one-half to one inch larger than pan with a pencil.

2. Cut out board with a knife.

3. Trace board shape onto foil wrap, making outlines three to four inches larger than board. Cut out foil cover. Cut deep slits at several points around foil leaving a half-inch uncut so it folds neatly around board.

4. Cover board with foil and tape to underside securely. If the cake is heavy, use two or more boards for added serving support. Stock up on strong Wilton cake boards, including circles and rectangles, and Fanci Foil Wrap on pages 154-155.

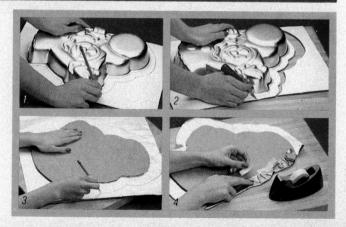

ICING GUIDE

Proper consistency is the key to making decorator icing that will shape the petals of a flower, show the details of a border or cover the surface of a cake. Therefore, it's important that you use the recommended icing and consistency for any technique. As a general rule, flowers require a stiff icing consistency, borders a medium-stiff consistency and writing or leaves a slightly thinned consistency. Icing that can peak to an inch or more is stiff, less than that is medium consistency. Icing that flows easily from a tip without running is a thin consistency. Every Wilton icing recipe is tested for taste and other important qualities. This chart will tell you each recipe's qualities, so you can determine which is the right one for your cake.

We are very excited to introduce New Wilton Icing Mix (p. 131)!
It offers you everything the best homemade buttercream does! Creamy TASTE, luscious TEXTURE and the CONVENIENCE of a mix. Ideal for both frosting and decorating. So easy to make—just add butter and milk, the shortening's already in the mix. The 14 oz. size makes 2 cups of buttercream icing. Complete instructions on bag. It's available in creamy white (easy to tint) or chocolate flavor. The Snow-White and Deluxe recipes that follow are delicious variations to try with Wilton Buttercream Mix. Remember, having the right icing consistency is a must for good decorating.

Icing	Recommended Uses	Tinting	Flavor & Consistency	Icing Storage	Special Features
Buttercream (Wilton Mix or Homemade)	• Borders, Writings • Roses, drop flowers & sweet peas • Icing cakes smooth	• Deep Colors • Most colors deepen upon setting	• Sweet, buttery flavor • Medium-to-stiff consistency	• Refrigerate icing in an air-tight container for 2 weeks	• Iced cake can be stored at room temperature for 2-3 days • Flowers remain soft enough to be cut with a knife
Snow-White Buttercream	• Borders, Writing • Roses, drop flowers & sweet peas • Icing cakes smooth	• Deep colors • Most colors deepen upon setting • Gives true colors	• Sweet, almond flavor • Medium-to-stiff consistency	• Refrigerate icing in an air-tight container for 2 weeks	• Iced cake may be stored for 2-3 days • Air dried flowers have translucent look • Flowers remain soft to be cut with a knife • Good for wedding cakes • Tints true colors due to pure white color
Deluxe Buttercream	• Borders, Writing • Drop flowers & sweet peas • Icing cakes smooth	• Deep colors	• Rich, creamy flavor • Medium-to-soft consistency	• Refrigerate icing in an air-tight container for 2 weeks	• Texture remains soft on decorated cake • Iced cake may be stored at room temperature
Cream Cheese	• Basic Borders, writing, stars, shells, drop flowers • Icing cake smooth	• Pastels	• Cream cheese • Medium-to-thin consistency	• Refrigerate icing in an air-tight container for 1 week	• Iced cake must be refrigerated • Cream cheese flavor is especially good with spice cakes, carrot cakes, etc.
Stabilized Whipped Cream	• Borders, writing • Icing cake smooth	• Pastels can be achieved • Paste colors are best to use	• Creamy, delicate sweetness • Light, medium-to-thin consistency	• Use immediately	• Iced cake must be refrigerated • Texture remains soft on decorated cake • Especially good on cakes decorated with fruits
French Buttercream	• Basic Borders • Writing • Icing cake smooth	• Pastels can be achieved	• Tastes similar to vanilla ice cream • Consistency similar to whipped cream	• Use immediately	• Store iced cake in refrigerator • Texture remains soft on decorated cake • Cooked icing gives a special flavor similar to vanilla ice cream
Easy Pour Fondant	• For icing cakes or cookies only	• Pastels	• Very sweet flavor • Pourable consistency	• Use immediately; excess fondant drippings can be reheated & poured again	• Dries to a shiny, smooth surface to coat petit fours and cookies • Seals in freshness
Royal	• Especially flower-making, figure piping, making flowers on wires • Decorating cookies & gingerbread houses	• Deep colors • Colors may fade upon setting	• Very sweet • Stiff consistency	• Store in air-tight grease-free container at room temperature for 2 weeks	• Dries candy hard for lasting decorations • Bowl & utensils must be grease-free • Cover icing with damp cloth to prevent crusting

Wilton
ICING MIX RECIPES

BUTTERCREAM ICING
Creamy White or Chocolate
1 pkg. Wilton Icing Mix (p.131)
6 Tbsps. butter or margarine
2-3 Tbsps. milk or water
Complete mixing instructions on packages.
YIELDS 2 cups.

SNOW-WHITE BUTTERCREAM
3 Tbsps. water
2 Tbsps. Wilton Meringue Powder (p.131)
1 pkg. Wilton Icing Mix (p.131)
1/4 cup solid vegetable shortening

Combine water and meringue powder, whip at high speed until peaks form. Add approximately half of the package of icing mix, beat well at medium-low speed. Add shortening; mix well. Add remaining icing mix; beat at medium-low speed until well blended.
YIELDS 1-3/4 cups.

DELUXE BUTTERCREAM
1 pkg. Wilton Icing Mix (p.131)
6 Tablespoons butter or margarine
1/4 cup whipping cream

Cream butter or margarine and icing mix together, beating at medium speed. Add whipping cream and beat at medium speed until light and fluffy. YIELDS 2 cups.

CAKE ICING RECIPES

SPECIALTY ICING RECIPES
Be sure to refer to icing chart (p. 81) for the advantages of each.

BUTTERCREAM ICING

1/2 cup solid vegetable shortening
1/2 cup butter or margarine*
1 tsp. Clear Vanilla Extract (p. 131)
4 cups sifted confectioners sugar (approx. 1 lb.)
2 Tbsps. milk**

Cream butter and shortening with electric mixer. Add vanilla. Gradually add sugar, one cup at a time, beating well on medium speed. Scrape sides and bottom of bowl often. When all sugar has been mixed in, icing will appear dry. Add milk and beat at medium speed until light and fluffy. Keep icing covered with a damp cloth until ready to use. For best results, keep icing bowl in refrigerator when not in use. Refrigerated in an airtight container, this icing can be stored 2 weeks. Rewhip before using.
YIELD: 3 cups

*Substitute all-vegetable shortening and ½ teaspoon Wilton Butter Extract (p. 131) for pure white icing and stiffer consistency.

**Add 2 additional Tbsps. milk per recipe to thin for icing cake or use 3-4 Tbsps. light corn syrup per recipe.

CHOCOLATE BUTTERCREAM

Add 3/4 cup cocoa or 3-1 oz. unsweetened chocolate squares, melted, and an additional 1 to 2 Tbsps. milk to recipe. Mix until well blended.

For a unique change of pace, add Wilton Candy Flavors (p. 120) in Rum, Orange or Cherry in place of vanilla extract.

FRENCH BUTTERCREAM ICING RECIPE

2/3 cup sugar
1/4 cup flour
1/4 tsp. salt
3/4 cup milk
1 cup cold butter
1 tsp. vanilla extract

Place sugar, flour and salt in saucepan and mix thoroughly, stir in milk. Cook over medium heat and stir constantly until very thick. Remove from heat and pour into a medium mixing bowl. Cool at room temperature. Add 1/2 cup butter at a time (cut into several pieces) and beat at medium-high speed until smooth. Add vanilla and beat well. Chill icing for a few minutes before decorating. Iced cake must be refrigerated until serving time.

YIELD: 2 cups

STABILIZED WHIPPED CREAM RECIPE

1 tsp. unflavored gelatin
4 tsps. cold water
1 cup heavy whipping cream (at least 24 hours old and very cold)
1/4 cup confectioners sugar
1/2 tsp. vanilla

Combine gelatin and cold water in small saucepan. Let stand until thick. Place over low heat, stirring constantly until gelatin dissolves (about 3 minutes). Remove from heat and cool slightly. Whip cream, sugar, and vanilla until slightly thickened. While beating slowly, gradually add gelatin to whipped cream mixture. Whip at high speed until stiff. YIELD: 2 cups. Cakes iced with whipped cream must be stored in the refrigerator.

CREAM CHEESE ICING

3-8 oz. packages slightly softened cream cheese
3 cups sifted confectioners sugar

Beat cream cheese until smooth. Add confectioners sugar and mix thoroughly. Beat at high speed until light and fluffy.

YIELD: 3½ cups

EASY POURED FONDANT

1 lb. Candy Wafer/Fondant Mix, p. 120
1/4 cup water
2 teaspoons vegetable oil
1/4 teaspoon flavoring
coloring, as desired

Mix dry fondant mix and water in top of double boiler; place over boiling water. Heat to 150°F, stir constantly. Remove from heat. Stir in vegetable oil, color and flavor until well blended. Continue to stir until mixture thickens slightly. To cover cake, ice with thin coating of buttercream icing or apricot glaze and allow to set. Place cakes on racks over a drip pan. Pour fondant starting at center of cake and work toward edges. Excess fondant can be reheated and poured again. Additional water may be added to obtain the proper pouring consistency.

YIELD: 1½ cups

CHOCOLATE QUICK-POUR FONDANT

Add 1 Tbsp. water to Fondant recipe. After heating, stir in 1 or 2 oz. melted unsweetened chocolate, then add vegetable oil and flavoring. Add brown color, if necessary. Chocolate Quick-Pour Fondant would be a nice alternative to using Candy Melts™ brand confectionery coating on the "berry" special cake, page 63.

DECORATING WITH PREPARED ICINGS & CREAMS

CANNED ICING

For best results, refrigerate icing before using. If icing becomes too soft, place decorating bag in refrigerator until icing is firm enough for decorating. Each can yields about 1½ cups icing.

FROZEN NON-DAIRY WHIPPED TOPPING

Non-dairy whipped topping must be thawed in the refrigerator before coloring or used for decorating. Can be used for decorating techniques similar to stabilized whipped cream. Do not allow to set at room temperature as it becomes too soft for decorating. After decorating, store cake in refrigerator.

PACKAGE TOPPING MIX

Whipped topping mix can be used for decorating similar to stabilized whipped cream. However, use immediately after preparing. Do not allow to set at room temperature as topping becomes too soft for well-defined decorations.

ROYAL AND COLOR FLOW ICING RECIPES

ROYAL ICING

This smooth, hard-drying icing makes decorations that last. Ideal for making flowers, piping figures, overpiping and decorating cookies. Flowers and decorations made from royal icing will last for months, if stored properly, without softening. Royal icing decorations should be air dried. Allow more drying time for larger decorations. Make sure bowl and utensils are grease free, since any trace of grease will cause royal icing to break down.

Royal Icing dries quickly, so keep icing bowl covered with a damp cloth at all times. Store in air tight container. Rebeat at low speed before using.

Note: Royal Icing is edible. Since it dries candy-hard, it is not recommended for icing your cakes. Use only for special effects you want to last.

To "paint" plastic cake trims with royal icing: Thin 1/2 cup icing with 1 Tablespoon water and add 1 teaspoon of Piping Gel (p.131) or light corn syrup for shine; to 1/4 cup icing, add 1/4 teaspoon piping gel when decorating confectionery coating candies.

ROYAL MERINGUE RECIPE

3 level Tbsps. Wilton Meringue Powder Mix (p.131)
4 cups sifted confectioners sugar (approx. 1 lb.)
6 Tbsps. water*

Beat all ingredients at low speed for 7 to 10 minutes (10 to 12 minutes at high speed for portable mixer) until icing forms peaks.
YIELD: 3 cups

*When using large counter top mixer or for stiffer icing, use 1 Tbsp. less water.

ROYAL EGG WHITE RECIPE

3 egg whites (room temperature)
4 cups confectioners sugar (approx. 1 lb.)
1/2 tsp. cream of tartar

Beat all ingredients at high speed for 7 to 10 minutes. Use immediately. Rebeating will not restore texture.
YIELD: 2½ cups

COLOR FLOW ICING

To create candy-hard decorations using an outline and filling in method of decorating, use this success-tested Color Flow recipe. You can trace emblems, insignias, original designs and patterns from Wilton Pattern Books (pp. 98-103) with this icing and the results will last.

1/4 cup water + 1 teaspoon
1 lb. sifted confectioners sugar (4 cups)
2 Tbsps. Wilton Color Flow Icing Mix (p.130)

In an electric mixer, blend all ingredients on low speed for 5 minutes. If using hand mixer use high speed. Color Flow icing "crusts" quickly so keep it covered with a damp cloth while using it. Stir in desired Paste Icing Colors. Use full strength for outlining. To fill in outlines, soften full-strength Color Flow icing by adding 1/2 teaspoon of water at a time, (just a few drops as you near proper consistency) per 1/4 cup icing, until it becomes the right texture. Use grease-free spoon or spatula to stir slowly. Color Flow is ready for filling in outlines when a small amount dropped into the mixture takes a full count of ten to disappear. Let outlines dry thoroughly (1-2 hours) before filling in. Let Color Flow decorations dry for at least 24 hours. For complete directions and step-by-step information about Color Flow, see the **Wilton Way of Cake Decorating Volume I**, Chapter XIV. (sold on page 98).

ICING YOUR CAKE

A beautifully decorated cake begins with a smooth, even coating of icing. This becomes the base to show off your pretty flowers and borders. Icing a cake properly is easy if you follow these basic steps. Tip: Most Yearbook cakes require 4-6 cups of icing to ice and decorate. See recipes on pages 81-83.

1. LEVEL CAKE

If you've followed the baking instructions on page 80, or the ones included with your Wilton pan, your layers should have a slight crown. However, if it is too high, or one side of the cake is raised more than the other, trim off the excess. Remove cake from pan, use a sharp, serrated knife, and move it sideways back and forth across the top of the cake in a saw-like fashion. A cake that's partially frozen is easier to trim.

2. FILL LAYERS

Place one cake layer on a cake board atop a cake stand, top side up. Fit bag with coupler and fill with icing. Make a dam by squeezing out a circle of icing about 3/4" high on cake top. Using a spatula, spread icing, jam, pudding or other filling on cake top. Next, position top layer, bottom side up.

3. ICE TOP

Thin your buttercream icing with milk or light corn syrup for easy spreading. The consistency is correct when the spatula glides over the icing. Put 3"-wide waxed paper strips under the edges of the bottom layer to keep the cake stand free of icing drips. With large spatula place mound of icing on center of cake and spread across cake top, pushing excess icing down onto cake sides. Always keep spatula on the iced surface, because once it touches the cake surface, crumbs will mix in with the icing.

4. ICE SIDES

Cover the sides of the cake with excess icing from the top, adding more icing if necessary. Work from top down, forcing any loose crumbs to the cake base. Again, make sure the spatula only touches the icing. Using an angled spatula (p. 118), can make icing the cake sides easier. For curved sides, hold the spatula upright against the side of the cake and, pressing lightly, turn cake stand slowly around with your free hand without lifting the spatula from the cake side surface. Return excess icing to bowl and repeat procedure until sides are smooth. For angled sides such as on cross cake, do each straight side individually; hold spatula firmly to smooth.

5. SMOOTH TOP

Place spatula flat on one edge of cake top and sweep it across to center of cake. Lift off, remove excess icing and repeat, starting from a new point on edge of cake top. Repeat procedure until entire top surface of cake is smooth. To smooth center of cake, apply an even pressure to spatula as you turn cake stand around in a full circle. Lift off spatula and any excess icing. Tip: For smoother cakes, thin buttercream icing with milk or light corn syrup. This makes consistency best for easy spreading. Running a spatula under hot water, then smoothing icing, is not recommended.

SHEET AND OTHER FLAT SURFACED CAKES

Use the same icing procedure as shown here for sheet cakes, heart, oval, square and other shaped cakes with flat surfaces.

SHAPED CAKES

Most Wilton character and 3-dimensional cakes do not require icing before they're decorated. The decorating instructions with your pan show what to do.

Tip: Certain shaped cakes (especially 3-dimensional cakes) do require an even icing surface. Ice smooth, then, after a slight crust has formed (about 15 min.), press plastic wrap against icing and smooth out spatula marks.

Note: Some cake designs require that you ice only small areas of the cake top smooth with a spatula. Make sure you ice slightly past area, so that edges will be covered with stars, etc.

CAKE ICER TIP

A fast and unique way to ice cakes, the Wilton Cake Icer Tip 789 (p. 114) fits into large Wilton Featherweight Decorating Bags, and allows you to cover flat-surfaced cakes with wide bands of icing. Hold tip flat against cake surface, serrated side up, and squeeze out a ribbed band of icing. Hold tip smooth side up, and squeeze out a smooth band of icing. For cake side, turn cake stand clockwise as you squeeze out a band of icing, wrapping it around the cake.

When the cake is completely iced use a fork to add ribbings and join ribbed icing band seams together, or a spatula for smooth icing bands.

COLOR TECHNIQUES

Color brings cake decorations to life, therefore it's essential that you learn how to tint icings to achieve different decorating effects. Liquid and paste are two kinds of color bases used to tint icing. Wilton Paste Icing Color is the favorite of most decorators because it's concentrated color in a creamy, rich base. It gives icing vivid or deep, rich color without changing icing consistency (especially when tinting). Wilton Liquid Icing Colors are also concentrated and blend easily in icing. They produce soft, pastel colors. See page 131 for a complete selection of quality Wilton Icing Colors. Paste icing color kits are also available.

HOW TO TINT ICING

1. Start with white icing and add the color a little at a time until you achieve the shade you desire. Use a toothpick to add paste color; add liquid color a drop at a time (use more depending on amount of icing). TIP: Tint a small amount of icing first, then mix in with remainder of white icing. Colors intensify or darken 1 to 2 hours after mixing, so keep this in mind when you're tinting buttercream icing. You can always add extra color to deepen the icing color, but it's difficult to lighten the color once it's already tinted. Use White-White Icing Color to make your buttercream icing the purest snow-white!

2. To mix deep or dark colored icing, (such as red for roses) you may need a larger amount of Wilton Paste Icing Color. The color should still be added gradually, but use a clean small spatula each time to add the color. TIP: When mixing red icing, you may want to add extract or flavoring to the icing to cover any taste given by the extra color. We recommend using red for an accent color rather than for large areas of a cake. Watermelon Icing Color is a good substitute for red when large areas are to be covered and a real deep red isn't necessary. If you plan to use flavorings, make icing stiff consistency, then use enough flavoring to improve taste.

3. Always mix enough of any one color icing. If you're going to decorate a cake with pink flowers and borders, color enough icing for both. It's difficult to duplicate an exact shade of any color. As you gain decorating experience, you will learn just how much of any one color icing you will need.

IMPORTANT HINTS

1. Royal icing requires more base color than buttercream to achieve the same intensity.

2. Use milk, not water, in buttercream icing recipe when using Violet Icing Color, otherwise the icing may turn blue.

3. Substitute chocolate icing for dark brown colors. Use just 6 Tablespoons unsweetened cocoa powder, or 2 one-ounce squares of melted unsweetened baking chocolate, 1 Tablespoon milk, and add to 1-1/2 cups white icing.

4. Add color to piping gel, color flow, gum paste, cookie dough, marzipan, cream cheese, sugar molds and even cake batter for striking decorating effects!

5. To restore the consistency of Wilton Paste Icing Colors that have dried out, add a few drops of Wilton Glycerin. Mix until proper consistency is reached. See page 131 for Glycerin.

6. Use a clean toothpick or spatula to add Wilton Paste Icing Colors each time, until you reach desired shade.

SPECIAL EFFECTS

Apply one or more stripes of full strength icing color to the inside of a parchment paper bag. (Paste icing color stains the plastic-coated bags.) Fill bag with white or pastel colored icing and squeeze out multicolored borders, flowers, even figure piped clowns. TIP: For deep color effects (red roses), brush the entire inside of the parchment paper decorating bag with any paste color. Fill the bag with icing in a medium shade of the same color, and squeeze out deep dramatic decorations.

BRUSH STRIPING

Striping is a method used to give multiple or deep color effects to icing. To do this, one or more colors are applied to the inside of the parchment paper bag with a brush. Then the bag is filled with white or pastel colored icing and, as the icing is squeezed past the color, out comes the striped decorations! See pictures below.

SPATULA STRIPING

Use a spatula to stripe the inside of a decorating bag with pastel colored icing. Then fill the bag with white icing, or another shade of the same color as the striping, and squeeze out decorations with pastel contrasts. Use the above color techniques when figure piping for exciting results. It's fun to experiment with color! Try to achieve natural-looking flower colors by using the spatula striping method. (Roses look especially beautiful with this effect.) Discover color — the key to decorating drama!

SPECIAL EFFECTS

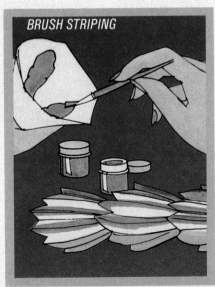

BRUSH STRIPING

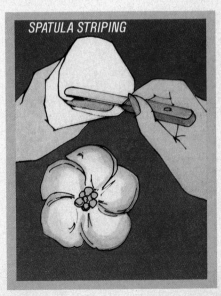

SPATULA STRIPING

TIERED CAKE ASSEMBLY

A tiered cake is a work of art and architecture, whether it's two tiers or a towering multi-tiered masterpiece. The tiers refer to the number of different size cake layers, each usually separated by a set of separator plates and pillars. It's these separator plates and pillars (p. 156-161), combined with a network of wooden dowel rods (p. 159), that give the tiered cake a foundation and framework on which to build. The classic tiered cake assembly shown here can be adapted for any multi-tiered cake. Each tier is two cake layers deep, with the base tier deeper if there are more than three tiers above it. For some elegant tiered wedding cakes see pages 26-31.

How To Assemble a Tiered Cake

1. Ice all tiers first. Place bottom tier on a sturdy base plate, or Tuk-N-Ruffle (p. 154) trimmed cake boards (2 or 3) cut 4" larger than tier diameter. On center top of this tier, press a cake board circle (p. 154) 2" smaller in diameter than the tier to be placed above it to imprint outline. Remove cake circle and push a dowel rod into lowest portion of cake within circular outline, until rod touches base plate. Lift up rod and use sharp pruning shears to cut off end at icing mark. Use this rod as a guide to cut six more dowel rods the same length. Push all seven rods into tier cake base so they're equally spaced within the circular outline and even with the cake top. NOTE: If you plan to position a small cake atop a novelty cake, ice the small cake on a cake board cut to fit. A dowel rod may be necessary to support the small cake. Ice all cakes on boards cut to fit when making any tiered cake.

2. With dowel rods in place, position next tier setting on cardboard base. Use cardboard circle 2" smaller in diameter to imprint an outline on second tier and repeat step 1 using five dowel rods. Now sharpen the end of another dowel rod with a kitchen knife or pencil sharpener and push through both layers of cake to cardboard circle base. Hit end of rod sharply with a tack hammer to drive rod through cardboard to bottom cake tier. Clip rod even with top of second tier using pruning shears. This serves to secure tiers, keeping them in place for transporting.

3. Insert pegs in base of separator plate, pillars on top; and push separator plate pegs into tier top.

4. Set top cake tier on corresponding size separator plate and position atop pillars for a three-tiered cake. Remove this top tier, and any tiers separated by plates, when transporting a cake.

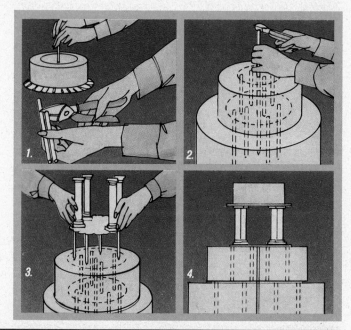

1. 2. 3. 4.

HELPFUL HINTS

FOR FASTER DECORATING:

1. Buy several of the bags and tips you use most. It'll save changing bags so you'll save time.

2. Tips from the same basic group that are close in size may be substituted for one another, such as tips 15 and 16, 18 and 19, 101 and 102, 66 and 67, etc. The effect is a slightly smaller or larger decoration.

3. Use tip 20 or 21 or the super fast Triple-Star Tip (p. 115), when you want to cover a cake quickly with stars. You can also use zigzags for filling in large areas.

4. When using parchment bags, you may place a tip with a smaller opening over the tip you're using and tape it in place. This saves time changing bags and tips when you're using the same color icing.

FOR BETTER CAKE BAKING:

1. Packaged, two-layer cake mixes usually yield 4 to 6 cups of batter, but formulas change, so always measure.

2. If you're in doubt as to how many cups of batter you need to fill a pan, measure the cups of water it will hold first and use this number as a guide. Then, if you want a cake with high sides, fill the pan 2/3 full of batter. For slightly thinner cake layers, fill 1/2 full. Never fill cake pans more than 2/3 full. Even if the batter doesn't overflow, the cake will have a heavy texture.

3. For pans 3" deep or more, we recommend pound or pudding-added cake batters. For best baking results, fill pan half full only. Use pound cake batter when baking 3-D, stand-up cakes.

4. For easy unmolding, line bottom of basic geometric pan shapes with waxed or parchment paper after greasing. The cake will be slightly lighter and have tender crusts, but may have more crumbs than cakes baked in greased and floured pans.

FOR EASIER ICING

1. Thin buttercream icing with milk or light corn syrup for easy spreading.

2. To smooth the icing surface on 3-dimensional cakes such as the ball, egg, lamb or bunny cakes, let buttercream icing crust slightly. Then place plastic wrap over the icing and smooth over the surface gently with your hands. Carefully remove wrap. For a textured surface, follow the same procedure with a cloth or paper towel. See page 84 for icing techniques.

3. Canned icing works well for most decorating techniques, and will withstand humidity better than buttercream. It must always be refrigerated before using, to stiffen consistency. However, canned icing is not for flowers that require a stiffer consistency like the rose, mum and lily.

4. To make clean-up easier and quicker when decorating with buttercream icing, use a degreaser cleaner to dissolve icing from tools. It is especially important to have grease-free utensils when using royal or color flow icings.

86

ESSENTIALS OF CAKE DECORATING

DECORATING BAGS

After preparing the proper icing for your decorating, the next step is to prepare the decorating bag.

There are three types of decorating bags you may choose to use. Wilton Featherweight bags are coated polyester cones and Parchment Triangles are grease-resistant, disposable paper shapes you roll into bags. Clear, plastic Wilton Disposable Decorating bags are convenient and easy to handle. Each serves as an excellent container for your decorating tip and icing.

Easy-to-follow instructions are included with all Wilton Decorating Bags.

See page 117 for a complete selection of Wilton quality Decorating Bags and Couplers. The coupler allows you to change decorating tips on the same bag. It's a real timesaver when you want to use several different tips and the same color icing. Use couplers with featherweight and Disposable Decorating Bags. Complete how to use coupler instructions are included with Wilton Decorating Bags.

HAND POSITION

The angle at which you hold your decorating bag and tip must be correct in order to produce a desired decoration. To hold the decorating bag correctly, grip the bag near the top with the twisted or folded end locked between your thumb and fingers.

Generally, there are two basic positions for the decorating bag: The 90° angle and the 45° angle. In 90° angle, the decorating bag is held perpendicular to the decorating surface (see picture A). In the 45° angle position, the decorating bag is held at a slant to the decorating surface (see picture B).

Since most decorating tips are symmetrical, their positioning corresponds to that of the decorating bag. However, some tips are wider or serrated on one side; such as ribbon decorating tips on page 114, and have a correct position of their own. You will become acquainted with these positions as you learn to decorate. Guide the bag with your free hand.

FOR LEFT-HANDERS ONLY

If you are left-handed, hold the decorating bag in your left hand and guide the decorating tip with the fingers of your right hand. (see picture C). If the instructions say to hold the decorating bag over to the right, you should hold your decorating bag over to the left. A right-handed person will always decorate from left to right. A left-handed person should always decorate from right to left. The only exception to this rule is when you are writing or printing. When decorating a cake on a turntable, rotate the stand counterclockwise.

For flower-making on a flower nail, turn nail clockwise in right hand as you pipe petals using left hand. Whether you're right or left handed, the amount of pressure and the steadiness with which it's applied to the decorating bag will determine the size

and uniformity of any icing design. Some decorations require an even pressure, others a varying application of light, medium or heavy pressure. The more controlled the pressure, the more exact your decorations will be. Only practice can teach you the proper pressure application for each technique. Practice decorating on a Wilton Practice Board (p. 119) or the back of a cookie sheet using buttercream icing. Scrape practice decorations back into bowl and rewhip for use again. Be sure to rewhip frequently and keep the icing bowl covered with a damp cloth to prevent icing from crusting. If icing becomes too soft, place in refrigerator. Now you're ready to try your hand at cake decorating!

DECORATING TIPS & TECHNIQUES

PRINTING AND WRITING
Use thin consistency icing. Letters are combinations of straight and slanted lines, circles, half-circles and curves. It's important to practice these motions individually before combining them to form words.

To Print: Hold bag at a 45° angle to surface with back of bag to the right for horizontal lines, toward you for vertical. Raise the tip slightly and squeeze out lines. To end outline, stop squeezing, touch tip to surface and pull away. **To Write:** Hold bag at a 45° angle to surface with back of bag to the right. Use your arm, not just fingers, to form every line, letter or word. The tip should lightly touch the cake as you write.

The size and shape of the opening on a decorating tip identifies the basic group to which the tip belongs and determines the type of decorations the tip will produce.

PLAIN OR ROUND TIPS

Use for outline details, filling or piping in areas, printing and writing messages, figure piping, stringwork, beads, dots, balls, stems, vines, flower centers, lattice, cornelli lace. These tips are smooth and round — small plain tips include numbers 1, 2, 3, 4; medium, 5, 6, 7, 8, 9, 10, 11, 12; large, 1A, 2A. For fine stringwork, use 1S, 1L, 2L, OL, OOL and 000; and oval tips for Philippine method flower making are 55 and 57.

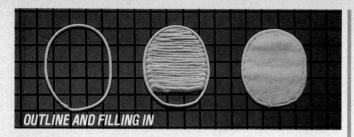

OUTLINE AND FILLING IN

To outline contours and details of shaped cake or for covering the marks transferred on your cake from a pattern...hold bag at a 45° angle and touch tip to surface. Now raise the tip slightly and continue to squeeze. The icing will flow out of the tip while you direct it along the surface. To end an outline, stop squeezing, touch tip to surface and pull away.

For Fill In: With thinned icing, squeeze out tip 2 or 3 side-by-side icing strings to fill area. For larger areas, use tip 4 or 5. Immediately smooth over strings with a dampened Decorator's Brush, fingertip or spatula dipped in cornstarch.

Piping In: Follow same procedure as Fill In, but do not thin icing. Squeeze with heavier pressure allowing icing to build up slightly. When necessary, shape with fingertip dipped in cornstarch.

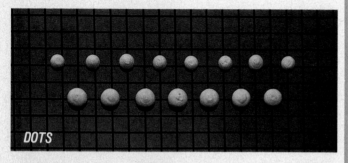

DOTS

Hold bag at a 90° angle with tip slightly above surface. Squeeze and keep point of the tip in icing until dot is the size you want. Stop pressure, pull away, use tip to clean point away or smooth with fingertip dipped in cornstarch. To make large dots or balls, lift tip as you squeeze to allow greater icing build-up.

BEADS, BEAD HEARTS AND SHAMROCKS

Hold bag at 45° angle with tip slightly above surface and end of bag pointing to the right. Squeeze and lift tip slightly so icing fans out into base. Relax pressure as you draw tip down and bring bead to point. Ideal for borders or piped in side-by-side rows to cover large areas.

For Hearts: Pipe two beads side by side and join points.

For Shamrocks: Pipe 3 bead hearts so points meet. Add tip 3 outline stems.

CORNELLI LACE

Use a 90° angle with tip slightly above surface. Pipe a continuous string of icing, curve it up, down and around until area is covered. Stop pressure, pull tip away. Make sure strings never touch or cross.

DROP STRINGS

With icing dots, mark 1½" horizontal intervals on your surface. Hold bag at 45° angle to the surface so that end of bag points slightly to the right. Touch tip to first mark and squeeze, holding bag in place momentarily so that icing sticks to surface.

Then pull tip straight out away from surface, allowing icing to drop into an arc. Stop pressure as you touch tip to second mark to end string.

Repeat procedure, attaching string to third mark and so on, forming row of drop strings. It's very important to let the string, not your hand, drop to form an arc. Try to keep your drop strings uniform in length and width.

For Double Drop Strings: Start at first mark again, squeeze bag. Let icing drop into a slightly shorter arc than arc in first row. Join end of string to end of corresponding string in first row and repeat procedure.

Always pipe longest drop strings first and add shorter ones. This technique is ideal for cake sides. Practice is important in making drop strings uniform.

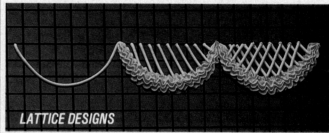

LATTICE DESIGNS

1. Starting at center of the shape to be covered with lattice, pipe tip 3 diagonal strings from top to bottom edge. Return to center and fill in rest of outline with diagonal strings, keeping them evenly spaced.

2. Starting at center of area again, pipe diagonal strings in the opposite direction. Repeat to fill in rest of outline. Cover edges of lattice with string or star tip border.

STAR TIPS

The star-shaped openings create the most popular decorations...stars, zigzags, shells, rosettes and more. The most often used star tips are numbers 13 through 22. Star tips range in size from small to extra large. For deep ribbed decorations, try tips 23-31, 132, 133, and 195. Large star tips include numbers 32, 96, 4B, 6B, and 8B. Fine cut star tips are numbers 362, 363, 364, 172 and 199.

STARS

Hold bag at 90° angle with tip slightly above surface. Squeeze bag to form a star, then stop pressure, and pull tip away. Increase or decrease pressure to change star size. An entire cake or just one area can be covered with stars made very close together so that no cake shows between stars. Use the triple-star tip (p. 115) or use larger star tip to cover areas of cake in less time.

For Pull-Out Stars: Hold bag at 45° angle to surface. As you squeeze out icing, pull tip down and away from cake. When strand is long enough, stop pressure and pull tip away. Work from bottom to top of area to be covered with pull-out stars.

ROSETTES

Hold bag at a 90° angle with tip slightly above surface. Squeeze and move hand to the left, up and around in a circular motion to starting point. Stop pressure and pull tip away. For a fancy effect, trim center with a star.

For Spirals: Following rosettes technique, starting at outer edge, move tip in a clockwise direction in a circular motion until center is reached. Stop pressure and pull tip away.

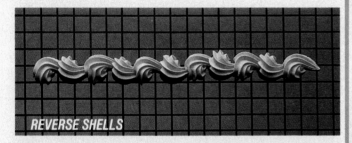

SHELLS

Hold bag at 45° angle with tip slightly above surface and end of bag pointing to the right. Squeeze with heavy pressure and slightly lift tip as icing builds and fans out into a full base. Relax pressure as you pull hand down towards you to make the tail. Stop pressure completely, pull tip away. When you make the shells, always work toward yourself starting each new shell slightly behind tail of previous shell.

For Elongated Shells: Extend tail while relaxing pressure, until desired length is achieved.

For Upright Shells: Hold bag at 90° angle to cake sides. Follow same procedure as elongated shells.

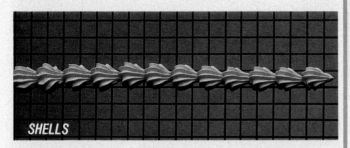

REVERSE SHELLS

Hold bag at 45° angle with tip slightly above surface. Squeeze to let icing fan out as if you were making a typical shell, then swing tip around to the left in a rosette shape as you relax pressure to form tail of a shell. Stop pressure, pull tip away. Repeat procedure, only this time, swing tip around to the right as you form tail of shell. Continue procedure alternating directions for a series of reverse shells.

FLEUR-DE-LIS

Make a shell. Keep bag at 45° angle and starting at the left of this shell, squeeze bag to fan icing into shell base. Then as you relax pressure to form tail, move tip up slightly around to the right, relaxing pressure, forming tail similar to reverse shells. Join to tail of the first shell. Repeat procedure to right side of first shell.

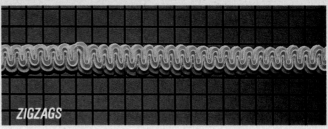

ZIGZAGS

Hold bag at 45° angle to surface, so that end of bag points out to the right, and fingertips gripping bag face you. Allow the tip to touch the surface lightly. Steadily squeeze out icing, move hand in tight side-to-side motion for zigzag. To end, stop pressure and pull tip away. Use tip 16 to 21 for large areas to be covered with zigzags, tip 3 or 4 for small areas.

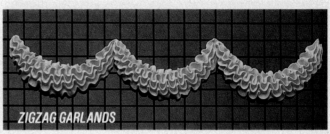

ZIGZAG GARLANDS

Hold bag as for basic zigzag procedure. Allow tip to touch the surface lightly and use light-to-heavy-to-light pressure to form curves of garland. To end, stop pressure, pull tip away. Practice for rhythmic pressure control so garlands are uniform.

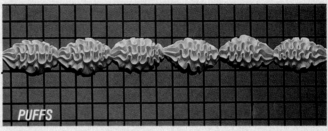

PUFFS

Hold bag at 45° angle to surface, fingertips on bag facing you. Touch tip to surface and use a light-to-heavy-to-light pressure and zigzag motion to form puff. Repeat procedure again and again as you move tip in a straight line to form row of puffs. To end row, stop pressure, pull tip away.

SCROLLS

Hold bag at 45° angle to surface so that end of bag points to the right. Use tip 3 to draw an inverted "C" center and use circular motion to cover inverted "C". (Overpipe scroll design with tip 13 or any small star tip). Use a heavy pressure to feather the scroll, relaxing pressure as you taper end. Add side petals like reverse shells.

REVERSE SCROLLS

With tip 3 squeeze out an inverted "C" scroll. Then, starting at the top of this "C" squeeze and move tip down, up and around for a backward "C". Cover outlines with tip 16. Add reverse shell side petals and you have a pair of reverse scrolls.

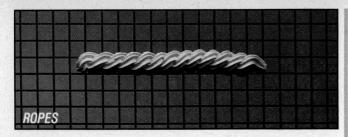

ROPES

Hold bag at 45° angle to surface with end of bag pointing over right shoulder. Touch tip to surface and squeezing bag, move tip down and up and around to the right forming a slight "s" curve. Stop pressure, pull tip away. Tuck tip under bottom arch of first "s" and repeat procedure. Continue joining "s" curves to form rope.

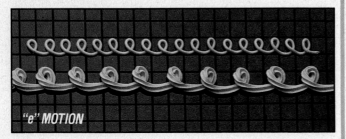

"e" MOTION

Hold bag at 45° angle to surface, fingertips on bag facing you. As you squeeze out icing, move tip down, up to the right and around as if writing the letter "e." Use a steady, even pressure as you repeat procedure over and over. To end, stop pressure, pull tip away.

DROP FLOWER TIPS

These are the easiest flowers for a beginning decorator to execute. The number of openings on end of the tip determines the number of petals the flower will have. Each drop flower tip can produce two different flower varieties—plain or swirled. Swirled drop flowers cannot be made directly on cake. Small tips include numbers 107, 129, 217, 220, 224, 225 (each form center holes), 135, 108, and 195. For large flowers, tips 1B, 1C, 1E, 1G, 2C, 2E and 2F. Use tip 190 or 225 and slightly stiffer consistency icing. Hold bag at a 90° angle with tip touching surface. For swirled flowers: Curve wrist around to the left and, as you squeeze out icing, bring hand back to the right. Stop pressure, pull tip away. For star flowers: Squeeze and keep tip in icing until star petals are formed. Stop pressure, pull away. Add tip 2 or 3 dot flower centers.

LEAF TIPS

The v-shaped openings of these tips give leaves pointed ends. With any leaf tip you can make plain, ruffled or stand-up leaves. Make leaves with center veins from small 65s, 65-70, to large, 112-115 and 355. Other popular leaf tips are numbers 71-76, 326, 349, 352.

BASIC LEAF

STAND UP LEAF

Hold bag at 45° angle to surface, back of bag facing you. Squeeze and hold tip in place to let icing fan out into base, then relax and stop pressure as you pull tip towards you and draw leaf to a point.

Hold bag at a 90° angle to surface. Touch tip lightly and squeeze, holding tip in place as icing fans out to form base. Relax and stop pressure as you pull tip straight up and away creating stand-up leaf effect.

PETAL TIPS

These tips have an opening that is wide at one end, narrow at the other. This teardrop-like shaped opening yields a variety of petals that form flowers like the rose, carnation, daisy, pansy and more (see pages 91-93). Petal tips can also make ribbons, drapes and swags; bows and streamers. Plain rose tips include numbers 101s, 101, 102, 103, 104, 124, 125, 126, 127 and giant roses, tip 127D. Swirled rose tips that make instant-curled petals are 97, 116, 118 and 119. Others include 59s, 59, 60, 61, 121, 122, 123, 62, 63, 64 and 150.

RIBBON DRAPE

Hold bag at a 45° angle to surface, fingertips on bag facing you. Touch wide end of tip to surface, angle narrow end out about ¼" away from surface. As you squeeze, swing tip down and up to the right forming ribbon drape.

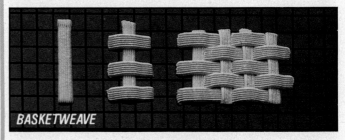

RUFFLE

Use same procedure as for ribbon drape. And, as you swing tip down and up to form a curve, move hand up and down slightly to ruffle the icing.

RIBBON TIPS

These are decorating tips with a smooth side for making smooth, wide icing stripes and/or one serrated side for making ribbed, wide icing stripes. When short ribbed horizontal stripes are interwoven in vertical rows the effect is that of a basketweave. Tips are 46 and 47. For smooth stripes, 44 and 45. For ribbed stripes, 48 and 327. Large ribbon tips include 1D, 2B and 789.

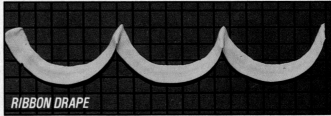

BASKETWEAVE

Use star or basketweave tip and medium consistency icing. You may use a small round tip as a vertical guide line if preferred.

1. Hold bag at 45° angle to cake with serrated side of tip facing up (or use round tip). Touch tip lightly to surface and squeeze out a vertical line of icing.

2. Next, hold bag at a 45° angle to surface, fingertips gripping bag facing you. Touch tip, serrated side facing up, to top left side of vertical line and squeeze out 3" horizontal bar. Add two more horizontal bars, each about a tip width apart, to cover vertical line.

3. With bag and tip at 45° angle, make another vertical line of icing to right of first one, overlapping ends of horizontal bars. Use same procedure as step two to cover this line with two horizontal bars, working them in spaces of bars in first row.

4. Repeat entire procedure, alternating vertical lines and horizontal bars, to create a basketweave effect. Other tips may be used for basketweave, but serrated tips 46-48 give icing a ribbed basket effect.

Making A Rose

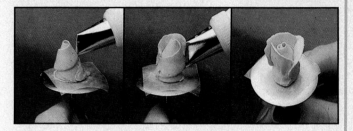

THE FLOWER NAIL

The flower nail is a decorating tool used to make the most popular flower of all, the rose. It is also used to make pretty flowers like the violet, apple blossom and the daisy (see p. 93).

The key to making any flower on the nail is to coordinate the turning of the nail with the formation of a petal. The stem of the nail is held between your left thumb and forefinger, so you can turn the flat nailhead surface at the same time you're piping a flower with your right hand. Using the flower nail takes practice, but the beautiful results are well worth the effort!

Note: Left-handed decorators should use the nail opposite of above instructions.

Make all flowers on the nail with royal or stiffened buttercream icing (see p. 81 and 83), and the tips specified for each flower. Air dry flowers made in royal icing, and freeze buttercream flowers (buttercream roses can also be placed directly on iced cake) until firm at least 2 hours. Then, when you're ready to decorate, remove the frozen flowers, a few at a time, and position them on the cake. (Snow White Buttercream Icing flowers can be air dried).

For each flower you make, attach a 2'' square of waxed paper to the nailhead with a dot of icing. Make a flower; remove waxed paper and flower together.

1ST ROW OF 3 PETALS

1. Hold bag at 45° angle with end of bag pointed over your shoulder. Touch wide end of tip 104 to midpoint of bud base. Turn nail counterclockwise and move tip up and back down to midpoint of bud base forming first petal of rose.

2. Start slightly behind end of 1st petal and squeeze out 2nd petal same as first.

3. Start slightly behind end of 2nd petal and add a 3rd petal, ending this petal overlapping starting point of 1st petal. Now you have a full rosebud made on a nail to use just as you would a rosebud made on a flat surface (see p. 92).

MAKE THE ROSE BASE

1. Use tip 10 or 12. Hold the bag perpendicular at a 90° angle to nail with tip slightly above center of nailhead.

2. Squeeze with a heavy pressure, keeping bottom of tip in icing until you've made a full, round base.

3. Ease pressure as you raise tip up and away from nailhead, narrowing base to a dome head. The base is very important for successful rose-making. Be sure that it is secure to nail and can support all the petals. Practice until you feel comfortable with the technique.

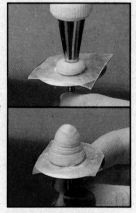

2ND ROW OF 5 PETALS

1. Touch wide end of tip 104 slightly below center of a petal in 1st row, angle narrow end of tip out slightly more than you did for 1st row of petals. Squeeze and turn nail counterclockwise, moving tip up then down to form 1st petal in second row.

2. Start slightly behind this last petal and make a 2nd petal. Repeat this procedure for a total of 5 petals, ending last petal overlapping the 1st petal's starting point.

THE CENTER BUD

1. Use tip 104. Hold bag at a 45° angle to nail with wide end of tip just below top of dome, and narrow end pointed in slightly. Back of bag should be pointed over your shoulder.

2. Now you must do three things simultaneously...squeeze, pull tip up and out away from top of dome stretching icing into a ribbon band, as you turn the nail counterclockwise.

3. Relax pressure as you bring band of icing down around dome, overlapping the point at which you started.

3RD ROW OF 7 PETALS

1. Touch wide end of tip 104 below center of petal in 2nd row, again angling narrow end of tip out a little more. Squeeze and turn nail counterclockwise and move tip up and down forming 1st petal. Repeat for a total of 7 petals.

2. Slip waxed paper and completed rose off nail. Attach another square of waxed paper and start again. Have several squares of waxed paper cut ahead of time so you can continue rose-making without stopping. TIP: An easy way to place a buttercream icing rose directly on your cake is to slide open scissors under base of rose and gently lift flower off waxed paper square and flower nail. Position flower on cake by slowly closing scissors and pushing base of flower with stem end of flower nail.

Practice is the key to perfect blooms!

FLOWERS

FLAT-SURFACE FLOWERS: ROSEBUDS, HALF ROSES AND SWEET PEAS

These are flowers you can make right on a cake, or any flat surface. To make all three, use tip 104 and royal, or stiffened buttercream icing, (see pages 81, 83 for recipes). Attach a sheet of waxed paper to the back of a cookie sheet with dots of icing or use Wilton Practice Board, p. 119.
Make your practice flowers in horizontal rows and when you've filled the entire sheet, loosen the waxed paper with a spatula to remove it and start again.

When you're decorating a cake with lots of flat-surface flowers, make all the ones you need ahead of time using this same cookie sheet method. Let them dry, and they're ready when you're ready to decorate! Air dry flowers made with royal icing and freeze flowers made with buttercream until hard (at least 2 hours). Remove buttercream flowers with your spatula, a few at a time as you decorate, so they stay firm (Snow White Buttercream Icing flowers may be air-dried).
To attach a flower to the top or the sides of a cake, dot the cake with stiffened icing and set in position. Whether used individually as a border design, or arranged in clusters, sprays or bouquets, flowers add beauty to cakes, candy and cookies.

ROSEBUD

1. Make base petal. Hold bag at a 45° angle so that the end of bag points over your right shoulder, fingertips gripping bag facing you. Touch wide end of tip 104 to surface, point narrow end to the right. Squeeze, move forward ¼", hesitate so icing fans out, then move back as you stop pressure.

2. Make overlapping center petal. Hold bag in same position as step 1 with wide end of tip touching inside right edge of base petal, narrow end of tip pointing slightly up above base petal. Squeeze as icing catches inside edge of base petal and rolls into interlocking center bud. Stop pressure, touch large end back to surface and pull tip away.

3. Make sepals and calyx with tip 3 and thinned icing. Hold bag at a 45° angle to base of bud with end of bag pointing towards you. Touch tip to bud. Squeeze and pull tip up and away from flower, relaxing pressure as you draw sepal to a point. Add three sepals and tip 3 calyx.

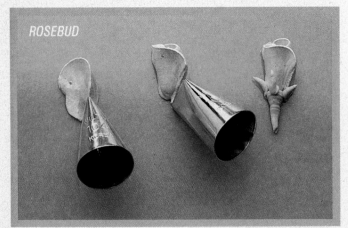

ROSEBUD

HALF ROSE

1. Make a rosebud without sepals and calyx. Hold bag at a 45° angle so that end of bag points to the right, fingertips gripping bag facing you. Touch wide end of tip 104 to bottom left side of bud. Squeeze, move it up, around to the right and down, relaxing pressure.

2. Make right petal. Hold bag in opposite position as far left petal. Touch wide end of tip to bottom right side of bud base. Squeeze, move up, around to the left and down to center of bud base. Stop pressure, pull tip away.

3. Make sepals and calyx with tip 3 thinned icing. Follow same procedure as for step 3 of rosebud, starting at bottom center of half rose.

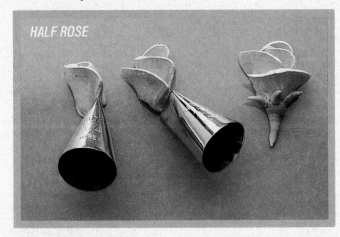

HALF ROSE

SWEET PEA

1. Make base petal. Hold bag at a 45° angle to surface, fingertips on bag facing you. Touch wide end of tip 104 to surface, point narrow end slightly up and away from surface. Squeeze, pivot tip around to the right forming cupped base petal.

2. Make center petal. Hold bag at a 45° angle to surface so that back end of bag points toward you. Touch wide end of the tip to bottom of base petal, just inside cupped edge, point narrow end of tip straight up. Squeeze, raise tip slightly and let icing roll into center petal. Stop pressure, lower tip, pull away.

3. Make side petals. Touch wide end of tip to bottom left edge of center rolled petal, point narrow end up and out to the left. Squeeze, lift tip slightly, stop pressure, lower tip, pull away. Repeat procedure for right petal, starting at bottom edge of center petal.

4. Add calyx to flower base with tip 3 and thinned icing. Hold bag at 45° angle to surface so that end of bag points toward you. Insert tip into flower base and hold in place as you squeeze to build up pressure as you draw tip down, narrowing calyx to a point.

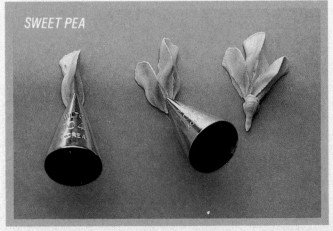

SWEET PEA

FLOWER NAIL FLOWERS

Use Royal or stiffened Buttercream Icing (see recipes p. 82-83) and the tips specified for each flower. We refer only to Buttercream Icing in the instructions that follow. If you use Snow-White Buttercream Icing for flowers, you may air dry them instead of freezing. When decorating with flowers or candy, always make extras to allow for breakage. Instructions usually call for more than you'll need.

Daisy

1. For best results, use Royal Icing (p. 83). Use tip 103 and dot center of nail with icing as guide for flower center. Hold bag at a 45° angle with tip almost parallel to nail surface, wide end of tip pointing to nail center, narrow end pointing out. Now, starting at any point near outer edge of nail, squeeze and move tip towards center icing dot. Stop pressure, pull tip away. Repeat procedure for a total of twelve or more petals.

2. Add tip 4 yellow flower center and press to flatten. For pollen-like effect dampen your finger, press in gold edible glitter, (see p. 130) and then flatten center.

Apple Blossom

1. Use tip 101 or 101s and hold bag at a 45° angle to flower nail with wide end of tip touching nail center, narrow end pointed out 1/8" away from nail surface.

2. Squeeze bag and turn nail as you move tip 1/8" out from nail center and back, relaxing pressure as you return to starting point.

3. Repeat procedure to make four more petals. Add five tip 1 dots for center.

Chrysanthemum

1. Hold bag at 90° angle to nail and pipe tip 6 mound of icing on nail center. Use tip 79 and very stiff royal icing for short petal effect. Hold bag at a 45° angle to outer base edge of mound, with half-moon opening of tip 79 pointing up. Squeeze row of 1/2" long cupped base petals.

2. Add second row of shorter petals atop and in between those in first row. Repeat procedure making each additional row of petals shorter than the previous row.

3. When entire mound is covered add a few stand-up petals to top and tip 1 center dots.

Daffodil and Jonquil

1. Use tip 104 for daffodil or tip 103 for jonquil. Hold bag at a 45° angle to nail, with large end of tip touching nail, narrow end pointed out and almost parallel to nail surface. Squeeze as you turn nail, move tip out about 1/2" and back to center of nail to form petal. Repeat procedure for five more petals.

2. Dip your fingers in cornstarch and pinch ends of petals to points.

3. Pipe row-upon-row of tip 2 string circles and top with tip 1 zigzag for center.

Narcissus

Use tip 102 and same procedure as for daffodil to make six 3/4" long petals. Add tip 1 coil center and tip 1 zigzag.

Violet

1. Use tip 59s and same procedure as for apple blossom to make three 1/4" long petals and two 1/8" base petals.

2. Add two tip 1 center dots.

Pansy

1. Fit two decorating bags with tip 104. Fill one with yellow icing, the other with violet. Hold bag with yellow icing at a 45° angle to nail center, squeeze and move tip out to edge of nail. Turn nail as you squeeze, relax pressure as you return to nail center. Repeat to form second yellow petal. Use same procedure to add two shorter yellow petals atop the first two.

2. Now with bag of violet icing, squeeze out a base petal that equals the width of the yellow petals, using a back and forth hand motion for a ruffled effect.

3. Use an art brush to add veins of violet food color after flower has air dried. Add tip 1 string loop center.

LILY NAIL FLOWERS

The Wilton lily nail (see p. 115) lets you make natural-looking flowers with bell-like shapes and cupped, turned-up petals. Different lily nail sizes relate to the size of flowers you can make. The larger the nail, the larger the flower. Always use royal icing for flowers made on the lily nail, (see p. 83 for recipe) since softer icing will not hold their deeply-cupped shapes. To make any flower on the lily nail, place a 2" aluminum foil square in bottom half of nail. Press in top half to form a foil cup. Remove the top half. Lightly spray foil with vegetable oil spray. This makes it easier to remove from foil after icing has dried and reduces breakage. Pipe a flower on the foil cup and lift out flower and foil to dry. Repeat procedure.

Easter Lily

1. Probably the most popular lily nail flower of all. Use tip 68 and 1-5/8" lily nail. Touch center well of nail with tip and squeeze, pulling petal up and over edge of foil cup. Decrease pressure as you reach tip of petal and hesitate before you stop pressure and pull tip away, drawing petal to a point.

2. Pipe 2 more petals as shown. then pipe 3 more petals in between the open spaces.

3. Add tip 14 star center and push in artificial stamens, (see p. 130).

Daisy   Apple Blossom   Chrysanthemum   Daffodil and Jonquil

Narcissus   Violet   Pansy   Easter Lily

FIGURE PIPING

Figure piping lets you create whimsical 3-dimensional figures and decorations out of icing. Unlike borders and flowers that require perfecting specific techniques, figure piping allows you to experiment and use your imagination. Since most of the figures you'll be making are a caricature, they do not have to be perfect. Icing consistency, pressure control and practice are essential to successful piping. Pipe most figures in Royal Icing (p. 83) on waxed paper. Let dry. Position on cake. Simple shapes can be made in Buttercream (recipe p. 82) directly on cake. If you choose to use buttercream, it does not withstand humidity or hold its shape as well as royal icing. Some buttercream icing figures may be frozen. Hint: Let buttercream icing set before shaping or flattening with fingertip dipped in cornstarch.

Noah's Ark Animals (p. 4)

For Elephants: Use tip 12 and royal icing. Hold bag at 90° angle over waxed paper surface. With even pressure, squeeze out kidney bean shaped heads (each about 2" wide) side-by-side. Pipe tip 12 smooth stripe on sides of heads and flatten with fingertip dipped in cornstarch). Add tip 2 facial features. Let dry. Pipe tip 12 trunks after attaching to cake with royal icing. Hold bag at 45° angle and with even pressure, pipe right trunk, then left (overlap end).

For Lions: Use tip 12. On waxed paper, hold bag at 90° angle and with even pressure, pipe out an oval-shaped ball. Gradually pull tip up to form a snout. Pull tip away. Add tip 16 zigzag curly mane (pipe several rows to build up dimension). Pipe tip 12 dot ears and tip 2 facial features. Let dry. Attach to cake with dots of icing.

Elephants & Donkeys (p. 71)

For Elephants: Use tips 2A, 3, 12 and 104. **For Donkeys:** Use tips 2A, 3, 6, 12. Use royal icing for best results. To pipe bodies: Use tip 2A, hold bag at 90° angle to surface. With heavy pressure, squeeze out icing until body builds to desired height. Stop pressure, then pull away. For support, gently twist a plastic straw cut to to fit into icing. Let dry.

For elephant head, tuck tip 2A into "neck" and squeeze out icing, gradually relaxing pressure as you form trunk. Stop pressure and pull tip away. For donkey head, follow same method, but move tip out and away from body to form snout (shape with fingertip dipped in cornstarch).

Insert tip 12 into bodies and pipe legs and "arms" using same method. Add tip 104 "rose petal ears" to elephant; tip 6 dot ears (pinch ends to form points) on donkeys. Trim faces with tip 3 dot eyes.

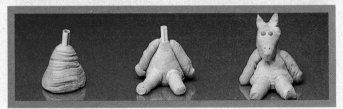

WIRED FLOWERS

To Put Flowers On Wire Stems: You'll need: 1" waxed paper squares, 4" or 6" florist wires and florist tape (p. 130), wire cutters, styrofoam block, round and leaf tips (p. 112-115) and royal icing flowers. Flowers and leaves must be made of royal icing for wired and taped arrangements.

1. Hold decorating bag perpendicular to a waxed paper square and squeeze out a small mound of icing with tip 6. This will be the calyx or flower base.

2. Make 1/8" hook on one end of florist wire and insert the hook into the calyx. Use a moistened decorator brush to smooth the places where icing and wire meet, tapering the calyx and securing it to the wire into styrofoam to let calyx dry. Repeat steps 1 and 2, making calyxes in different sizes proportionate to the flowers you're using.

3. When dry, remove waxed paper, dot calyxes with tip 3 royal icing and attach flowers. Push wire stems into a styrofoam to dry.

MARBELOUS MARBLE CHEESECAKE

Crumb crust: 1 cup finely crushed vanilla wafers
        1/4 cup sugar
        3 Tbsps. butter or margarine, melted
Filling:
2 Tbsp. gelatin
1/2 cup cold water
1/3 cup milk
4 eggs, separated
3/4 cup sugar
1/2 tsp. vanilla
1/4 tsp. salt
Three 8-oz packages cream cheese, softened
1/2 cup sugar
1 cup whipping cream
1 oz. square semi-sweet chocolate, melted

For crust: Combine crumbs and sugar. Add melted butter and stir until well blended. Pat evenly in bottom of springform pan.
For filling: Soak gelatin in water. Scald milk in heavy 1 quart saucepan or double boiler. Beat yolks, 3/4 cup sugar, vanilla and salt until well-blended. Gradually add milk to beaten egg mixture. Heat and stir over medium low heat or boiling water until mixture is bubbling and thickened. Stir softened gelatin into hot custard mixture until dissolved. Remove from heat and cool slightly. Beat cream cheese until smooth. Gradually add custard mixture to the cheese, mix until blended. Whip egg whites until stiff but not dry. Continue to beat and gradually add 1/2 cup sugar. Fold whites into custard-cheese mixture. Beat whipping cream until stiff, fold into cheese mixture. Reserve 1/2 cup mixture. Pour remaining mixture into pan. Mix 1/2 cup cheese mixture with melted chocolate. Add chocolate mixture by dropping spoonfuls on top in 3-4 different spots. Use knife to swirl chocolate through cheesecake in zigzag motion. Refrigerate several hours until firm. (See p. 32 for decorating instructions.)

Candy Cut-Outs

You'll need melted Candy Melts™ brand confectionery coating and aluminum foil. Cover counter top with 7'' x 11'' aluminum foil. To confine coating, tape two strips of corrugated cardboard in thickness of coating desired to vertical sides of foil. Pour melted coating at top of aluminum foil sheet. Take a metal ruler or spatula and pull coating towards you to evenly spread across sheet. Let set at room temperature until firm. Score with spatula into triangles, rectangles, hearts or any geometric shape. Break into shapes and cut away excess coating. Trim cake tops and sides with these intriguing candy wafers.

MERINGUE RECIPE

2 Tablespoons Wilton Meringue Powder (p. 130)
1/2 cup cold water
6 Tablespoons + 2 teaspoons granulated sugar
6 Tablespoons + 2 teaspoons granulated sugar
1/4 teaspoon almond extract

Place meringue powder, water and 6 Tablespoons plus 2 teaspoons sugar in a mixing bowl. Whip at high speed for 5 minutes. Gradually add remaining 6 Tablespoons plus 2 teaspoons and flavor. Continue to whip at high speed for 5 minutes more until meringue is stiff and dry. Pipe decorations according to specific instructions. Bake per directions on pages 12 and 51.

CANDY CUT-OUTS AND BAKING RECIPES

EASY APRICOT GLAZE

Add a slight tangy flavor and glistening effect to cakes you plan to decorate simply with fruit and minimal icing trims.

RECIPE

Heat apricot preserves to boiling and strain. Use the ''juice'' to glaze cake or fruit according to directions below.
For cakes: Apricot Glaze may be used as a coating under fondant as well as a shiny glaze for cakes to be decorated with fruit. Prepare cake by brushing all loose crumbs from surface. Use a pastry brush to evenly coat completely cooled cake with warmed glaze.
For fruit: Drain canned, thawed or fresh fruit. Blot fruit dry with paper toweling if necessary. Place fruit on rack over drip pan. Spoon glaze over fruit to coat evenly. Let set until dry. Arrange on cake top.

ROLL-OUT COOKIES

Here's a success-tested, firm vanilla sugar cookie dough for cut-out cookies.

1/2 cup butter or margarine, softened
1/2 cup sugar
2 large eggs

ROLL-OUT COOKIES cont.

1 tsp. vanilla
2 tsps. baking powder
2-3/4 cups flour

Preheat oven to 400°.

In a large bowl, cream butter and sugar with an electric mixer. Beat in eggs and vanilla. Add baking powder and flour one cup at a time, mixing after each addition. The dough will be very stiff; blend last flour in by hand. Do not chill dough.

Divide dough into 2 balls. On a floured surface, roll each ball in a circle approximately 12'' in diameter and 1/8'' thick. Dip cutters in flour before each use. Bake cookies on ungreased cookie sheet on top rack of oven for 6 to 7 minutes, or until cookies are lightly browned.

COOKIE DECORATING & SPECIAL ICING RECIPE

Here is an icing that dries to a shiny, hard finish and tastes good, too. It works well for filling in cookie top designs that have been outlined with this special icing or royal icing. Do outlining and filling in with tip 2 or 3. When dry, cookies can easily be stacked. **NEW! COOKIEMAKER COOKIE ICING MIX** is ideal for all cookie decorating! So versatile...can be flavored and made to different consistencies for icing, piping and filling. See p. 108 for more details.

COOKIE ICING RECIPE

1 cup sifted confectioners sugar
2 tsps. milk
2 tsps. light corn syrup

Place sugar and milk in bowl. Stir until mixed thoroughly. Add corn syrup and mix well. For filling in areas, use thinned icing (add small amounts of light corn syrup until desired consistency is reached.)

MOUTHWATERING BUTTER COOKIES

May be made in mixer or food processor. This cookie dough is ideal for molds or for piping. To use for cut-out cookies just chill and roll out.

1 cup butter
1 cup sugar
2 large eggs
3 cups flour
1 teaspoon cinnamon or 1 teaspoon grated lemon rind

Preheat oven to 375°.

Cream butter; add sugar gradually. Blend until very light and creamy; beat in eggs. Add flour and cinnamon (or lemon rind). Stir until blended. Press dough into ungreased mold and prick 2 or 3 times with fork (to keep dough from puffing while baking). Dough should be level with top of mold. Bake 10-15 minutes. Remove from molds immediately. Recipe yields 5 dozen molded or 7 dozen piped cookies.

BROWN BUTTER COOKIES

Sweet cake-like cookies with a delicate almond flavor.

3/4 cup butter
1-2/3 cups confectioners sugar
1 cup powdered almonds
1/3 cup flour
5 egg whites

Preheat oven to 350° F.

Cook butter over medium heat just until light brown. Watch closely, butter burns easily. Mix the sugar, powdered almonds and flour together. Gently stir in egg whites, then the hot butter.

Baking: Generously butter the Tartlet molds. Fill each mold halfway with the batter and place on cookie sheet. Bake at 350° for 13-15 minutes. Remove immediately. Yields approximately 2 dozen.

WILTON CANDY MELTS™ *brand confectionery coating (p. 120) are the key ingredient to successful, easy candy making. They melt easily, right to the ideal consistency for molding, dipping, filling and more. They have a creamy, rich flavor or for a change of taste can be flavored with Wilton Candy Flavors (p. 120). See pages 120-128 for all the Wilton CandyMaker™ products. For more about candy making get the* **Candy Making for Beginners Book** *or the* **Complete Wilton Book of Candy** *on p. 120. The New Candy Making Home Study Course has it all, see p. 128.*

CANDY MELTS™ BASICS

MELTING. *There are two popular ways to melt Candy Melts for molding or dipping.*

Double Boiler Method — *Fill lower pan of double boiler with water to a depth below level of top pan. Bring to a simmer, then remove from heat. Put Candy Melts in top pan and set in position on lower pan. Stir constantly (do not beat) until smooth and completely melted.*

Microwave Method — *Place 1 lb. Candy Melts in microwave-safe container. Microwave at ½ power or defrost setting for 1 minute, stir thoroughly. Reduce times to microwave less than 1 lb. of Candy Melts. Microwave and stir at 30-second intervals until smooth and completely melted.*

Important: *Do not add water, milk or any liquid to "thin" your coating. This will cause it to thicken and harden immediately. If coating is thick, add 1 Tablespoon of hydrogenated vegetable shortening to 1 pound coating. Stir well.*

MOLDING. *Pour or spoon melted Candy Melts into dry molds (p. 123-127). Tap molds until all air bubbles are gone. Refrigerate until firm. Unmold by gently tapping mold. Remove excess coating from candies with a sharp knife or vegetable peeler.*
Hint: *Fill an uncut parchment or disposable decorating bag (p. 117) with melted coating, cut tip away and fill molds.*

TO MOLD STAND-UP CANDY. *For stand-up candy use Wilton 2-pc. molds on p. 124. Cut mold in half along dotted line and snap together. Stand upright. Fill mold with melted coating and gently tap mold to release air bubbles. To make hollow candy, place in refrigerator for about 5-10 minutes to harden the outside of mold. Pour out excess. Return mold to refrigerator; harden completely. Unmold. To seal the bottom, cover cookie sheet with waxed paper. Pour a pool of melted Candy Melts that's larger than the opening. Position hollowed candy on top of pool. Let set. Trim excess coating away. For solid, stand-up candy, fill as for hollow candy and refrigerate until firm, approx. 1½ hours. Unmold and trim excess. To make a candy box, fill both halves of the Heart Box mold on (p. 124) with melted Candy Melts and gently tap to release air bubbles. Place in refrigerator. After a few minutes, when outside is hardened, remove bottom half and pour out excess. Return to refrigerator to harden completely. Unmold. Fill with candy.*

CANDY MELTS VARIATIONS

How to Flavor: *Add approximately 1/4 teaspoon Wilton oil-based Candy Flavor (p. 120) to 1 lb. of melted Candy Melts. Never use alcohol based flavorings. They will cause coatings to harden.*

How to Color: *Add Wilton Candy Colors (p. 120) to melted Candy Melts a little at a time. Mix thoroughly before adding more color. Colors tend to deepen as they're mixed. Pastel colored candies are most appetizing, so keep this in mind when tinting.*

Decorating with Candy Melts: *To 1 cup of melted coating, add ¼ teaspoon light corn syrup. More corn syrup may be added until coating is of piping consistency. Mix well. Fill decorating bag and pipe decorations on candy. Work quickly. Allow to set until firm. Remove bottom half and pour out excess. Return to refrigerator to harden completely. Unmold. Fill with candies.*

Kids will love 'em...create a cast of candy characters for table favors! Molds sold on page 123.

DIPPING CENTERS AND MORE

Melt Candy Melts. When completely melted, place a delicious CandyMaker™ center (Center Mixes sold on p. 120), nuts, blotted fruit bits, mini-pretzels, cookies and more, one at a time into coating.

Roll around gently but quickly with Dipping Spoon or Fork (p. 120) until well-covered (use a spoon if cluster-type). Slip the dipper under the center. Scrape off excess coating against edge of bowl or pan. Drop right side up on waxed paper. As candy drops from dipper, twist the thread of coating clinging to dipper and make a swirl on top. Let set until firm.

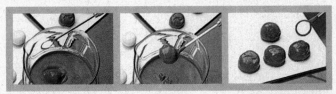

TO CREATE MULTI-COLOR EFFECTS

"Painting" method. Use a Decorator's Brush dipped in melted Candy Melts. Paint features or details desired. Let set. Fill mold. Refrigerate until set. Unmold.

"Layering" method. Pour melted coating in dry molds to desired height. Refrigerate until partially set. Fill mold with contrasting color melted coating. Refrigerate until partially set. Repeat until desired numbers of layers are formed and hardened. Unmold. Wilton Classic Candy Molds are available in a wonderful variety of unique and traditional shapes. Their generous depth makes painting and layering fun and easy. See pages 125-127 for the complete story.

HOW TO MAKE HARD CANDY

New Wilton Easy Melts™ (p. 122) make creating colorful, jewel-like hard candies so easy. No thermometer is needed! Use with Wilton quality Hard Candy/Lollipop Molds.

1. Lightly brush or spray Wilton Hard Candy or Lollipop Molds (p. 122) with vegetable oil.

2. To Melt. There are two ways to melt your Easy Melts.

Saucepan Method:
Place one package of Easy Melts in a heavy saucepan over medium low heat. When wafers begin to melt, stir occasionally (about 10 minutes). Continue stirring until candy is completely melted and pourable. Let stand 1 to 2 minutes to allow bubbles to disappear.

Microwave Method — *Place 1 lb. Candy Melts in microwave-safe container. Microwave at ½ power or defrost setting for 1 minute, stir thoroughly. Repeat. Microwave and stir at 30-second intervals until smooth and completely melted. Reduce times to microwave less than 1 lb. of Candy Melts.*

3. To Mold:
Pour melted Easy Melts into oiled molds. Unmold. Let set at room temperature.

NEW! EASY MELTS *make it so quick and easy to make luscious lollipops and delightful bite-size treats! Wilton Hard Candy Molds, available in a wonderful variety of shapes and sizes, will create tasty surprises that are bound to please!*

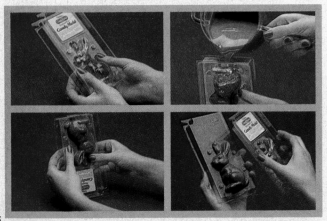

NEW! EASY MELTS™!
Now, it's easy to make luscious lollipops and delightful bite-size treats.

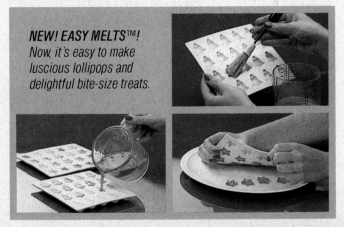

WILTON SCHOOL

The Wilton school is accredited by the Illinois State Board of Education under the provisions of the Illinois Private Business and Vocational Schools Act. Skilled instructors offer personalized guidance and take you step-by-step to accomplishment.

The class agenda includes 5 important courses.

MASTER COURSE. 2 weeks — 70 hours. Cake decorating fundamentals that will turn you into a professional decorator. You'll go from basic stars to lavish wedding cakes.
Course fee, $500.00

FOREIGN METHOD. 2 weeks — 80 hours. Includes a detailed Gum Paste course, the Australian, Nirvana, South African methods and more. Previous decorating experience essential.
Course fee, $500.00

LAMBETH COURSE. 2 weeks — 80 hours. You'll become an expert at the impressive English over-piped style of cake decorating. Previous decorating experience required.
Course fee, $500.00

BEGINNERS GUM PASTE. 15 hours. A mini-course that teaches the basics of the art of gum paste.
Course fee, $125.00

CANDY MAKING COURSE. 1 week — 30 hours. You will learn hollow molding, center making and hand dipping as well as how to make fondant, marzipan, truffles, liqueur and candy cups and other fabulous confections. You will work with confectionery coatings and real chocolate.
Course fee, $300.00

The Wilton School of Cake Decorating and Confectionary Art is located in Woodridge, Illinois (a suburb of Chicago). Course enrollment is limited, so don't delay. To enroll or for more information, call or write to Manuel Lopez, Wilton School of Cake Decorating and Confectionary Art, 2240 W. 75th Street, Woodridge, IL. Or call 312/963/7100. A free catalog will be sent upon request.

You may charge your courses. VISA and MasterCard welcome.

SPECIALTY HOME STUDY LESSONS

1. Flower Making

2. Color Flow

3. Figure Piping

Now you can learn advanced decorating methods at home, at your convenience! Send for Flower Making, Figure Piping or Color Flow Lessons today. Basic skills are all you need to start. And you'll earn a certificate of completion from Wilton when you finish each course. The necessary tools you'll need come with each course. Each course is $19.99. Save by buying two for only $36.99. The total course program of 3 lessons is $49.99 complete. Use the convenient tear-out coupon between pages 128-129 to order. Charge them on VISA or MasterCard.

1. FLOWER MAKING. 902-M-1094. $19.99
Learn to make icing blossoms galore! You get 37 pages of illustrated instructions. Includes Artificial Flower Stamens, Flower Formers, Lily Nails, Meringue Powder Mix. All products shown are included.

2. COLOR FLOW. 902-M-1078. $19.99
Learn how to outline and fill in with a special icing to create perfect designs. The essential ingredient is Wilton Color Flow Mix. You'll also get Wilton

Hold-A-Cone, Decorator's Brushes, 8 in. spatula, 8-1/2 x 11 in. plastic-coated Practice Sheets. All products shown are included.

3. FIGURE PIPING. 902-M-1086. $19.99
Discover how to make fun figures atop your cakes. It's easy to do with step-by-step directions. Course provides six plastic clown heads. 8-1/2 x 11 in. plastic-coated Practice Sheet. 3 vinyl Decorating Bags, 3 Couplers. All products shown are included.

THE WILTON METHOD OF CAKE DECORATING

Three Magnificent Volumes — All You Need to Master Every Method of Cake Decorating Popular Throughout the World!

The Wilton Way of Cake Decorating, Volume One — The Beautiful Basic!

The one book you should own if you could own but one book on cake decorating! Provides the best groundwork on the basics, but adds a touch of magic even to simple techniques. It has helped many thousands of decorators achieve master status.

Starts right at the beginning and assumes no previous knowledge of cake decorating. It's a treasury of facts and ideas, a magnificent reference, a stimulating teaching tool covering all phases of Wilton-American decorating. Handsomely bound treasury will expand your basic knowledge of cake decorating to the fullest!

Over 600 full-color photos display the Wilton-American Method of Cake Decorating. This hard-cover book will take you from fast children's one-squeeze star cakes to gala tiered cakes, from icing borders and color techniques to lettering, flowers and color flow. Individual chapters cover sugar molding, 3-dimensional figure piping and working with marzipan. You'll discover ways to mold and decorate candy, ice cream and other foods for parties. Easy and delicious recipes, all tested by Wilton professionals, are included.

Hard-cover, 328 color pages; 9 x 11-1/4 in. Printed in Italy.
904-M-100. $29.99 each

Learn to pipe advanced trims like pretty Picot Lace!

Learn the techniques for making realistic Marzipan Treats!

Learn to make dozens of beautiful, lifelike Icing Flowers!

Learn to make artistic centerpieces and Sugar Mold Creations!

PATTERN BOOKS

VOLUME ONE PATTERN BOOK.
Includes all the necessary patterns for cakes shown in *The Wilton Way of Cake Decorating, Volume One.*
9-1/2 x 11-1/2 in.
408-M-3007. $5.99 each

VOLUME TWO PATTERN BOOK.
Over 70 patterns covering the cakes shown in *The Wilton Way of Cake Decorating, Volume Two.*
9-1/2 x 11-1/2 in.
408-M-1195. $5.99 each

VOLUME THREE PATTERN BOOK.
Includes all patterns needed for cakes shown in *The Wilton Way of Cake Decorating, Volume Three.*
9-1/2 x 11-1/2 in.
408-M-1306. $5.99 each

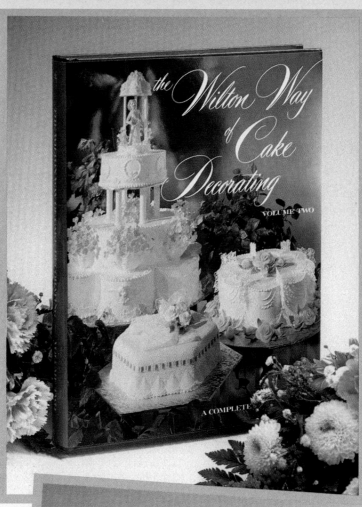

The Wilton Way of Cake Decorating, Volume Two — All Advanced Techniques!

Every experienced decorator will want to own this magnificent sequel to Volume One. This 328-page encyclopedia contains the world's most breathtaking cake decorating techniques. It describes in great detail advanced Wilton-American methods, as well as all major foreign techniques: English (Nirvana and over-piped), Australian, Continental, Mexican, Philippine and South African. Over 670 color photos display every important detail close-up so you can master them all.

Volume Two is also a wonderful guide to piped and shaped flowers; it covers flowers from every state in the Union, 23 varieties of icing roses. Shows cakes with air-borne icing loops and icing lace…photos enlarged to show details.

Learn to make gum paste flowers that look like live blooms! A new method makes it easy, fast and fun. Make realistic gum paste figures and more! See how Wilton People Molds take all the trouble and guess-work out of molding figures — leaving you just the pleasure and creativity!

Explore shimmering pulled sugar techniques as taught by Norman Wilton. He shows you, step-by-step, how to make glistening masterpiece cakes — even a romantic pulled sugar swan!

Volume Two presents an endless array of ideas decorators can adapt to their own masterpieces!

Hard-cover, 328 color pages: 9 x 11-1/4 in. Printed in U.S.A.
904-M-119. $29.99 each

*PLEASE NOTE:
All prices, certain products and services reflect the U.S.A. domestic market and do not apply in Australia or Canada.*

The Wilton Way of Cake Decorating, Volume Three — Uses of All 180 Tips!

There's never been a book like this — there's always been a need for one. Decorating tips are explained in depth! Knowing what each tip is capable of creating will make it possible for you to achieve your fullest decorating potential. It's a marvelous reference for every decorator — novice to advanced. Each tip, and its many piped effects, is shown actual size.

You'll be amazed at the fascinating discoveries you'll make! The 180 tips are divided into several families for easy learning. No other book teaches you so simply how to choose precisely the right tip to decorate a masterpiece!

Volume Three contains more than 400 color photos, covering over 40 beautiful borders, scores of flowers and many decorative motifs piped using various tips. A section on desserts, cookies and hors d'oeuvres offers beautiful party ideas to use all year round. New ideas for figuring piping and gum paste are explained and demonstrated. Full-color photos and instructions show you how to use your newly mastered techniques on decorated cakes.

Hard-cover, 328 color pages: 9 x 11-1/4 in. Printed in U.S.A.
904-M-348. $29.99 each

1.

2.

1. CELEBRATE! WEDDING CAKES BY WILTON. You'll find large and small cakes, flowery and lacy cakes, simple cakes and ones to challenge you. Scores of exciting designs include some using foreign methods, many using staircases and fountains. Directions and patterns included. Hard-cover, 192 color pages: 8-3/4 x 11-1/4 in.
916-M-847. $12.99 each

2. BEAUTIFUL BRIDAL CAKES THE WILTON WAY. A most impressive collection of wedding cake ideas! Select from an array of tiered wedding cakes designed using the Wilton method, plus continental, English, Australian and Philippine styles, too. You'll find cakes for intimate gatherings and gala affairs. Directions and patterns included for each cake. Hard-cover, 144 color pages: 8-1/2 x 11-1/4 in.
908-M-117. $12.99 each

Select one or several! These expert volumes are perfect for new ideas, reference and how-to's!

3.

4.

5.

3. THE WILTON BOOK OF WEDDING CAKES. All about weddings, showers, rehersal dinners, bachelor parties, anniversaries, more! Includes modern and traditional designs, towering tiers and simple creations. Information on planning, choosing flowers, selecting music and making arrangements included for bride-to-be. Hard-cover, 112 color pages: 8-7/8 x 11-1/4 in.
908-M-109. $10.99 each

4. THE WILTON WAY TO DECORATE FOR CHRISTMAS. Make this your merriest Christmas ever! Includes delicious recipes and holiday decorating ideas: festive cakes, candy, cookies, fruit cake, cream puffs plus ornaments and ideas for table centerpieces. Includes patterns, instructions and close-up photographs to make these fun projects easy to do! Soft-cover, 96 color pages: 8-1/2 x 11 in. Printed in Italy.
911-M-224. $6.99 each

5. CELEBRATE! CHRISTMAS. An idea book of Christmas magic! Gingerbread house designs cover many pages. We'll show you how to make candy trims and add icing decorations. We'll even show you how to light your dream house electrically. Includes centerpiece cookie and cake creations, delicious recipes and patterns. Soft-cover, 80 color pages: 8-1/2 x 11 in.
916-M-774. $6.99 each

INTRODUCING AN ALL NEW BOOK IN THE CELEBRATE! SERIES...spectacular party cakes and specialties to highlight every occasion from A to Z! This outstanding treasury is a must for experienced decorators, a valuable reference for beginners!

1. NEW! CELEBRATE! WITH PARTY SPECTACULARS FROM A TO Z. *A star-studded collection of over 150 all new cakes and treats from Anniversary cakes to Zany creatures. Complete instructions tell you how to decorate each cake, how to combine shapes for lifelike stand-up animal cakes, and how to construct a lighted gingerbread house! Learn new ways to use Candy Melts coating, quick pour fondant, cookies, gum paste, even popcorn and ice cream! Hard-cover, 160 color pages: 8-5/8 x 11-1/4 in.*
916-M-936. $12.99 each

Celebrate! A to Z Pattern Book.
408-M-446. $5.99 each

NEW!

2. CELEBRATE! III. *Introduces the Sugar Plum Shop with exciting birthday cakes plus Valentine's, Mother's and Father's Day cakes. Covers flowers-of-the-month for birthdays, marzipan and bread dough designs plus the Philippine and Australian methods. Soft-cover, 160 color pages: 8-1/2 x 10-7/8 in.*
916-M-308. $10.99 each

Celebrate! III Pattern Book.
408-M-229. $5.99 each

3. CELEBRATE! IV. *Sugar Plum Shop offers 43 new birthday cakes including a circus wagon! Elegant wedding cakes are included — one features a gum paste bridal couple. Discover the art of pulled sugar and learn to make Color Flow, candy and gingerbread! Hard-cover, 160 color pages: 8-7/8 x 11-1/4 in.*
916-M-456. $10.99 each

Celebrate! IV Pattern Book.
408-M-253. $5.99 each

4. CELEBRATE! V. *Wilton Golden Anniversary edition features half a century of cake decorating know-how and helpful hints. Offers nearly 200 cake designs with ideas for birthdays, weddings, holidays and more! Soft-cover, 160 color pages: 8-1/2 x 10-7/8 in.*
916-M-553. $10.99 each

Celebrate! V Pattern Book.
408-M-2019. $5.99 each

5. CELEBRATE! VI. *Discover glorious cake, candy and cookie ideas — fun, fancy and unique! Weddings and showers, holidays and birthdays are presented. Even the Australian, Philippine and English overpiped styles. Hard-cover, 160 color pages: 8-7/8 x 11-1/4 in.*
916-M-618. $10.99 each

Celebrate! VI Pattern Book.
408-M-407. $5.99 each

1. THE COMPLETE WILTON BOOK OF CANDY. Wilton candy specialists will teach you to make luscious molded and dipped chocolates, fudges, truffles, confectionery coating candies, marzipan, hard candies and more! Recipes with helpful hints clearly explain how to make dozens of different candies you never would have thought possible to make in your own kitchen. This beautiful book is packed with exciting ideas and how-to's that make it a wise investment for both beginning and advanced candy makers. Makes a creative gift, too! Hard-cover, 176 color pages: 7-7/8 x 10-7/8 in.
902-M-1243. $12.99 each

EXPLORE THE EXCITING WORLD OF CAKE DECORATING, CANDY MAKING AND MORE! WILTON PUBLICATIONS OFFER YOU THE BEST IN PROFESSIONAL, INFORMATIVE, EASY-TO-FOLLOW HOW-TO BOOKS. THEY'RE PACKED WITH ORIGINAL IDEAS, COLOR PHOTOS AND INSTRUCTIONS THAT APPEAL TO BOTH BEGINNING AND ADVANCED LEVELS.

PUBLICATIONS

2. 1984 WILTON YEARBOOK.
Introduce someone to the fun of cake decorating... order a copy for a friend! Soft-cover, 184 color pages: 8-1/4 x 11 in.
1701-M-847. $3.50 each

3. 1984 WILTON PATTERN BOOK.
All the patterns needed for '84 Yearbook cakes. Neatly bound and organized. Soft-cover, 8-7/8 x 11 in.
408-M-8408. $3.99 each

4. 1983 WILTON YEARBOOK. Filled with exciting ideas from cakes and cookies to candies made with Wilton products. Soft-cover, 192 color pages: 8-1/4 x 11 in.
1701-M-836. $3.50 each

5. 1983 WILTON PATTERN BOOK. Detailed patterns for unique designs in '83 Yearbook. Soft-cover, 8-7/8 x 11 in.
408-M-1829. $3.99 each

6. DISCOVER THE FUN OF CAKE DECORATING. Over 100 unique cake ideas, from fast and easy sheet cakes to glorious tiered wedding cakes, are shown with easy-to-follow, step-by-step instructions. A must for beginners, an indispensable reference for advanced decorators. Covers Basic Borders, Flowers, Figure Piping, Marzipan, Color Flow, more! Includes patterns and cake serving ideas. Hard-cover, 184 color pages: 8-7/8 x 11 in.
904-M-206. Was $15.95. Now $12.99 each

7. THE WILTON METHOD ON FILM! The Wilton film "The Art of Cake Decorating" is a great way to demonstrate Wilton Method cake decorating techniques to customers, clubs, classes. Full-color, 30-minute film features Norman Wilton skillfully piping icing decorations. Connie Riherd, professional instructor, creates lifelike gum paste flowers. Write for free information: **Wilton Enterprises, Film Productions 2240 West 75th Street, Woodridge, IL 60517**

2.

3. **NEW!**

4. **NEW!**
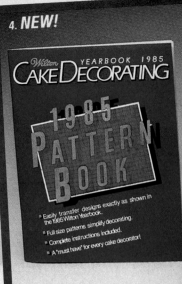

1-2. WILTON BEGINNERS GUIDE TO CAKE DECORATING. *Clearly shows and explains Wilton cake decorating basics. You get ideas for beautifully decorated cakes and children's party treats. Most* take less than 1 hour to decorate! Soft-cover, 34 color pages: 5-1/2 x 8-1/2 in.
1. ENGLISH VERSION.
902-M-1183. $1.99 each
2. SPANISH VERSION.
902-M-1418. $1.99 each

3. NEW! 1985 WILTON YEARBOOK. *New cake design ideas (and instructions!) let you add that special touch that means so much! Ideas cover cake decorating occasions from January to December. Includes mail-order product sections. Soft-cover, 192 color pages: 8-1/4 x 11 in.*
1701-M-857. $3.99 each

4. NEW! 1985 WILTON PATTERN BOOK. *Includes all of the patterns you'll need to dupli-cate your favorite designs from the 1985 Yearbook. Soft-cover, 8-7/8 x 11 in.*
408-M-8571. $3.99 each

5.

6. **NEW!**
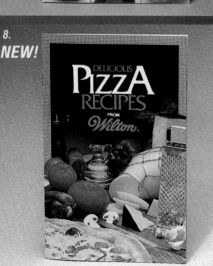

7.

8. **NEW!**

5. WILTON CANDY MAKING FOR BEGINNERS — REVISED EDITION. *Filled with delicious candy recipes, ideas and products. Basic candy making techniques, like molding and dipping, are explained in detail. Learn how to make lollipops, coat fruit and create candy treats with Wilton candy molds. It's fun, it's easy! Soft-cover, 44 color pages: 5-1/2 x 8-1/2 in.*
902-M-1361. $1.99 each

6. NEW! HOW TO MAKE GREAT TASTING FANCY COOKIES. *Learn to bake fancy cookies as good (or better) than the ones at the bakery! New book is packed with kitchen-tested recipes, helpful hints, detailed instructions. We'll show you how to get the best results using cookie cutters, new cookie molds or a pastry bag and decorating tip. Explore the possibilities using jams, jellies and fillings; glazes, drizzles and dips; nuts, fruits and piped icing decorations. Soft-cover, 44 color pages: 5-1/2 x 8-1/2 in.*
902-M-3600. $1.99 each

7. HOW TO GIVE GREAT PARTIES FOR KIDS. *Fun ideas, delicious, nutritious recipes kids will love, even party games to play! With this idea-packed book you can be sure your next children's party will be a big success. Soft-cover, 32 color pages: 5-1/2 x 8-1/2 in.*
909-M-499. $1.50 each

8. NEW! DELICIOUS PIZZA RECIPES FROM WILTON. *Flavorful, nutritious recipes, both classic and modern. Includes deep dish, spinach stuffed, barbeque, taco, more. Soft-cover, 10 pages: 5-1/2 x 8-1/2 in.*
1808-M-1250. $.99 each

Now you can make cookies

Wilton Cookie Maker

Wilton Introduces An Entirely New Line of Helpful Cookie-Making Products...

Homemade cookies can say so much for so many occasions. Because millions of people bake cookies and want them to be extra special, Wilton has created Cookie Maker, the line that helps you make cookies look as good as they taste.

Wilton Cookie Maker products make it easier than ever before for you to create impressive, fancy, great-tasting cookies that are sure to win you compliments. Cookie Maker has the molds, tips, cutters, decorating accessories and tools to help you make your cookies the best in town.

Elegant, specially-designed cookie molds help you create classic shaped cookies that look as if they came from the most exclusive continental bakeries. Each mold includes a special kitchen-tested recipe created exclusively for that mold. Once you make your dough, just press it into the molds, bake and unmold. And you have a delicious conti-

nental cookie. Or you may use one of the other recipes included with the mold, or perhaps your family favorite.

There are dozens of easy-to-use cookie cutters to help you quickly cut out delightful holiday, party and all-occasion cookies to enchant everyone.

Holiday and specialty cookie kits include charming ideas with the instructions and tools necessary to create dramatic, decorative and delicious centerpieces.

Quality pastry bags and metal tips pipe out dozens of beautiful, appetizing shaped cookies and pastries in no time.

And, exclusively from Wilton! Cookie Dips, Cookie Icing Mix, Sprinkle Tops, Cookie Colors...and other exciting new products to help you decorate your cookies in a very special way.

look as good as they taste!

902-M-3600 $1.99 each

And This Fabulous, New 44-Page Book Makes It All Easy!

It's the perfect book for anyone wanting to learn the techniques of fancy cookie making, baking and decorating!

You'll be thrilled with the amount of helpful information and creative ideas we've packed into its beautiful, full-color pages.

You'll review the basics of cookie making, such as what you need to get started, plus helpful cookie baking and storing hints. Next comes an array of wonderful, quality helpful cookie-making products that you'll want to have in your kitchen. Then we show you how to add the special touch to your cookies by dipping, drizzling and decorating. And of course we include great-tasting recipes for all kinds of

cookies—molded, pastry bag, drop and cut-outs. Many recipes were specially developed at the Wilton kitchens and introduce new taste sensations; they'll soon become your specialties. We've included some traditional favorites as well. Finally, to make your cookies unique and very special, we have lots of exciting fancy cookie decorating ideas with easy-to-follow instructions.

All your cookie making, from baking to decorating, will be fun and easy with the great selection of Wilton Cookie Maker products available now. We've included them in this book. You'll want to collect them all and make fancy cookie making an ongoing tradition in your home.

Wilton presents Classic Cookie Molds. Each has its own exclusive recipe.

Now, you can make cookies look as good as they taste!

Bring some of the flavor of the continent into your own home. Treat yourself, your family and friends to the exciting, unique taste and beauty of homemade molded cookies like those you find in fabulous foreign cities and in the finest American gourmet bakeries. This gourmet flavor has been captured in the exclusive continental recipes included on the labels. Just prepare the recipe, press the dough into the molds, bake, and unmold.

Six exceptional Classic Cookie Molds are available: Barcelona, Bavarian, Marseilles, Parisian, Venetian, Viennese. Each top-quality mold includes two continental designs and bakes 16 or 18 (depends on the mold) evenly-sized cookies that are perfect just as they are or may be dipped in chocolate or decorated for added elegance, or make your own sandwich cookies. In addition to the continental recipe, which is different for each mold, each label includes two other recipes plus decorating ideas.

These quality molds are made of durable, professional quality, heavy gauge aluminum for even browning. They're also dishwasher safe and rustproof.

1. PRESS DOUGH INTO MOLD   **2. BAKE**   **3. UNMOLD**

Marseilles

Calm waters, blue skies, fishing boats in the mist. Late breakfast outdoors and Marseilles cookies! A refreshing treat!

MARSEILLES CLASSIC COOKIE MOLD
2306-M-101 $6.99 each

Bavaria

White wine, flickering candles, rich, creamy dessert and Bavarian cookies.

BAVARIAN CLASSIC COOKIE MOLD
2306-M-104 $6.99 each

106

Barcelona 🇪🇸

Flamenco dancers, castanets, strumming guitars. Serve Barcelona cookies at a colorful fiesta!

BARCELONA CLASSIC COOKIE MOLD
2306-M-106 $6.99 each

Venice 🇮🇹

Winding canals, gliding gondolas. a walk on the Bridge of Sighs. Coffee and Venetian cookies at St. Mark's Square. A delicious coffee break anywhere.

VENETIAN MOLD
2306-M-105 $6.99 each

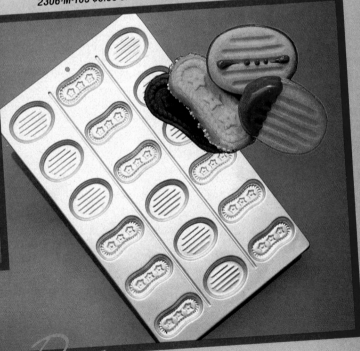

Vienna 🇦🇹

Violins humming a waltz, glittering chandeliers, a midnight buffet and rich Viennese cookies! The cookie that makes every event romantic.

VIENNESE MOLD
2306-M-102 $6.99 each

Paris 🇫🇷

Jaunty berets, honking cabs, a cafe in the shadow of the Eiffel Tower. The ideal luncheon dessert? Parisian cookies...abroad or at home!

PARISIAN CLASSIC COOKIE MOLD
2306-M-103 $6.99 each

Cookie molds made in Korea.

Wilton Cookie Maker

COOKIE DECORATING PRODUCTS

NEW!

1. **Cookie Icing Mix**
- Rich, creamy taste
- Easy to mix-just add milk and butter, recipes on back
- Yields about 2 cups

Perfect for decorating and frosting cookies. And for making sandwich cookie centers!

Recipes and instructions on back.

Chocolate FLAVOR

NET WT. 14 OZ. (39...)

NEW!

Cookie Icing Mix
Now, you can make cookies look as good as they taste!
- Rich, creamy taste
- Easy to mix-just add milk and butter, recipes on back
- Yields about 2 cups

Perfect for decorating and frosting cookies. And for making sandwich cookie centers!

Recipes and instructions on back.

Creamy White
Easy to tint with Wilton Co...

NET WT. 14 OZ. (3...)

2. **NEW!**

Cookie Dips ™
- Easy-to-melt wafers
- Ideal for dipping and decorating fancy cookies
- Rich, creamy taste
- Easy to follow instructions on back

3. **NEW!**

Cookie Color
Green

4. **NEW!**

Sprinkle·Tops
Multicolored Decorating Trims

Five festive trims for all your desserts... the quick and easy way!

NET WT. 4¼ OZ. (120...)

Easy-to-use quality products for making fancy cookies to your taste. Decorate simply or elaborately...all your cookies will rate rave reviews and repeat performances!

1. NEW! COOKIE ICING MIX. Make creamy cookie icing or filling easily with this convenient mix. Just add butter and milk. Complete recipes and instructions on package. White and chocolate flavored. Tint white with Wilton Cookie Colors. 14 oz. packages.
WHITE. 2302-M-139. $1.99 each
CHOCOLATE FLAVORED. 2302-M-137. $1.99 each

2. NEW! COOKIE DIPS. Rich, creamy, fast and easy-melting candy wafers perfect for dipping and drizzling cookies and pastries. White and light cocoa. Tint white a variety of colors with Wilton Cookie Colors. 12 oz. packages.
WHITE. 2302-M-133. $1.99 each
LIGHT COCOA. 2302-M-131. $1.99 each

3. NEW! COOKIE COLOR. Oil-based cookie color to tint white Wilton Icing Mix and Cookie Dips. Add a drop at a time to icing or melted coating until the desired color is reached. 3/4 oz. jars.
PINK. 2302-M-142. $1.99 each
RED. 2302-M-144. $1.99 each
YELLOW. 2302-M-146. $1.99 each
GREEN. 2302-M-148. $1.99 each

4. NEW! SPRINKLE TOPS — MULTI-COLORED DECORATING TRIMS. Delightfully decorative cookie trims that easily add the festive look to any cookie. Chocolate Sprinkles, Rainbow Mix, Non-Pareils, Red Crystals, Green Crystals.
2302-M-120. $1.59 per package

COOKIE MAKING ACCESSORIES & KITS

5.

6. **NEW!**

7.

8.

Wilton Featherweight Decorating Bag 12"

5. 8 IN. TAPERED SPATULA. Perfect for frosting cookies and pastries. Flexible stainless steel blade and rosewood handle.
409-M-517. $2.59 each

6. NEW! COOKIE PICKUP. Ideal for removing cookies from cookie sheet or pan. Quality stainless steel.
2305-M-134 $1.99 each

7. 12 IN. FEATHERWEIGHT DECORATING BAG. Lightweight polyester bag to hold icing.
404-M-5125 $3.99 each

8. 16 IN. COOKIE MAKING AND PASTRY BAG. Heavy-duty, reusable bag to use with cookie tips. Easy to handle, flexible, soft and workable. Specially coated so grease won't go through. Boilable. Dishwasher safe, too.
404-M-1201. $5.99 each

FANCY COOKIE TIPS.
Professional quality, long-lasting nickel-plated metal tips pipe out many cookie sizes and shapes easily.

1. **Tip 230.** Perfect for doughnuts, rolls, tarts, cream puffs and eclairs.
2305-M-120. **$1.49 each**

2. **Tip 1C.** Ideal for cookie logs and jelly-filled shapes: meringue and whipped cream shells, too!
2305-M-114. **$1.49 each**

3. **Tip 1A.** Perfect for drop cookies. meringue mushrooms, and for piping and filling cream puffs and eclairs.
2305-M-112. **$1.49 each**

4. **Tip 6B.** Great for meringue and whipped cream shells. cream puffs and more!
2305-M-118. **$1.49 each**

5. **Tip 1D.** Pipes straight or zigzag bar shaped cookies. Make smooth or striped tops. Just turn tip.
2305-M-116. **$1.49 each**

6. **LARGE COUPLER.** Make different cookie sizes and shapes with the same pastry bagful of dough. Change just the tips. Fits Wilton 14". 16". 18" decorating and pastry bags.
2305-M-117. **$1.49 each**

7. **COUPLER SET.** Decorate cookies with more than one tip without changing the bag. Use a coupler. Fast and easy. Follow directions on package. Includes two durable, washable standard couplers for use with standard decorating bags.
2104-M-4175. **$1.29 set**

8. **STAR DECORATING TIP SET.**
Includes three nickel-plated metal star decorating tips: 14, 16, 18. Perfect for star, shell and zigzag designs. Decorate cookies from simple to elaborate.
2104-M-4094. **$1.79 set**

9. **ROUND DECORATING TIP SET.**
Includes three nickel-plated metal round decorating tips: 2.3.4. Great for outlining. decorating and printing on cookies and pastries. Use with Wilton coupler and decorating bag for quick decorating.
2104-M-4035. **$1.79 set**

10. **NEW! FANCY COOKIE MAKING AND PASTRY KIT.** The perfect kit to turn your kitchen into a gourmet pastry shop. You get the tools. recipes and instructions to create unique. luscious pastries. cookies. meringue. fillings and icings in 1 kit. Includes one 16 in. pastry bag: cookie tips 1A. 1C. 1D. 6B. 230: one large coupler, plus 8 pages of recipes and step-by-step instructions. A great time-saver, convenience and bargain!
2301-M-125. **$9.99 kit**

NEW! HOLIDAY COOKIE MAKING AND DECORATING KITS. Get into the holiday spirit with a family cookie making, baking and decorating party. You'll love the fun and the cookies. And they're oh so easy to make with our kits. Choose the Santa and Angel or Christmas Tree and Wreath kits or both! Each kit includes two cookie cutters. two decorating tips. three disposable decorating bags. three liquid icing colors and an 8-page easy-to-follow recipe and instruction book for decorating 6 designs. Some are simple enough to make even your most inexperienced decorator proud. Be sure to make some for hanging on your tree!

11. **SANTA AND ANGEL KIT.**
2301-M-117. **$3.99 kit**

12. **CHRISTMAS TREE AND WREATH KIT.** 2301-M-119. **$3.99 kit**

COOKIE CUTTERS & SETS

COOKIE CUTTERS, SETS AND SUPPLIES

Get ready for lots of cookie making and eating fun with these super products. Cookies really shape up great with quality, quick-cut cookie cutters and other supplies. Make bunches of cookies for birthdays, school treats, the holidays, or just for munching.

NUMBER SET. It's number one for birthdays, anniversaries, showers, school treats. Idea Tip: Teach youngsters easy addition, subtraction, multiplication! 13-pc. set includes 0 thru 9, =, + and ? symbols. 2 x 1-1/8 each.
2304-M-103. $4.99 set

ALPHABET SET. The sweetest way to spell out a good cheer message or teach toddlers how to read easy words, including their names. Set of 26 washable cutters. 2 x 1-1/8 in. each
2304-M-102. $6.99 set

NEW! HORSE. Bake up a corral of these toy treats and the party crowd will giddyap to the kitchen for more. Decorate each cookie differently for individual party favors! 4-1/4 x 4-3/4 in.
2304-M-136. $.69 each

NEW! TOY TRAIN. Make individual birthday expresses, bon voyage treats and more! 3-3/4 x 4-1/4 in.
2304-M-138. $.69 each

NEW! TEDDY BEAR. Decorate him cuddly and they'll want to hug him. Great for baby shower place cards. 5 x 4-1/8 in.
2304-M-134. $.69 each

NEW! GIRAFFE. The tallest member of the cookie animal menagerie. Fun to decorate...and eat! 5-1/2 in. high.
2304-M-133. $.69 each

NEW! CIRCUS CLOWN. No clowning around. He's fun to make and decorate. He'll shape up great with the giraffe, hobby horse and elephant for real circus fun. 5-5/8 x 4-1/2 in.
2304-M-137. $.69 each

NEW! ELEPHANT. Make a pretty pachyderm. He'll be the beauty of your cookie circus. Great party treats! 4-3/8 in. high.
2304-M-132. $.69 each

NEW! ICE CREAM CONE. A delicious favorite. Bake up a big batch, frost in favorite ice cream flavor frosting, and let them choose. A real treat. 5-1/8 in. high.
2304-M-135. $.69 each

NEW! DOLL HOUSE. Perfect for children's parties, or as a unique way to welcome new neighbors. Decorate to resemble home. 5-5/8 x 3-1/2 in.
2304-M-131. $.69 each

GINGERBREAD SET. Bake and decorate yummy gingerbread family. Perfect with doll house cookies for a family surprise. 4-pc. set includes two 5-1/2 x 4 in. high and two 2-1/2 x 1-1/2 in. high figures.
2304-M-121. $2.59 set

Plastic cutters made in Hong Kong.

NEW! CRINKLE CUT SET. Fancy shapes are perfect for every occasion, including cookie gift-giving. Three sizes: 1-1/2 in., 2-1/2 in., 3 in. Washable plastic.
2304-M-125. $1.59 set

NEW! PLAYING CARD SET. Four cutters in the playing card symbols. Perfect for hors d'oeuvres, breads, cookies, especially for bridge parties and other entertaining. 2-1/2 x 2-7/8 in.
2304-M-127. $1.59 set

NEW! CHILDREN'S ALPHABET A to Z SET. Adorable alphabet cutters with delightful figures peeking in and around them. Perky birthday treats! Set of 26 washable, plastic cutters. 1-2-1/2 in. wide, 5/16 in. deep.
2304-M-104. $4.99 set

HOLIDAY SHAPES SET. All the festive shapes to make merry holiday eating and decorating. 5-pc. set includes Tree, Angel, Santa, Boy and Girl. Washable plastic. 3-5/8 in. to 6 in. high.
2304-M-105. $2.59 set

HEART SET. Six different sizes for all sorts of lovely cookies. Perfect for Mother's Day, Valentine's Day, birthdays, anniversaries, more! Sizes range from 1-1/4 in. to 4-1/8 in. Package of 6.
2304-M-115. $2.59 set

STAR SET. Six super stars in graduated sizes. Great for all holiday and any day baking. You'll shine. 1-5/8 in. to 4-5/8 in. Washable plastic.
2304-M-111. $2.59 set

ROUND SET. Favorite, versatile shape in six graduated sizes for cookies, hors d'oeuvres and more. From 1-1/2 in. to 4 in.
2304-M-113. $2.59 set

MINIATURE VARIETY SET. Tiny cutters for cookies, hors d'oeuvres, breads, more. Shapes for every occasion. Washable plastic. 1 in. to 1-5/8 in. high. Includes star, flower, heart, round and diamond.
2304-M-101. $1.59 set

1. 12 in. x 18 in. COOKIE PAN. Time-saving size bakes more cookies, biscuits, brownies at one time.
2105-M-4854. $8.50 each

2. NEW! 10-1/2 x 15-1/2 in. COOKIE/ JELLY ROLL PAN. Perfect for drop cookies, biscuits, bar and filled cookies, brownies, jelly rolls.
2105-M-1269. $7.50 each

3. NEW! MINI MUFFIN PAN. Ideal for special treats, muffins, more!
2105-M-2125. $5.99 each

4. 16-1/2 x 12-1/2 in. COOKIE SHEET. Long grip for easier handling. Extra large size holds more cookies.
2105-M-2975. $6.50 each

5. NEW! 10 in. x 15 in. COOKIE SHEET. Easy-to-use, easy-grip. Roll dough and cut out cookies right on sheet.
2105-M-1265. $5.50 each

6. NEW! TARTLET MOLD SET. Fabulous for filled cookies, mini fruit and custard pies, tarts and pastries. Set of 6.
2105-M-3794. $3.99 set

PERFORMANCE PANS™ PREMIUM BAKEWARE!

Pans made in Korea.

111

COLLECT QUALITY DECORATING TIPS AT BUDGET-MINDED PRICES!

A. ROUND TIPS. Smooth, circular openings. See pages 87-88 for how to use.
TIPS 1-12.
Order 402-M-number. $.59 each
Tips 000, OL, OOL, IL, 2L use parchment bags only.
TIP 000. For finest stringwork, lattice.
402-M-1010. $.99 each

TIP OL. 402-M-903. $1.29 each
TIP OOL. 402-M-903. $1.29 each
TIP IL. 402-M-901. $1.29 each
TIP 2L. 402-M-902. $1.29 each
For fine icing lacework.
TIP Is. 402-M-1009. $.99 each
Figure-piping tips.
TIP 1A. 402-M-1001. $1.29 each
TIP 2A. 402-M-2001. $1.09 each

Pastry size for filling buns, etc.
TIP 230. 402-M-230. $1.89 each
Philippine flower-making tips.
TIP 55. 402-M-55. $.59 each
TIP 57. 402-M-57. $.59 each

B. MULTIPLE OPENING TIPS. More than one round opening for multiple icing string effects. For grass, hair, lattice, musical staff designs.
TWIN LINE TIPS 41, 42, 43.

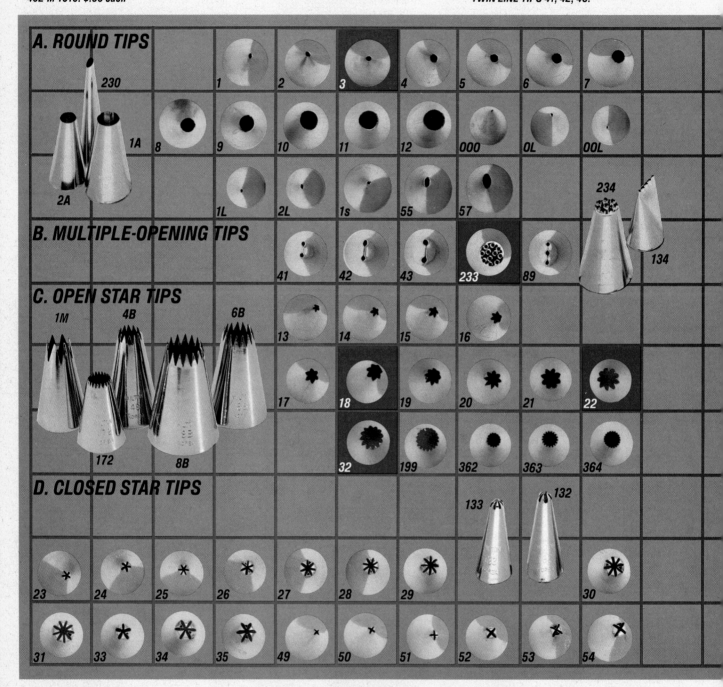

A. ROUND TIPS
230 · 1 · 2 · 3 · 4 · 5 · 6 · 7
1A · 8 · 9 · 10 · 11 · 12 · 000 · OL · OOL
2A · 1L · 2L · 1s · 55 · 57 · 234 · 134

B. MULTIPLE-OPENING TIPS
41 · 42 · 43 · 233 · 89

C. OPEN STAR TIPS
1M · 4B · 6B · 13 · 14 · 15 · 16
172 · 8B · 17 · 18 · 19 · 20 · 21 · 22
32 · 199 · 362 · 363 · 364

D. CLOSED STAR TIPS
23 · 24 · 25 · 26 · 27 · 28 · 29 · 133 · 132 · 30
31 · 33 · 34 · 35 · 49 · 50 · 51 · 52 · 53 · 54

402-M-41. Small $.59 each
402-M-42. Medium $.59 each
402-M-43. Large $.59 each
TIP 134. Five holes.
402-M-134. $1.29 each
TIP 233. Eleven pinholes.
402-M-233. $1.09 each
TIP 234. Eight openings.
402-M-234. $1.29 each
TIP 89. Three holes.
402-M-89. $.59 each

C. OPEN STAR TIPS. Pipe star techniques and some drop flowers. See pages 88-90 for how to use.

TIPS 13-22, 32. 402-M-number. $.59 each
TIP 4B. 402-M-4400. $1.09 each
TIP 6B. 402-M-6600. $1.09 each
TIP 8B. 402-M-8800. $1.29 each
Fine-Cut Open Star Tips
TIP 1M. Large star shape decorations in icing or pastry dough.
402-M-2110 $1.09 each
TIP 172. Large for lavish shells and borders. Ideal for pastries.
402-M-172. $1.09 each
TIPS 362, 363, 364, 199.
Order 402-M-number. $1.09 each
For shells and puffs with many ridges.

Deep-Cut Stellar Tip Set.
Not Shown. Graduated sizes for tier shells, puffs and more. Tips 501, 502, 504, 506, 508 included.
401-M-502. $3.59 set

D. CLOSED STAR TIPS. Make well-defined stars, shells and fleur-de-lis. Drop flowers have fine petals. See pages 88-90 for how to use.
TIPS 23-35, 49-54, 132, 133. The number of cuts in the tip opening determines how many petals or ridges your decoration will have.
Order 402-M-number. $.59 each

MAKE VERSATILE AND PRETTY ICING DECORATIONS EFFORTLESSLY!

E. RUFFLE TIPS. Pipe smooth, sleek, icing ribbons, ruffles and stripes with these unique tips. See page 90 for attractive ruffle-tip techniques.
Ripple Ribbon Tips
For garlands, ribbons, and ripple-type borders. Select various sizes.
TIP 401. 402-M-401. $.79 each

TIP 402. 402-M-402. $1.09 each
TIP 403. 402-M-403. $1.29 each
TIP 339. 402-M-339. $.99 each
TIP 340. 402-M-340. $.99 each
TIP 99. 402-M-99. $.59 each
TIP 100. 402-M-100. $.59 each
Create unusual effects with these special ruffle tips!
TIP 87. 402-M-87. $.59 each
TIP 88. 402-M-88. $.59 each
TIP 353. 402-M-353. $.99 each

F. PETAL TIPS. Pipe everyone's favorite flower — the rose! Plus make daffodils, apple blossoms, pansies and more. See pages 91-93 for specific flower-making instructions. Choose many different sizes to create life-like flower sprays and bouquets.
PETAL TIPS 101, 102, 103, 104.
Most popular sizes; large to very small. Order several.
Order 402-M-number. $.59 each
Petal Tips for Special Effects
TIP 97. 402-M-97. $.59 each

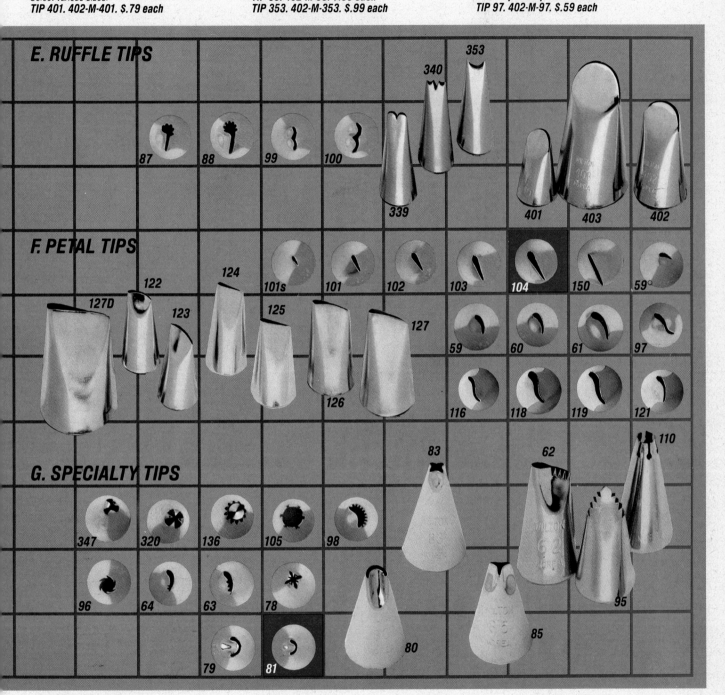

E. RUFFLE TIPS

87 88 99 100 340 353 339 401 403 402

F. PETAL TIPS

127D 122 123 124 125 126 127 101s 101 102 103 104 150 59° 59 60 61 97 116 118 119 121

G. SPECIALTY TIPS

347 320 136 105 98 96 64 63 78 79 81 80 83 85 62 110 95

TIP 101s. 402-M-1019. $.99 each
TIP 59s or 59°. 402-M-594. $.59 each
TIP 150. Carnation tip makes broken petal effect the easy way.
402-M-150. $1.09 each
TIPS 59, 60, 61. For pretty carnations.
Order 402-M-number. $.59 each
TIPS 116, 118, 119, 121, 122, 123, 124, 125, 126, 127. Large petal tips.
Order 402-M-number. $1.09 each
TIP 127D. Extra large rose.
402-M-1274. $1.29 each

G. SPECIALTY TIPS. Pipe shells, ropes, basket-weaves with interesting, exciting effects. It's fun to experiment and create your own original borders with this variety tip group. Get the **Wilton Way of Cake Decorating, Volume Three.** (See page 99.) It shows you the many uses of Wilton tips.
TIP 320, 402-M-320. $1.09 each
TIP 347. 402-M-347. $1.09 each
TIPS 77, 78, 79, 80, 81, 83, 85, 95, 96, 98, 105, 110, 62, 63, 64 (tip 77 not shown).

Order 402-M-number. $.59 each
TIP 136. Instantly pipe little candleholder ringlets of icing.
402-M-136. $1.29 each

Complete Decorating Tip Kits on Page 119.

Metal tips made in Korea.

DENOTES POPULAR BEGINNERS TIP ORDER SEVERAL

LET YOUR DECORATING TALENTS TAKE BLOOM!
Pipe any size drop flower, ribbon or basketweave stripes with these essential Wilton tips.

H. DROP FLOWER TIPS. *You'll want to have a varied collection on hand for creating pretty, easy one-step flowers in royal or buttercream icing. See how to make drop flowers on page 90.*
TIPS 106, 107, 108, 129, 131, 177, 191, 193, 195, 217, 220, 224 and 225.

Order 402-M-number. $1.09 each
TIPS 109, 135, 140, 190, 194.
Order 402-M-number. $1.29 each
Large Drop Flower Tips. *Pipe large diameter flowers. Use 14 in. decorating bag and large coupler (see page 117). To create beautiful icing arrangements, you'll want to collect them all.*
TIP 2C. 402-M-2003. $1.09 each
TIP 2D. 402-M-2004. $1.09 each
TIP 2E. 402-M-2005. $1.09 each

TIP 2F. 402-M-2006. $1.09 each
X-Large Drop Flower Tips. *Make giant blooms for large cakes with these special tips. Use 14 in. decorating bag and large coupler, p. 117.*
TIP 1B. 402-M-1002. $1.29 each
TIP 1C. 402-M-1003. $1.29 each
TIP 1E. 402-M-1005. $1.29 each
TIP 1F. 402-M-1006. $1.29 each
TIP 1G. 402-M-1007. $1.29 each

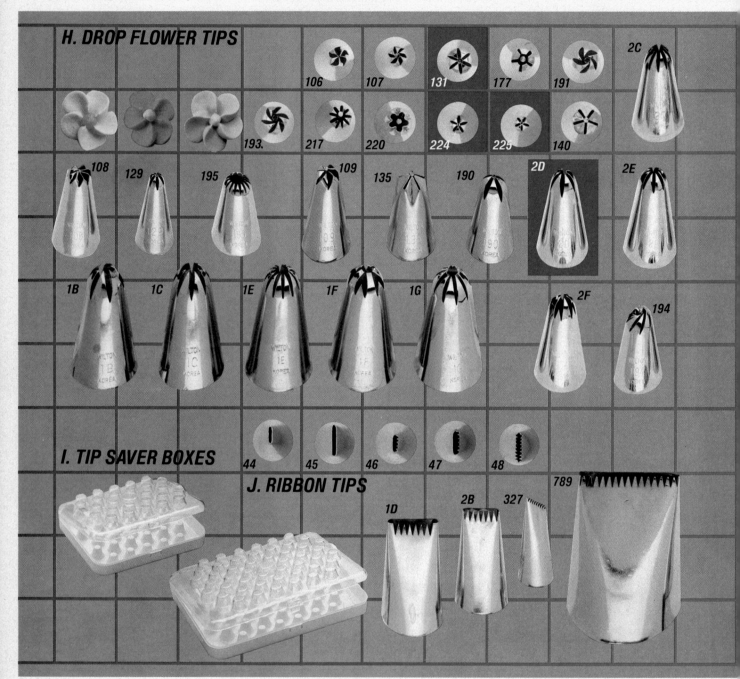

H. DROP FLOWER TIPS
106 107 131 177 191 2C
193 217 220 224 225 140
108 129 195 109 135 190 2D 2E
1B 1C 1E 1F 1G 2F 194

I. TIP SAVER BOXES
44 45 46 47 48

J. RIBBON TIPS
1D 2B 327 789

I. TIP SAVER BOXES. *Keep your decorating clean and organized in these quality plastic boxes. Select from two sizes.*
26 tip capacity.
405-M-8773. $4.59 each
52 tip capacity.
405-M-7777. $6.59 each

J. RIBBON TIPS. *Pipe smooth and serrated stripes for basketweave technique, ribbons and bows. Tips 44 and 45 make smooth stripes, while all the rest create smooth ribbed decorations.*

TIPS 44-48
Order 402-M-number. $.59 each
TIP 1D. 402-M-1004. $1.29 each
TIP 2B. 402-M-2002. $1.09 each
TIP 327. 402-M-327. $.99 each

CAKE ICER TIP. *Pipe 2 in. wide smooth or ribbed decorations or ice sides of a cake super fast. Use 16 in. or large decorating bag with this tip. 2 x 2-1/2 in.*
TIP 789. 409-M-789. $2.09 each

PLEASE NOTE: All prices, certain products and services reflect the U.S.A. domestic market and do not apply in Australia and Canada.

Invest In The Wilton Way of Cake Decorating Volume Three On Page 99. It's A Complete Encyclopedia Of Tips And Their Usage.

Metal tips and nails made in Korea.
Plastic lily nail set and Tip Saver Boxes made in Hong Kong.

PIPE OUT UNIQUE, IMPRESSIVE ICING DECORATIONS!

These nickel-plated tips pipe out any size leaf you desire. Sturdy flower nails make it easy to create flowers that rival nature. Specialty nails let you make intricate designs.

K. LEAF TIPS. Collect several to make various leaf styles...plain, stand-up or ruffled variations. See page 90 for how to use.

TIPS 65-76.
Order 402-M-number. $.59 each
Small Leaf Tips.
Trim flowers with dainty icing leaves.
TIP 65s. 402-M-659. $.99 each
TIP 352s/349. 402-M-349. $.99 each
Special Leaf Tips
Pipe flatter, scalloped-edge leaves.
TIP 326. 402-M-326. $.99 each
TIP 352. 402-M-352. $.99 each

TIP 355. 402-M-355. $.99 each
Large Leaf Tips
Trim icing vines and flowers on large cakes or design eye-catching borders.
TIP 112. 402-M-112. $1.09 each
TIP 113. 402-M-113. $1.09 each
TIP 114. 402-M-114. $1.09 each
TIP 115. 402-M-115. $1.09 each

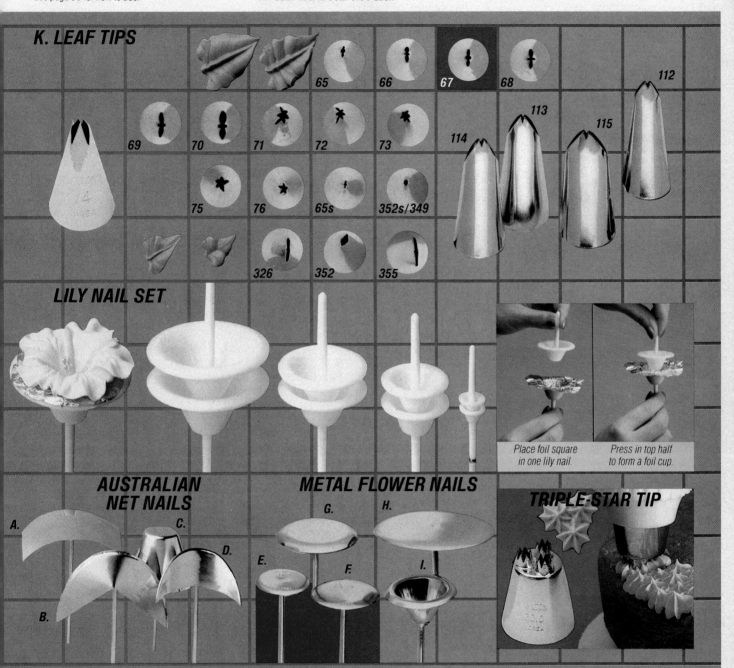

K. LEAF TIPS

65 66 67 68 112

69 70 71 72 73 114 113 115

75 76 65s 352s/349

326 352 355

LILY NAIL SET

Place foil square in one lily nail.   Press in top half to form a foil cup.

AUSTRALIAN NET NAILS

A. C. D. B.

METAL FLOWER NAILS

G. H. E. F. I.

TRIPLE-STAR TIP

LILY NAIL SET. For making cup flowers such as lilies (see page 93) and more! Four sizes. Here's how to use 2-pc. nails. Place aluminum foil in bottom half of nail and press in top half to form cup. Pipe 1/2 in., 1-1/4 in., 1-5/8 in. and 2-1/2 in. diam. cups. Sturdy white plastic.
403-M-9444. $1.99 8-pc. set

NEW! AUSTRALIAN NET NAILS.
Just rub a little oil on these curved nails and pipe latticework designs. Let dry. Then lift off intricate, dimensional decorations.

A. AUSTRALIAN ARCH NAIL.
402-M-822. $1.79 each

B. AUSTRALIAN LARGE BORDER NAIL.
402-M-863. $1.99 each

C. AUSTRALIAN BASKET NAIL.
402-M-803. $1.09 each

D. AUSTRALIAN CRESCENT NAIL.
402-M-805. $1.79 each

METAL FLOWER NAILS. Turntables for piping glorious icing flowers such as the rose.

E. FLOWER NAIL NO. 9. 1-1/4 in. diameter.
402-M-3009. $.59 each

F. FLOWER NAIL NO. 7. 1-1/2 in. diameter.
402-M-3007. $.59 each

G. 2 IN. FLOWER NAIL. Use tips 116-123 to make large blooms.
402-M-3002. $.99

H. 3 IN. FLOWER NAIL. For use with tips 123-127 D. Has extra large piping surface.
402-M-3003. $1.09 each

I. 1-PC. LILY NAIL. 1-5/8 in. diameter.
402-M-3012. $.79 each

TRIPLE-STAR TIP.
Tip pipes three stars at once (size of tip 17 decorations). Use with any size bag and cut to fit or use with large coupler and bag.
402-M-2010. $2.09 each

**TOOLS THAT SIMPLIFY DECORATING...
MOLDS THAT MAKE WONDERFUL
CONFECTIONS!**

1. DECORATOR'S BRUSHES. Set of 3. Essential for smoothing, glazing, candy making and more! 2104-M-846. **$1.49 set**

2. DECORATING COMB. Add interesting designs to simply iced cakes. White plastic. 12 in. long. 409-M-8259. **$1.29 each.**

3. EGG MOLD SET. Create candy, ice cream or sugar surprises year 'round with these 2-pc. plastic molds. One mold in each size included: 5 x 4 in., 4-1/2 x 3 in. and 3 x 2 in. 1404-M-1040. **$3.99 set**

4. CAKE DIVIDING SET. Wheel chart marks 2 in. intervals on 6 thru 18 in. diameter cakes. Triangle marker marks garlands and more, is 6 in. high. Instructions. 409-M-800. **$8.99 set**

5. CAKE STENCILS. Coated cardboard sheets feature popular year 'round designs. 8 x 10 in. 408-M-814. **$4.99 set**

6. 3-PC. CAKE TOP PATTERN PRESS. Set of 3, 8 in. diam. patterns. Sturdy plastic. 2104-M-3128. **$5.99 set**

7. DECORATING TRIANGLE. Each side creates a different effect in icing. 5 x 5-1/2 in. 409-M-990. **$.99 each**

PATTERN PRESSES. TOOLS & MOLDS

8. DIAL DIVIDER. Divide cake tops fast. Use on cakes 6 in. thru 16 inches in diameter. 409-M-8607. **$2.79 each**

9. 15-PC. DECORATOR PATTERN PRESS SET. Fast and easy way to decorate! Contemporary designs to imprint on cake top or sides. Then just outline with one tip or several. Some two-sides for reversing pattern. Sturdy plastic. 2104-M-2172. **$4.99 set**

10. 9-PC. PATTERN PRESS SET. Traditional designs from 2-1/2 to 5 inches high. Durable plastic. 2104-M-3101. **$4.29 set**

11. PANDA MOLD. Bakes cakes, molds sugar, luscious ice cream desserts or Candy Melts™ brand confectionery coating. 3-dimensional, 2-pc. aluminum pan/mold makes a darling topper for cakes (see p. 5). 518-M-489. **$4.99 each**

Aluminum Panda Mold made in Korea. Plastic products and brushes made in Hong Kong (except cake stencils, garland marker and wheel.) All decorating bags made in Japan.

PLEASE NOTE: All prices, certain products and services, reflect the U.S.A. domestic market and do not apply in Australia and Canada.

1. FEATHERWEIGHT DECORATING BAGS.

Lightweight, strong and flexible polyester bags contain your icing and are easy to handle, especially for beginners. Soft and workable, never stiff. Specially coated so grease won't go through. These bags may be boiled to thoroughly clean after use. Dishwasher-safe, too! Complete instructions included.

Size	Stock No.	Each
8 IN.	404-M-5087.	$1.89
10 IN.	404-M-5109	$2.99
12 IN.	404-M-5125.	$3.99
14 IN.	404-M-5140.	$4.99
16 IN.	404-M-5168.	$5.99
18 IN.	404-M-5184.	$6.99

CAKE DECORATING COUPLERS. Important decorating timesavers. They let you change tips without changing bags when using one color of icing. Instructions for using on Featherweight and Disposable Decorating bags. Three sizes, all white plastic.

2. LARGE COUPLER. Fits 14 in. to 18 in. Featherweight Bags. Use this coupler with large decorating tips. 1-1/2 x 2-1/2 in.
411-M-1006. $1.19 each

3. ANGLED COUPLER. Reaches around tricky angles. Fits all bags and standard decorating tips. 1-1/4 x 1-3/4 in.
411-M-7365. $.79 each

BAGS AND COUPLERS

4. DISPOSABLE DECORATING BAGS.
Popular 12 in. size bags of heavy duty, transparent plastic — flexible and easy to handle. Fit standard tips and couplers.
2104-M-358. $2.99 pack of 12.
NEW! 24 COUNT VALUE PACK. A good buy for busy decorators.
2104-M-1358. $5.49 pack of 24.

5. STANDARD COUPLER. Fits all decorating bags and standard tips.
411-M-1987. $.59 each

6. HOLD-A-CONE. Plastic organizer rack holds extra filled bags while you decorate. After washing bags, invert in holes to dry. White plastic. 5-1/2 x 3-5/8 in.
408-M-8769. $2.59 each

7. PARCHMENT TRIANGLES. It's easy to make your own disposable decorating bags with our quality, grease-resistant vegetable parchment paper. Pre-cut in triangles for easy rolling. Complete instructions on package. Essential for color flow, piping gel and color striping techniques.

12 IN.	2104-M-1206.	$ 3.99 pack 100
15 IN.	2104-M-1508.	$ 4.79 pack 100
15 IN.	406-M-1528.	$11.99 pack 300

8. TIP BRUSH. Plastic bristle brush cleans tips thoroughly. 4 in.
414-M-1123. $.99 each

9. TIP SAVER. A good investment! Reshapes bent tips and straightens prongs of metal. Directions included. Sturdy plastic.
414-M-909. $2.79 each

117

1. NEW!

2. NEW!

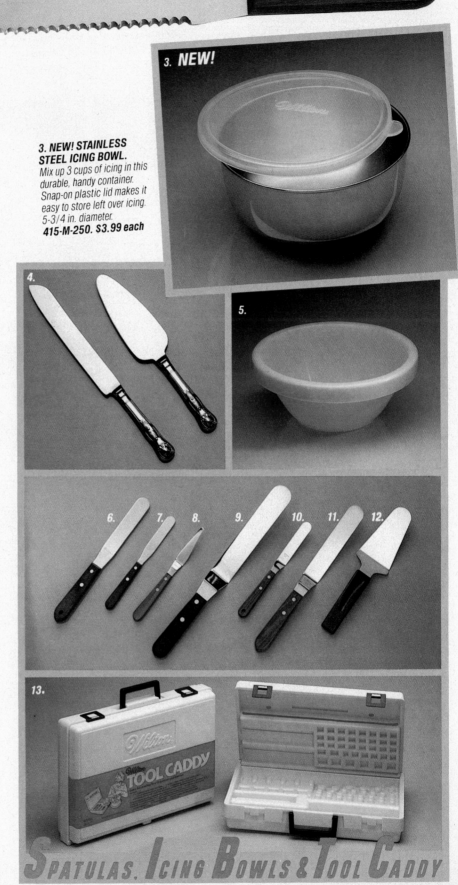

3. NEW!

1. NEW! LEVELER/SPREADER. *Ideal for leveling small cakes and ingredients. Handy for buttering and filling. Rosewood handle with 9-1/2 in. metal blade.*
409-M-1014. $4.99 each

2. NEW! SERRATED LEVELER. *Indispensable for preparing cake layers for icing and to level out recipe ingredients. Polished rosewood handle with 12 in. long stainless steel blade.*
409-M-1016. $5.99 each

4. WEDDING KNIFE & SERVER SET. *A lovely couple. Gleaming stainless steel with serrated blades and handsome fluted shell patterned handles. The perfect shower gift for a bride-to-be. Packaged in a gift box.*
409-M-1211. $20.99 set

5. ICING BOWL. *Holds up to 2-1/2 cups of icing. Handy size for mixing your tinted icing. Dishwasher safe plastic.*
415-M-775. $1.29 each

PROFESSIONAL QUALITY STAINLESS STEEL SPATULAS. *Essential for spreading icing and filling. All have flexible metal blades with rosewood handles.*

6. 11 IN. SPATULA. *Makes short work of icing any tempting treat.*
409-M-7694. $3.99 each

7. 8 IN. SPATULA. *Straight blade for putting icing on cake top and sides. Great for canapes, too!*
409-M-6043. $2.59 each

8. 8 IN. TAPERED SPATULA. *Ideal for icing hard-to-reach corners, sides and small areas.*
409-M-517. $2.59 each

9. 14 IN. ANGLED SPATULA. *Perfect for covering large cake areas with icing or filling.*
409-M-274. $5.99 each

10. 8 IN. ANGLED SPATULA. *Handy size, especially when smoothing icing around sides.*
409-M-738. $2.59 each

11. 12 IN. ANGLED SPATULA. *Essential when icing large areas on cake top or sides.*
409-M-134. $4.59 each

12. STAINLESS STEEL CAKE SERVER. *Polished rosewood-look handle with wide 10-1/4 in. long metal blade. Elegant and tasteful!*
409-M-2145. $4.99 each

13. TOOL CADDY. *Take your tools along or keep them organized at home. It will hold 38 tips, 10 paste color jars, couplers, spatulas, practice board, books and more! Lightweight, stain resistant, mold polyethylene. A teacher's must. 16-5/8 x 11-1/4 x 3-1/2 in.*
2104-M-2237. $16.99 each

Tips and flower nails made in Korea. Bags and spatulas made in Japan. Plastic couplers, boxes, bowl, practice board and stand made in Hong Kong.

3. NEW! STAINLESS STEEL ICING BOWL. *Mix up 3 cups of icing in this durable, handy container. Snap-on plastic lid makes it easy to store left over icing. 5-3/4 in. diameter.*
415-M-250. $3.99 each

SPATULAS, ICING BOWLS & TOOL CADDY

1. DELUXE TIP SET. *33 pc. kit contains 26 nickel-plated metal tips for writing, borders, leaves, flowers and more. Also, two no. 9 flower nails, standard coupler for easy tip changes, 10 in. and 12 in. Featherweight decorating bags. Beginners Guide To Cake Decorating Book and plastic tipsaver box. Individually $27.86.*
401-M-6667. $22.99 set
DELUXE TIP SET. *26 decorating tips and tip saver box only.*
2104-M-6666. $17.99 set

PLEASE NOTE: All prices and services reflect the U.S.A. domestic market and do not apply in Australia and Canada.

2. MASTER TIP SET. *60 pc. kit contains 52 nickel-plated metal tips that let you create practically every decorating technique. Tips for writing, figure-piping, leaf and flower making, basketweave and other special effects. Also includes standard and angled couplers, two no. 9 flower nails, 10 in. and 12 in. washable Featherweight decorating bags; Beginners Guide To Cake Decorating Book and plastic tipsaver box. Individually $46.39.*
401-M-7779. $38.99 set
MASTER TIP SET. *52 decorating tips and tip saver box only.*
2104-M-7778. $30.99 set

3. 15-PIECE TIP SET. *Excellent choice for a new decorator. Ten nickel-plated metal tips, two 12 in. vinyl decorating bags, coupler, no. 7 flower nail and Beginners Guide To Cake Decorating Book. All in plastic storage box. Individually $17.16.*
401-M-4443. $12.99 set

COLLECT ESSENTIAL CAKE DECORATING TOOLS AND TAKE ADVANTAGE OF THE SAVINGS ON COMPLETE SETS!

DECORATING SETS

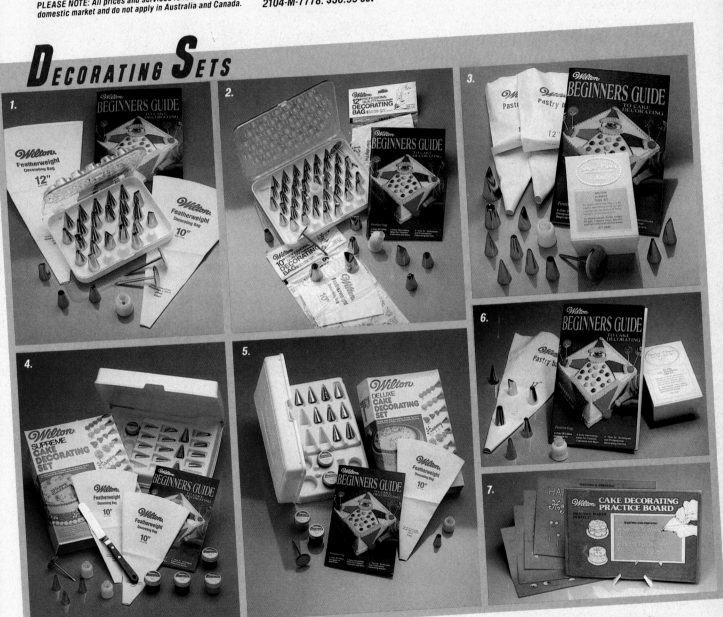

4. THE SUPREME SET. *Filled with 30 indispensable decorating tools, this set is an important investment for any level of cake decorator. You get 18 metal tips, two 10 in. Featherweight decorating bags, two couplers, five 1/2 oz. paste icing colors, no. 9 flower nail, 8 in. angled spatula, Beginners Guide To Cake Decorating Book and plastic storage box. An excellent gift idea for your favorite decorator!*
2104-M-3047. $27.99 set

5. THE DELUXE CAKE DECORATING SET. *Designed to meet the needs of any decorator — beginner as well as expert. Contains 18 important pieces a talented decorator needs. Ten nickel-plated metal tips, 10 in. Featherweight decorating bag; coupler, no. 9 flower nail, four 1/2 oz. paste icing colors, Beginners Guide to Cake Decorating Book and plastic storage box.*
2104-M-3063. $17.99 set

6. 9-PC. BASIC TIP SET AND BOOK. *Super starter set contains 6 metal tips, 12 in. vinyl bag, coupler and 40-page Beginners Guide To Cake Decorating Book.*
401-M-2221. $7.99 set

7. PRACTICE BOARD WITH PATTERNS. *A handy guide and surface on which to learn and improve your decorating skills. Just slip a practice sheet under wipeclean vinyl overlay and trace pattern in icing. Includes stand and patterns for flowers, leaves, borders, lettering (31 designs).*
406-M-9464. $6.99 each

119

Wilton CandyMaker™

1. CANDY MELTS™ BRAND CONFECTIONERY COATING. *Sold in 1 lb. bags.* **$2.50 each**
LIGHT COCOA. *(Cocoa flavor)* 1911-M-544
DARK COCOA. *(Cocoa flavor)* 1911-M-358
GREEN. 1911-M-404.
PINK. 1911-M-447.
YELLOW. 1911-M-463.
WHITE. 1911-M-498.
NEW! PEANUT BUTTER. 1911-M-562.
NEW! ORANGE. *(Available fall only, supply limited)* 1911-M-584.

2. CANDY WAFER & FONDANT MIX. *1 lb. can.* 1911-M-1427. **$3.99 each**

3. CANDY CENTER MIXES. *1 lb.* **$3.99 each**
CREME CENTER MIX. 1911-M-943.
CHOCOLATE-FLAVORED. 1911-M-1460.
MARSHMALLOW. 1911-M-1443.
MAPLE. 1911-M-2032.
RASPBERRY. 1911-M-2091.
STRAWBERRY. 1911-M-2075.
LEMON. 1911-M-2059.
CHERRY. 1911-M-2113.
ORANGE. 1911-M-2130.

4. NEW! CANDY CRUNCHES. *Adds texture and flavor to your homemade candy.* **8 oz. bag.**
TOASTED COCONUT. 1913-M-994. *$1.99 each*
GOLDEN CRUNCH. 1913-M-996. *$1.99 each*

5. CANDY FILLINGS. *16 oz. tubs.* **$3.50 each**
CARAMEL FILLING. 1911-M-1400.
COCONUT FILLING. 1911-M-1028.
NEW! NOUGAT FILLING. 1911-M-1488. *10 oz.*

6. CANDY FLAVOR. *Oil-based formula for flavoring Candy Melts.™ 1 oz. bottles.* **$1.99 each**
PEPPERMINT. 1913-M-403.
LEMON. 1913-M-431.
LIME. 1913-M-454.
ORANGE. 1913-M-535.
SPEARMINT. 1913-M-616.
CINNAMON. 1913-M-470.
BUTTERSCOTCH. 1913-M-497.
CHERRY. 1913-M-519.
RUM. 1913-M-705.
APRICOT. 1913-M-772.
PINEAPPLE. 1913-M-799.
ALMOND. 1913-M-802.
CREME DE MENTHE. 1913-M-821.
ROOT BEER. 1913-M-551.
WINTERGREEN. 1913-M-632.
MAPLE. 1913-M-720.
CARAMEL. 1913-M-845.
STRAWBERRY. 1913-M-861.
PEPPERMINT HARD CANDY FLAVOR. 604-M-1176.

7. CANDY COLORS. *3/4 oz. bottles.* **$1.99 each**
RED. 1913-M-1124.
YELLOW. 1913-M-1248.
GREEN. 1913-M-1183.
VIOLET. 1913-M-1221.
BLUE. 1913-M-1167.
ORANGE. 1913-M-1205.
PINK. 1913-M-1140.

8. EASY-POUR FUNNEL. *5" long x 4" wide at top. Nylon.*
1904-M-552. *$3.99 each*
NOT SHOWN: MINT PATTY FUNNEL. *Stainless steel with wooden stopper. 7 x 4-1/2 x 1/4".*
1904-M-528. *$12.99 each*

9. CANDY THERMOMETER. *Lower temperature for tempering chocolate.*
1904-M-1168. *$9.99 each*

CANDY DIPPING TOOLS. *White plastic, 7-3/4 in. long.* **$1.99 each**
10. DIPPING FORK. 1904-M-749.
11. DIPPING SPOON. 1904-M-714.

12. 4-PC. DIPPING SET. *Sturdy metal with wooden handles. 9 in. long.*
1904-M-838. *$12.99 set*
NOT SHOWN: 2-PC. DIPPING SET. *Includes a 2-prong fork and spoon. (Shown above in #12.)*
1904-M-925. *$6.99 set*

13. THE COMPLETE WILTON BOOK OF CANDY.
902-M-1243. *$12.99 each*

14. CANDY MAKING FOR BEGINNERS—REVISED EDITION. 902-M-1361. *$1.99 each*

15. FONDANT BARS. *2 each: 18 and 12 in. steel.*
1901-M-1148. *$45.00 set*

16. TRUFFLE CUTTER SET. *Average size 1/2 x 5/8". Plastic.*
1902-M-1398. *$.99 set*
NOT SHOWN: 6 IN. SQUARE PAN. *2 in. deep.*
507-M-2180. *$4.99 each*

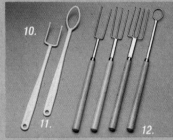

CANDY MAKING BOOKS. *Details on pp. 102, 103.*

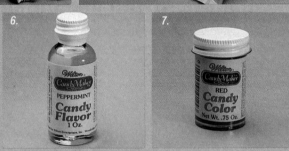

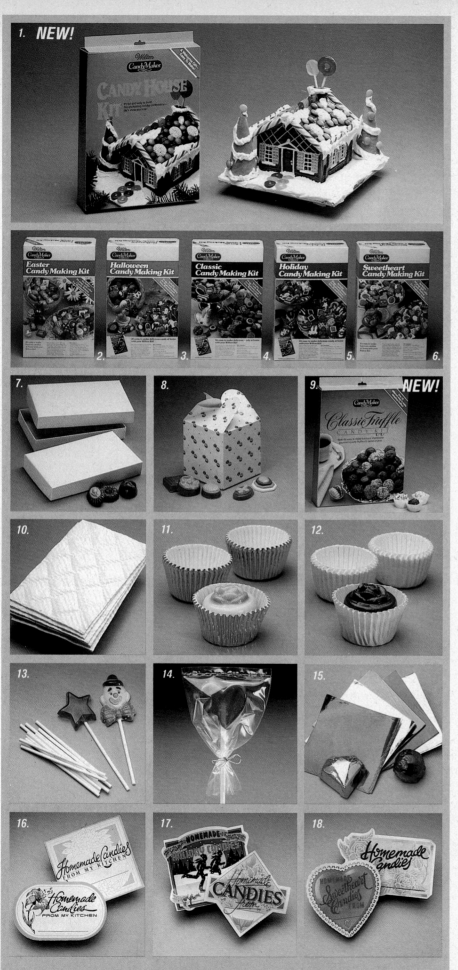

WILTON CANDY MAKING KITS. *Discover how easy it is to make delicious, luscious candy to serve or give. Create an enchanting candy centerpiece that's sure to impress. Each kit contains the molds, tools and instructions you'll need. Ingredients not included. For best results, use Wilton Candy Melts™ brand confectionery coating (sold on facing page).*

1. NEW! CANDY HOUSE KIT. *Three magical houses to make for occasions year 'round.*
2114-M-1992. $4.99 kit

2. EASTER CANDY KIT.
2114-M-3130. $6.99 kit

3. HALLOWEEN CANDY KIT.
2114-M-3350. $6.99 kit

4. CLASSIC CANDY KIT.
2114-M-1978. $6.99 kit

5. HOLIDAY CANDY KIT.
2114-M-3296. $6.99 kit

6. SWEETHEART CANDY KIT.
2114-M-4322. $6.99 kit

7. CANDY GIFT BOXES. *Elegantly textured white boxes make homemade candy so presentable. Three different sizes.*
1/2 LB. BOX. *7-5/8 x 4 x 1 in. deep.*
1912-M-2100. $1.99 set of 3
1 LB. BOX. *9-3/4 x 5-1/2 x 1 in. deep.*
1912-M-2240. $2.79 set of 3
GREETING CARD BOX. *6-3/4 x 5-1/ x 1 in. deep.*
1912-M-2223. $.69 each

8. NEW! 1/2 LB. CANDY GIFT BOX. *Attractive finish to complement your homemade candy delights. 3-1/2 x 3-1/2 x 3-1/2 in. deep.*
1912-M-1114. $2.29 set of 3

9. NEW! CLASSIC TRUFFLE CANDY KIT. *Includes delectable recipes, too.*
2114-M-2517. $4.99 kit

10. CANDY BOX LINERS. *Waffle-padded paper sheets protect candy. Six 9-1/4 x 5-1/2 in. sheets per pack.*
1912-M-1543. $.99 pack
CANDY CUPS. *1 in. diam. cups. Pack of 100. Choose from gold foil or white glassine-coated paper.*

11. GOLD FOIL.
1912-M-1227. $3.99 pack

12. WHITE.
1912-M-1243. $.99 pack

13. LOLLIPOP STICKS. *50 white sticks per pack.*
1912-M-1006. $.99 pack

14. LOLLIPOP BAGS. *Transparent plastic wrappers, 3 x 4". 50 per pack. Add your own ribbon ties.*
1912-M-2347. $1.99 pack

15. FANCY CANDY WRAPPERS. *Vibrant foil to enhance and protect your candy gifts. Five colors included — purple, blue, green, red and gold. 125 sheet. 3 x 3".*
1912-M-2290. $2.59 per pack
CANDY BOX LABELS. *Personalize white candy boxes or containers with these colorful stick-ons. 8 gummed labels. $1.59 pack*

16. ALL OCCASION CANDY LABELS.
1912-M-2428.

17. CHRISTMAS CANDY LABELS.
1912-M-2479.

18. VALENTINE CANDY LABELS.
1912-M-1936.

Plastic cutters, dipping fork and spoon made in Hong Kong. Dipping set, thermometer made in Japan. Metal funnel and pan made in Korea.

EASY MELTS & MOLDS

1. NEW!

2. NEW!

1. NEW! EASY MELTS.™ Melt these candy squares and only use with hard candy molds (see below). Sold in 16 oz. bags. **$2.50 each**
CHERRY 1911-M-1109.
GRAPE 1911-M-1119.
LEMON 1911-M-1107.
LIME 1911-M-1103.
ORANGE 1911-M-1105.
RASPBERRY 1911-M-1117.
ROOT BEER 1911-M-1115.
BLUE PEPPERMINT 1911-M-1113.

2. NEW! CANDY POPS KIT. Includes mold, tools and instructions. Use with new Easy Melts!
2114-M-2491. **$4.99 kit**

3.  4.

5.  6.  7. 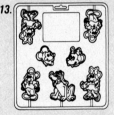 8.  9. 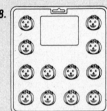 10.

11. 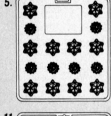 12.  13.  14.  15.  16.

17.  18.  19.  20.  21.  22.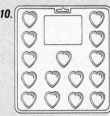

NEW! HARD CANDY & LOLLIPOP MOLDS. Ideal to use with Easy Melts! Made to withstand higher temperatures required for hard candy. Durable plastic sheets. 7-9/16" x 8-1/4".

3. STARS.
16 molds per sheet.
2115-M-336. **$1.99 each**

4. CHRISTMAS TREES.
13 molds per sheet.
2115-M-334. **$1.99 each**

5. SNOWFLAKES.
16 molds per sheet.
2115-M-332. **$1.99 each**

6. RABBITS. 12 molds per sheet.
2115-M-330. **$1.99 each**

7. CHICK IN EGG. 12 molds per sheet.
2115-M-328. **$1.99 each**

8. PUMPKIN. 12 molds per sheet.
2115-M-326. **$1.99 each**

9. HALLOWEEN LOLLIPOPS.
5 molds per sheet.
2115-M-324. **$1.99 each**

10. HEARTS. 15 molds per sheet.
2115-M-322. **$1.99 each**

11. ROSE CAMEO. 13 molds per sheet.
2115-M-320. **$1.99 each**

12. SMURF™ LOLLIPOPS.
7 lollipops per sheet.
2115-M-318. **$1.99 each**
© 1984 Peyo
Licensed by Wallace Berrie & Co., Inc. Van Nuys, CA

13. MICKEY MOUSE & FRIENDS.
5 lollipops and 2 molds per sheet.
2115-M-316. **$1.99 each**
Walt Disney's Mickey Mouse
Walt Disney Productions.

14. STRAWBERRY SHORTCAKE™.
5 lollipops and 2 bite-size molds per sheet.
2115-M-348. **$1.99**
© MCMLXXXIV
American Greetings Corp.

15. STAR WARS LOLLIPOPS.
7 molds per sheet.
2115-M-346. **$1.99 each**
™ and © Lucasfilm Ltd. (LFL) 1984
All Rights Reserved.
Wilton Enterprises Authorized User.

16. CLOWNS LOLLIPOPS.
5 molds per sheet.
2115-M-344. **$1.99 each**

17. FAIRYTALE ANIMALS.
One cat, one puppy and two bear molds on sheet.
2115-M-342. **$1.99 each**

18. VARIETY I LOLLIPOPS.
One each; a heart, round, diamond, tree and tulip shape per sheet.
2115-M-340. **$1.99 each**

19. VARIETY II LOLLIPOPS.
On each; a heart, round, flower, star and diamond per sheet.
2115-M-338. **$1.99 each**

20. ANIMAL LOLLIPOPS.
5 molds per sheet.
2115-M-350. **$1.99 each**

21. TREATS LOLLIPOPS.
5 molds per sheet.
2114-M-352. **$1.99 each**

22. BELLS.
16 molds per sheet.
2115-M-314. **$1.99 each**

1.
2.
3.
4.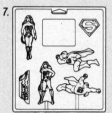
5.
6.
7.
8.
9.
10.
11.
12.
13.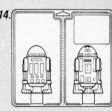
14.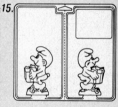
15.
16.
17.
18.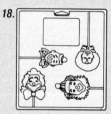
19.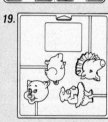
20.
21.

1.
2.
3.

SESAME STREET DESSERT MOLDS. Favorite friends, delicious treats!

1. NEW! BIG BIRD STAND-UP MOLD. A happy sight, sure to delight! 2114-M-2145. $2.49 each

2. SESAME STREET II. Cookie Monster, Big Bird, Oscar and Grouch, Grover, Bert and Ernie. 2114-M-1740. $2.29 each

3. SESAME STREET I. Bert, Ernie, Big Bird and Cookie Monster. 2114-M-1765. $2.29 each

© 1983 Children's Television Workshop. BIG BIRD, COOKIE MONSTER, OSCAR THE GROUCH, BERT AND ERNIE AND GROVER © 1983 Muppets, Inc. All rights reserved. Sesame Street and the Sesame Street sign are trademark and service marks of the Children's Television Workshop.

CHARACTER MOLDS. A star-studded cast that's sure to get rave review. Most are 7-9/16'' x 8-1/4'' plastic sheets. Made in U.S.A.

1. NEW! BABY SMURF. Adorable for birthdays and baby showers. 2114-M-2143. $2.49 each
*© 1983 Peyo Licensed by Wallace Berrie & Co., Inc. Van Nuys, CA

2. NEW! RAINBOW BRITE. A friendly new face all will enjoy seeing. 2114-M-2147. $2.29 each
© 1983 Hallmark Cards, Inc.

3. MICKEY MOUSE & FRIENDS. Minnie, and Pluto keep Mickey company. 2114-M-1781. $2.29 each

4. STAR WARS I.* Darth Vader™ & Storm Trooper™ full-figure and faces. 2114-M-1854. $2.29 each

5. STAR WARS II.* Yoda,™ Chewbacca,™ R2-D2,™ C-3PO.™ 2114-1870. $2.29 each
TM** & © Lucasfilm Ltd. (LFL) 1983 All Rights Reserved. Wilton Enterprises Authorized User

6. RAGGEDY ANN™ & ANDY.™ Full-figures and faces. Includes their dog too. 2114-M-1650. $2.29 each
© 1983 The Bobbs-Merrill Company, Inc.

7. SUPER HEROES II†. Batman†, Robin† and Emblems. 2114-M-1900. $2.29 each

8. SUPER HEROES I†. Wonder Woman†, Superman† and Emblems. 2114-M-1927. $2.29 each
† indicates Trademarks of DC Comics, Inc. © 1983

9. STRAWBERRY SHORTCAKE.™ Full-figures and faces of this adorable sweetheart with her friends. 2114-M-1676. $2.29 each
© MCMLXXXIII*** American Greetings Corp.

10. SMURFS II.™* Features Papa Smurf,™ Smurfette,™ Arial,™ Gargimel™ and Emblem. 2114-M-1633. $2.29 each

11. SMURFS I.™* Features Smurf,™ Smurfette,™ Mushroom Cottage™ and Emblem. 2114-M-1617. $2.29 each

12. CATHY.™ A collage of Cathy all can relate to. 2114-M-1706. $2.29 each

13. STAND-UP CATHY.™ Her happy smile makes life a lot more bearable. 2114-M-1722. $2.49 each
TM 1983 Universal Press Syndicate Company.

14. STAR WARS STAND-UP MOLD.** Everyone's favorite droid, R2-D2.™ 2114-M-2010. $2.49 each

15. SMURF STAND-UP MOLD.* Jolly Jokey™ is very gifted and sure to please. 2114-M-2036. $2.49 each

16. STRAWBERRY SHORTCAKE™* STAND-UP MOLD.** So pretty and perky! 2114-M-1692. $2.49 each

LOLLIPOP MOLDS. Pour melted coating into molds, position Lollipop Sticks (p. 121), let set and unmold. 4 molds on each 7-9/16 x 8-1/4 in. clear plastic sheet. $1.89 each

17. FRUITS. 2114-M-4098.

18. CLOWNS. 2114-M-4110.

19. LITTLE PIGS. 2114-M-4071.

20. BEARS. 2114-M-4055.

21. CAT & MOUSE. 2114-M-4039.

123

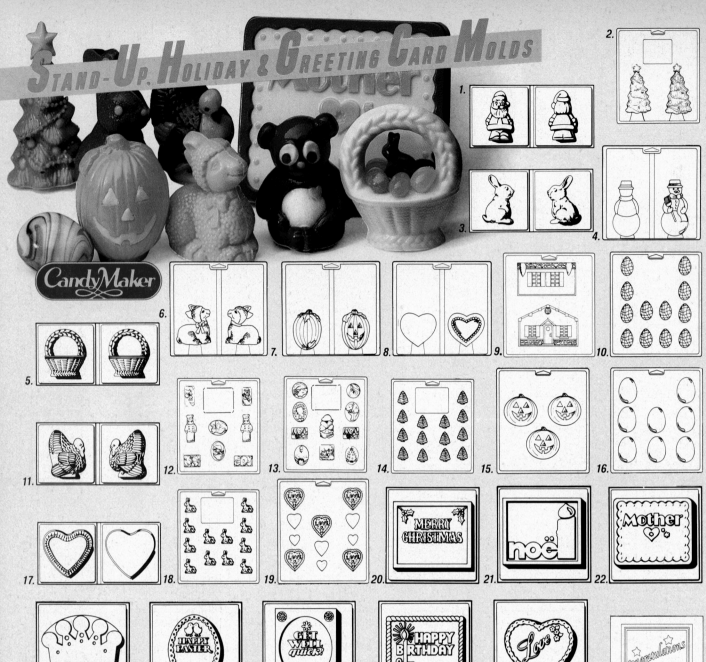

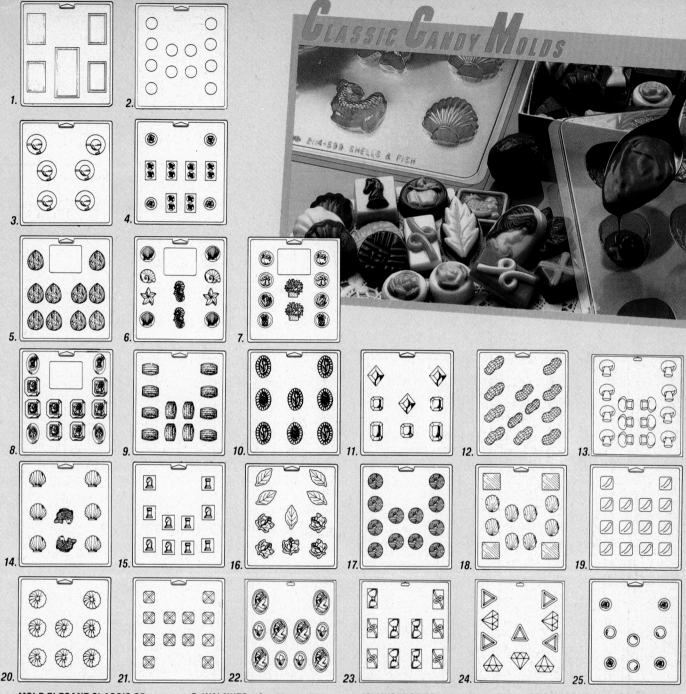

Classic Candy Molds

2114-599 SHELLS & FISH

1.

2.

3.

4.

5.

6.

7.

8.

9.

10.

11.

12.

13.

14.

15.

16.

17.

18.

19.

20.

21.

22.

23.

24.

25.

MOLD ELEGANT CLASSIC OR UNIQUE BITE-SIZE CANDY FOR YEAR 'ROUND DELIGHTING!

CLEAR MINI CANDY MOLDS.
Traditional shapes that are bound to impress. So easy to mold. Combine with delicious centers and fillings (see p. 120), too. 7-9/16 x 8-1/4 in. clear plastic sheets.

1. CANDY BARS. *5 molds per sheet.*
2114-M-1331. $1.89 each

2. RUFFLES. *12 molds per sheet.*
2114-M-910. $1.89 each

3. CORDIAL GLASSES. *6 molds per sheet.*
2114-M-1242. $1.89 each

4. ROSES. *10 molds per sheet.*
2114-M-1511. $1.89 each

5. WALNUTS. *10 molds per sheet.*
2114-M-2729. $1.89 each

6. SEA LIFE. *10 molds per sheet.*
2114-M-2702. $1.89 each

7. HARVEST I. *10 molds per sheet.*
2114-M-2699. $1.89 each

8. HARVEST II. *12 molds per sheet.*
2114-M-2672. $1.89 each

9. BARRELS. *12 molds per sheet.*
2114-M-483. $1.89 each

10. PINEAPPLES & FLOWERS. *8 molds per sheet.*
2114-M-513. $1.89 each

11. DIAMONDS II. *8 molds per sheet.*
2114-M-531. $1.89 each

12. PEANUTS. *12 molds per sheet.*
2114-M-556. $1.89 each

13. MUSHROOMS. *14 molds per sheet.*
2114-M-572. $1.89 each

14. SHELLS & FISH. *8 molds per sheet.*
2114-M-599. $1.89 each

15. CHESS PIECES. *10 molds per sheet.*
2114-M-602. $1.89 each

16. LEAVES. *10 molds per sheet.*
2114-M-629. $1.89 each

17. MINT DISCS. *12 molds per sheet.*
2114-M-1226. $1.89 each

18. FANCY CHOCOLATES I. *12 molds per sheet.*
2114-M-1269. $1.89 each

19. FANCY CHOCOLATES II. *14 molds per sheet.*
2114-M-1285. $1.89 each

20. FANCY CHOCOLATES III. *8 molds per sheet.*
2114-M-1315. $1.89 each

21. SQUARES. *12 molds per sheet.*
2114-M-955. $1.89 each

22. CAMEOS. *10 molds per sheet.*
2114-M-408. $1.89 each

23. RIBBONS & SCROLLS. *10 molds per sheet.*
2114-M-424. $1.89 each

24. DIAMONDS I. *10 molds per sheet.*
2114-M-440. $1.89 each

25. ROUNDS. *8 molds per sheet.*
2114-M-466. $1.89 each

CLASSIC CANDY MOLDS

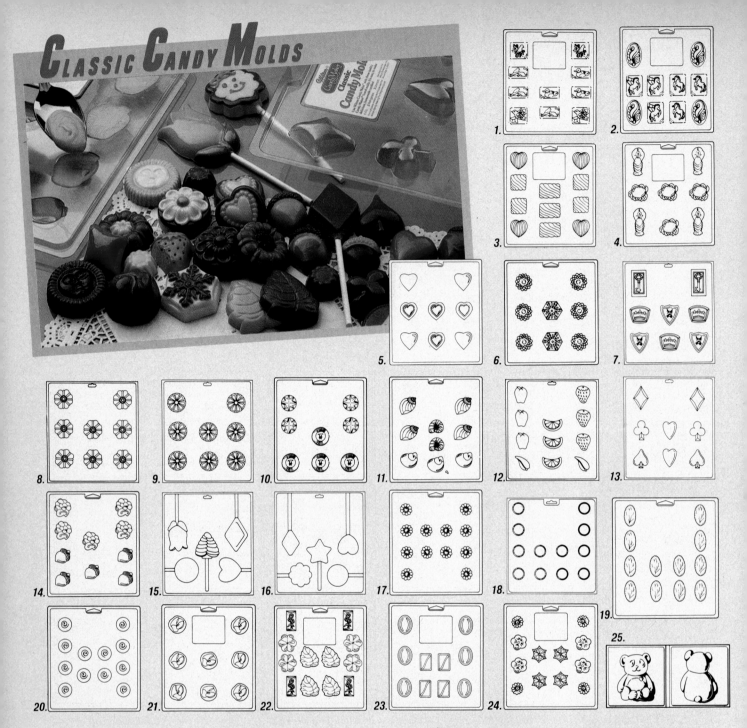

MOLD A DELECTABLE VARIETY OF CANDY FOR ALL-SEASONS & SO MANY REASONS!

Classic and fantasy shapes for bite-size eye-catchers and luscious lollipops. Clear, durable plastic sheets, each 7-9/16 x 8-1/4". Made in U.S.A.

1. WILDLIFE. 10 molds per sheet.
2114-M-2567. *$1.89 each*

2. FANTASY. 10 molds per sheet.
2114-M-2540. *$1.89 each*

3. RIPPLES. 11 molds per sheet.
2114-M-2524. *$1.89 each*

4. SHELLFISH. 8 molds per sheet.
2114-M-2508. *$1.89 each*

5. HEARTS II. 8 molds per sheet.
2114-M-645. *$1.89 each*

6. SNOWFLAKES. 8 molds per sheet.
2114-M-661. *$1.89 each*

7. COAT OF ARMS. 8 molds per sheet.
2114-M-688. *$1.89 each*

8. ROSETTES I. 8 molds per sheet.
2114-M-718. *$1.89 each*

9. ROSETTES II. 8 molds per sheet.
2114-M-750. *$1.89 each*

10. STARS & SUNS.
8 molds per sheet.
2114-M-734. *$1.89 each*

11. SHELLS. 9 molds per sheet.
2114-M-777. *$1.89 each*

12. FRUITS. 11 molds per sheet.
2114-M-793. *$1.89 each*

13. PLAYING CARD SUIT SYMBOLS. 8 molds per sheet.
2114-M-807. *$1.89 each*

14. ACORNS & FLOWERS.
10 molds per sheet.
2114-M-823. *$1.89 each*

15. LOLLIPOPS I. 5 molds per sheet.
2114-M-882. *$1.89 each*

16. LOLLIPOPS II.
5 molds per sheet.
2114-M-861. *$1.89 each*

17. OVALS. 10 molds per sheet.
2114-M-971. *$1.89 each*

18. ACCORDIAN RUFFLES.
10 molds per sheet.
2114-M-1013. *$1.89 each*

19. FLUTES. 12 molds per sheet.
2114-M-939. *$1.89 each*

20. BON BONS. 12 molds per sheet.
2114-M-1072. *$1.89 each*

21. LARGE BON BONS.
8 molds per sheet.
2114-M-2656. *$1.89 each*

22. FLOWERS & LEAVES.
12 molds per sheet.
2114-M-2630. *$1.89 each*

23. OVALS & RECTANGLES.
10 molds per sheet.
2114-M-2613. *$1.89 each*

24. FANCY CHOCOLATES IV.
12 molds per sheet.
2114-M-2583. *$1.89 each*

25. PANDA STAND-UP MOLD.
Perky pal ideal for birthday, baby showers and more! (See p. 124 for more Stand-up Candy Molds.)
2114-M-1463. *$2.49 each*

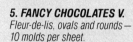

NEW! CLASSIC CANDY MOLDS

1.
2.
3.
4.
5.
6.
7.
8.
9.
10.
11.
12.
13.
14.
15.
16.
17.
18.
19.
20.

Learn all about candy making! Take the NEW Wilton Candy Home Study Course. See page 128 for all the details.

NEW! EXCITING! DELIGHTING!
It's easy to mold elegant candy for all occasions or fantasy shapes that suit someone special to a T! Clear plastic sheets, 7-9/16 x 8-1/4".

1. GEOMETRICS. Triangles, rounds, octagons — 8 molds per sheet.
2114-M-4230. **$1.89 each**

2. CRYSTALS. Stars and leaves — 8 molds per sheet.
2114-M-4228. **$1.89 each**

3. OCTAGONS. 16 molds per sheet.
2114-M-4226. **$1.89 each**

4. BALLET SLIPPERS & CAMEOS. 10 molds per sheet.
2114-M-4214. **$1.89 each**

5. FANCY CHOCOLATES V.
Fleur-de-lis, ovals and rounds — 10 molds per sheet.
2114-M-4242. **$1.89 each**

6. HAZELNUTS & ALMONDS.
12 molds per sheet.
2114-M-4240. **$1.89 each**

7. HEARTS & FLOWERS.
10 molds per sheet.
2114-M-4236. **$1.89 each**

8. LIONS & TIGERS.
8 molds per sheet.
2114-M-4234. **$1.89 each**

9. SWIRLS. 11 molds per sheet.
2114-M-4222. **$1.89 each**

10. TEDDY BEARS & GUM BALL MACHINES. 8 molds per sheet.
2114-M-4232. **$1.89 each**

11. PIANOS & TREBLE CLEF.
9 molds per sheet.
2114-M-4206. **$1.89 each**

12. LOCKETS. Square, oval and round — 12 molds per sheet.
2114-M-4208. **$1.89 each**

13. SPORTS. Golf clubs, tennis rackets, snow skis — 12 molds per sheet.
2114-M-4210. **$1.89 each**

14. MEDIEVAL. Knights, dragons, lions, coat of arms — 10 molds per sheet.
2114-M-4212. **$1.89 each**

15. CLASSIC CARS.
10 molds per sheet.
2114-M-4238. **$1.89 each**

16. LOCOMOTIVES & HOT AIR BALLOONS. 10 molds per sheet.
2114-M-4218. **$1.89 each**

17. CHINESE SYMBOLS. Good fortune, prosperity and happiness — 12 molds per sheet.
2114-M-4220. **$1.89 each**

18. OCEANIA. Penguins, dolphins, whales — 11 molds per sheet.
2114-M-4216. **$1.89 each**

19. NAUTICAL. 10 molds per sheet.
2114-M-4204. **$1.89 each**

20. WATER FOWL. Ducks and swans. 11 molds per sheet.
2114-M-4224. **$1.89 each**

PLEASE NOTE: All prices. certain products and services. reflect the U.S.A. domestic market and do not apply in Australia and Canada.

LEARN HOW TO MAKE AND MOLD DOZENS OF DELICIOUS CANDIES IN JUST 5 EASY LESSONS! The Wilton Candy Maker™ Home Study Course is designed to teach even the most inexperienced student how to make and mold eye-catching, taste tempting candies like these! Step-by-step instructions, illustrations and photographs will take you from basic melting and molding techniques to advanced cooked candies. Special Candy Maker™ tools, supplies and ingredients are included.

TRY IT FREE FOR 15 DAYS—RETURN COUPON AT RIGHT AND WE'LL SEND LESSON 1 TO YOU ON APPROVAL!

LESSON 1
Melt and mold an assortment of candy treats in various shapes, flavors and colors. Make candy clusters and candies with nut centers. Combine creamy caramel, pecans and chocolatey coating to create chewy Caramel Turtles!

Lesson 1 includes:
Notebook Easel and Lesson Pages
3 lbs. Candy Melts brand confectionery coating
3 Plastic Sheet Molds
Disposable Decorating Bags
Lollipop Sticks
Pink Candy Color
Peppermint Candy Flavor
Caramel Filling (full 16 oz. container).

LESSON 2
Shape and dip creme center candies! Learn to use Wilton Creme Center Mix to make vanilla, peppermint and peanut butter creme centers. It's easy to mold and dip these candies! Covered cherries are another tasty treat you'll learn to make.

Lesson 2 includes:
Lesson Pages
4 lbs. Candy Melts brand confectionery coating
2 Plastic Sheet Molds
Panda 3-D Stand-Up Mold
Two Canisters Creme Center Mix
Disposable Decorating Bags

Plastic Dipping Spoon
Decorator's Art Brush
Candy Box, Liner and Label
Paper Candy Cups.

LESSON 3
Learn to turn plain candies into extraordinary treats by decorating with melted coating. Learn to make molded, layered and piped truffle candies — so very creamy and rich! Try your hand at making ice cream candies to thrill a sweet tooth!

Lesson 3 includes:
Lesson Pages
5 lbs. Candy Melts brand confectionery coating
Heart Box 3-D Mold
Plastic Coupler and Decorating Tips
Disposable Decorating Bags
Green and Yellow Candy Colors
Lollipop Sticks
Lemon Candy Flavor
Foil Candy Cups.

LESSON 4
Mix and fix the most delicious candies! Mold candy cups to fill with liqueur or brandy. Learn how to make two cooked candies — light as air divinities and chewy nougats. Learn to shape an edible rose from special modeling candy recipe.

Lesson 4 includes:
Lesson Pages
3 lbs. Candy Melts brand confectionery coating
Cordial Cup Plastic Sheet Mold
Candy Box and Liner
Professional Quality Candy Thermometer.

LESSON 5
Make some super, sensational sweets! Learn how to make chewy jellied candies and shimmering hard candies in Super Flex candy molds. Make delicate mints and petits fours with their smooth and creamy fondant-like icing.

Lesson 5 includes:
Lesson Pages
Two Super Flex Candy Molds
Nylon Candy Funnel
Candy Wafer & Fondant Mix
Disposable Decorating Bags
Lollipop Sticks
1 lb. Candy Melts brand confectionery coating.

128

LEARN CAKE DECORATING AT YOUR OWN PACE, AT YOUR CONVENIENCE! Even if you've never tried cake decorating before, the Wilton Home Study Course will show you how to decorate beautiful cakes for every occasion. Easy-to-follow 5-lesson course includes the specialty tools you need plus the step-by-step instructions, illustrations and photographs that make it easy! Products sent to complete your lessons would cost $89.50 if purchased separately.

TRY IT FREE FOR 15 DAYS — COMPLETE COUPON AT LEFT AND WE'LL SEND LESSON 1 TO YOU ON APPROVAL!

CAKE DECORATING HOME STUDY COURSE

LESSON 1
Discover the easy way to pipe buttercream icing stars, zigzag borders and more! Learn how to prepare and color icing for your decorating bag, the correct angle to use, and how to control the pressure for expert results. Make a "Happy Birthday" cake!

Lesson 1 includes:
Notebook Easel and Lesson Pages
Decorating tips 4, 16 and 18
Quick-Change Plastic Coupler
Two Jars of Paste Icing Color
Shaped "Happy Birthday" Cake Pan
12" Featherweight Decorating Bag
Practice Sheets and Practice Board
Cardboard Cake Circle.

LESSON 2
Learn to make royal icing drop flowers, star flowers and leaves. Mold a sugar basket. Create a blooming basket cake. Learn how to acheive special effects with color and floral sprays plus how to print or write personalized messages!

Lesson 2 includes:
Lesson Pages
Flower Basket Sugar Mold
Stainless Steel Angled Spatula
Decorating Tips 3, 20, 67 and 131
Two Jars of Paste Icing Color
Meringue Powder (4 oz. canister)
Pack of 50 Parchment Paper Triangles
Cardboard Cake Circle
Six Pattern Sheets.

LESSON 3
Discover the techniques for making shells, rosebuds, sweet peas, ruffles, bows and more! Learn to make bouquets on a heart-shaped cake ideal for anniversaries, birthdays, Valentine's Day, weddings, showers.

Lesson 3 includes:
Lesson Pages
Five Pattern Sheets
Two 9" Aluminum Heart-Shaped Pans
Decorating Tips 22, 103 and 104
12" Featherweight Decorating Bag
Quick-Change Plastic Coupler
Cardboard Cake Circle
Jar of Paste Icing Color.

LESSON 4
Learn to make daisies and chrysanthemums using a flower nail. Weave basketweave stripes. Create symmetrical cake designs, pipe rope borders and more. Use your new cake turntable to decorate a round cake.

Lesson 4 includes:
Lesson Pages
Trim 'N Turn Cake Stand
Decorating Tips 48 and 81
Cardboard Cake Circle
Flower Nails 7 and 9
Jar of Paste Icing Color
Six Pattern Sheets
Wilton Cake Marker.

LESSON 5
Learn to shape the magnificent icing rose! Pipe stringwork and create a mini-tiered cake using the pans and separator set we'll send. After this lesson you'll qualify for your Wilton Certificate of Completion!

Lesson 5 includes:
Round Mini-Tier Kit (includes 3 cake pans, separator plates and columns)
Four Pattern Sheets
Decorating Tips 2, 12, 87 and 102
Cardboard Cake Circle.

GUM PASTE & SPECIALTY SUPPLIES

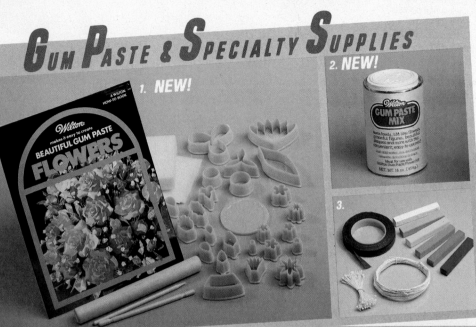

1. NEW! GUM PASTE FLOWERS KIT. Make beautiful, breathtaking flowers that almost look real in gum paste! Create bouquets or single blooms for cakes, centerpieces, favors and more. Full-color how-to book gives you step-by-step instructions and wonderful ideas. You also get 24 plastic cutters, 1 leaf mold, 3 wooden modeling tools and 2 squares of foam for modeling.
1907-M-117. $14.99 30-pc. set

2. NEW! GUM PASTE MIX. Easy-to-use...just add water and knead! Soon you'll have a workable, pliable dough-like mixture to mold into beautiful flowers and figures. 1 lb. can.
707-M-124. $4.99 each

3. GUM PASTE ACCESSORY KIT. Contains the tools you'll need to make fascinating gum paste blooms. Green florist tape, fine florist wire, pastel chalk and stamens.
1907-M-227. $9.99 kit

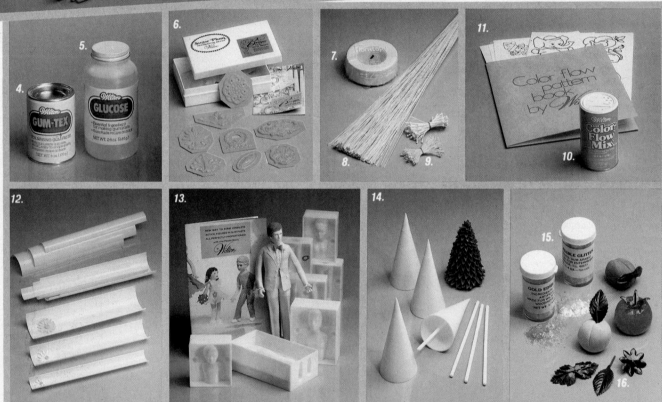

4. GUM-TEX™ KARAYA. Gives gum paste a pliable, elastic, easy-to-shape quality. 6 oz. can.
707-M-117. $5.29 each

5. GLUCOSE. Essential ingredient in making gum paste. 24 oz. plastic jar. **707-M-109. $4.29 each**

6. BAROQUE GUM PASTE MOLDS. Includes 12 classic molds, full-color instruction/idea booklet in a plastic box. **1906-M-1299. $10.99 set**

7. FLORIST TAPE. 1/2 in. wide. Two 90 ft. rolls per package. White. **409-M-614. $2.29 each**

8. FLORIST WIRE. Medium weight. 18 in. long. 175 wires per pack. White. **409-M-622. $5.59 pack**

9. STAMENS. 144 per bunch.
1005-M-7875. Yellow. $1.29
1005-M-102. Pearl White. $1.29

10. COLOR FLOW MIX. Add water and confectioners sugar to this mix to make a smooth icing for outlining and filling in favorite designs. 4 oz. can yields about ten 1-1/2 cup batches. (Refer to page 83 for more about Color Flow) **701-M-47. $6.99 each**

11. COLOR FLOW PATTERN BOOK. Over 70 unique, all-occasion designs to outline and fill in.
408-M-350. $5.99 each

12. FLOWER FORMERS. Sturdy plastic stands that allow icing leaves and flowers to dry convexed or concaved. Set of five. 11 in. long in 3 different widths: 1-1/2, 2, 2-1/2 in. **417-M-9500. $5.99 set**

13. WILTON PEOPLE MOLDS. Four 3-part molds (man, woman, two children) and instruction book. Create a whole family out of gum paste.
1906-M-5154. $13.99 set

14. TREE FORMERS. Make a forest of icing pine trees (see p. 73 for how-to's). Great stands for drying icing or gum paste decorations. 6-1/2 in. high. Set of 4. **417-M-1150. $1.99 each**

15. EDIBLE GLITTER. 1/2 oz. plastic jar.
703-M-1204. White. $2.29 each
703-M-1212. Gold. $2.29 each

16. MARZIPAN LEAVES. 100 per pack, 4 designs.
1005-M-1000. $5.99 pack

Stamens made in Korea. Plastic flower formers, tree formers, cutters, storage box, people molds made in Hong Kong. Gum paste book printed in U.S.A.

130

1. NEW! WILTON ICING MIX. *It offers you everything the best homemade buttercream icing does: rich taste, luscious, smooth texture — PLUS it's convenient! All you do is add butter and milk, the shortening is already in the mix. It's ideal for frosting as well as decorating! So easy-to-use …complete instructions on package. For icing variations with Wilton Icing Mix, see page 81. 14 oz. size yields 2 cups of icing. In two delicious flavors — try them both!*
CREAMY WHITE. *710-M-112. $1.99 each*
CHOCOLATE FLAVORED. *710-M-114. $1.99 each*

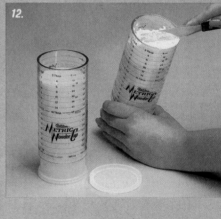

ICING MIX, COLORS & TOOLS

2. 10-ICING COLOR KIT. *1 oz. jars of paste colors: Violet, Leaf Green, Royal Blue, Brown, Black, Pink, Watermelon, Moss Green, Orange and Lemon Yellow.*
601-M-5569. *$11.99 10-color kit*

3. 8-ICING COLOR KIT. *1/2 oz. jars of paste color. Christmas Red, Lemon Yellow, Leaf Green, Sky Blue, Brown, Orange, Pink and Violet.*
601-M-5577. *$7.99 8-color kit*

4. PASTE ICING COLORS. *Concentrated colors in a creamy, rich base for fast mixing and no thinning. 1 oz. plastic jars.*
Each $1.29, except Red-Red and Burgundy, $1.89

Lemon Yellow.	610-M-108.	Violet.	610-M-604.
Golden Yellow.	610-M-159.	Royal Blue.	610-M-655.
Orange.	610-M-205.	Burgundy.	610-M-698.
Pink.	610-M-256.	Sky Blue.	610-M-700.
Christmas Red.	610-M-302.	Kelly Green.	610-M-752.
Watermelon.	610-M-353.	Leaf Green.	610-M-809.
Rose.	610-M-401.	Moss Green.	610-M-851.
Copper.	610-M-450.	Red-Red.	610-M-906.
Brown.	610-M-507.	Black.	610-M-981.

5. LIQUID ICING COLORS. *Concentrated colors in unbreakable plastic bottles with drop control spouts. Tint icings to bright pastel shades. 2 oz.*
Each $2.59, except Red-Red, $2.79

Lemon Yellow.	603-M-108.	Royal Blue.	603-M-655.
Orange.	603-M-205.	Sky Blue.	603-M-700.
Pink.	603-M-256.	Leaf Green.	603-M-809.
Copper.	603-M-450.	Red-Red.	603-M-906.
Brown.	603-M-507.	Black.	603-M-981.

6. WHITE-WHITE ICING COLOR. *Now you can make your buttercream icing pure white with just a few drops. Great for wedding cakes. 2 oz. plastic bottle.*
603-M-1236. *$2.99 each*

7. BUTTER EXTRACT. *For a rich buttery taste. 2 oz.*
604-M-2040. *$1.39 each*

8. CLEAR VANILLA EXTRACT. *Won't change icing color. 2 oz.* **604-M-2237.** *$1.39 each*

9. GLYCERIN. *A few drops stirred into dried-out paste color restores consistency. A money-saver. 2 oz.*
708-M-14. *$1.99 each*

10. MERINGUE POWDER MIX. *For royal icing and meringue (see recipes on pages 83 and 95).*
4 oz. *702-M-6007. $4.29 each*
8 oz. *702-M-6015. $6.79 each*

11. PIPING GEL. *Clear gel for glazing or can be tinted with paste color for writing, color striping, stringwork, filling and more. 10 oz. container.*
704-M-105. *$3.29 each*

12. METRIC WONDER CUP. *2 cup capacity with measures of cups, ounces and millimeters. Neat for measuring shortening. With plastic shaker lid. 6 x 3 in.*
415-M-105. *$5.59 each*

131

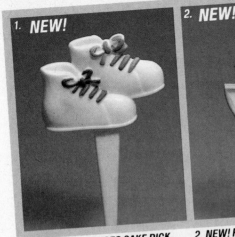

1. NEW!

2. NEW!

3. NEW!

1. NEW! BABY SHOES CAKE PICK. Scatter these tiny shoes around your shower cake to tell moms the patter of little feet is near.
2113-M-3811. $1.29 pack of 6

2. NEW! ROCKING HORSE CAKE PICK. Round up these rockin' ponies to trim your cake and you'll have time to rock at the party!
2113-M-3809. $1.29 pack of 6

3. NEW! STORK CAKE PICK. Land this fellow with his bundle of joy on your cake top and fly through the decorating.
2113-M-3805. $1.29 pack of 6

BABY SHOWER & CHRISTENING CAKE TOPS

4.

5.

6.

7.

8.

4. BABY RATTLES. Don't be rattled about decorating your baby shower cake if you have these adorable add-ons in hand. Lay flat on cake top or sides.
2113-M-3283. $.99 pack of 2

5. SLEEPING ANGELS. Sweet slumbering cherubs for a simply beautiful cake. Pink and blue gowned infants. 2-3/4 in. x 1-1/2 in.
2113-M-2325. $1.59 pack of 2

6. MR. STORK. He's preparing for his very special delivery. Perfect shower cake surprise for the mom-to-be.
115-M-1502. $4.99 each

7. DAINTY BASSINETTE. Perfect for your cake, party favors or place cards. Fill with candy and attach name card with pink and blue ribbons.
2111-M-9381. $.99 each

8. BABY CHRISTENING. Add a gentle touch to baby's first celebration cake. Pink or blue cradle. 3-1/2 in. long.
1103-M-7909. Pink. $1.59 each
1103-M-7895. Blue. $1.59 each

9.

10.

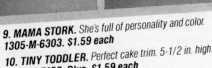
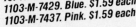

11.

12.

13.

14.

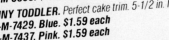

9. MAMA STORK. She's full of personality and color.
1305-M-6303. $1.59 each

10. TINY TODDLER. Perfect cake trim. 5-1/2 in. high.
1103-M-7429. Blue. $1.59 each
1103-M-7437. Pink. $1.59 each

11. BABY BRACELET. Pink and blue. 1 in. diameter.
2111-M-72. $1.59 pack of 4

12. LULLABY ORNAMENTS. 6 in. high.
115-M-921. Blue. $4.99 each
115-M-948. Pink. $4.99 each

13. CRYSTAL-CLEAR BOOTIES. Lace these dainty booties with pastel ribbon and fill with candy or flowers. 4-1/4 in. long.
1103-M-9332. $1.59 pack of 2

14. BOOTIE ORNAMENT. Capture hearts with crystal clear booties on filigree heart. Add pink or blue trim.
111-M-2500. $6.99 each

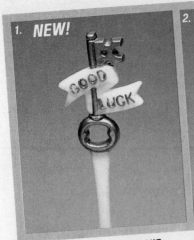

1. NEW!

2. NEW!

3. NEW!

**1. NEW! GOOD LUCK KEY CAKE
PICK.** *The key to success. It's also
your key to fast, successful decorating.*
2113-M-3801. $1.29 pack of 6

**2. NEW! MORTARBOARD AND
DIPLOMA CAKE PICK.** *Perk up your
graduate's cake and you'll both be
congratulated for a job well-done.*
2113-M-3803. $1.29 pack of 6

**3. NEW! RINGS AND RIBBON
CAKE PICK.** *Transform a simple cake
into a joyful celebration of love. Quick
and easy trimming.*
2113-M-3807 $1.29 pack of 6

Graduation & Wedding Shower Cake Tops

4. **5.** **6.** **7.**

4. SUCCESSFUL GRAD. *He's got his
future in his hands. Perfect tribute to
the proud grad. 4-1/2 in. high.*
2113-M-4549. $1.59 each

5. GLOWING GRAD. *She's radiant
with happiness and success. Place her
on your grad's cake to share her joy.
4-1/2 in. high.*
2113-M-1833. $1.59 each

6. GLAD GRADUATE. *Eager and ready
for the world, he's made it! And he'll
make your cake too. 4-3/4 in. high.*
2113-M-1817. $1.99 each

7. PROUD GRADUATES. *Rosy
cheeked and serious, they're ready for
bigger and better things. 4-1/2 in. high.*
Girl in white.
2811-M-160. $1.59 each
Boy in black.
2811-M-152 $1.59 each

8. **9.** **10.** **11.** **12.**

8. SPRINKLING CANS. *Fill
with nuts, candies, more. Two each/
pink and blue per package. 2 x 4 in.*
2110-M-9709. $1.59 pack of 4

9. PARTY PARASOLS. *Perfect
party favors, cake tops, gift ties.
4 in. parasols, 5 in. snap-on
handles.*
2110-M-9296. $1.59 pack of 4

10. FLOWER BASKETS. *Fill
with fresh flowers, mints, homemade candy for a treasured favor.
3 x 3 in.*
1008-M-904. $1.79 pack of 6

11. CHAMPAGNE GLASSES.
*Fill with homemade candy or pip-
ing gel to resemble champagne.
Ideal for New Year's Eve parties,
anniversaries, more! 2 in.*
2110-M-4162. $1.59 pack of 6

**12. RELUCTANT GROOM
COUPLE.** *Add a humorous touch
to the engagement or wedding
shower cake. 5-1/2 in. high.*
1316-M-9520.
$4.99 each couple

All products made in Hong Kong

133

LIVELY, ENCHANTING CAKE TOPS TO MAKE LITTLE EYES SPARKLE!

1. HONEY BEAR. You'll have a ball trimming your cake with this character. Hand-painted. 5 in. high.
2113-M-2031. **$1.99 each**

2. BIKER BOY. It's happy times when this little guy parks on your cake. 3 in. high.
2113-M-2678. **$2.59 each**

3. APPALOOSA ROCKING HORSES. Four painted ponies are ready to rock around your happiness cake. Set of 4, each 2-1/2 in. high.
2113-M-2015. **$2.99 set**

4. NUMBER 1 KID. Tell kids any age they're first with you. This super-fast cake trimmer lies flat on cake top or side. 3-1/2 in. high.
2113-M-4565. **S.99 each**

5. LI'L COWPOKE. Wee buckaroo will lasso cheers from the birthday kid. 5-1/8 in. high.
2113-M-2406. **$2.59 each**

6. DOLLY DRESS-UP. Little and big girls alike will like her style. Necklace is detachable. 4-1/2 in. high.
2113-M-1485. **$2.59 each**

7. MISS PONYTAIL. This little lady will win hearts with her charm. 4-1/2 in. high.
2113-M-500. **$1.59 each**

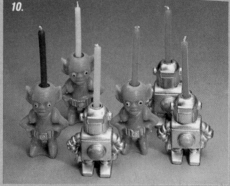

Young Children's Cake Tops

8. DANCING BALLERINA. Graceful dancer will star on celebration cakes. 6 in. high.
1301-M-7042. **$1.99 each**

9. SPACESHIP TOPPER SET. Create an adventure cake. Silver-toned spacecraft with clear dome is 3-3/4 in. high and 4-1/8 in. wide on 1-1/4 in. platform. One each 2-1/4 in. robot and 2-1/8 in. spaceman hold standard candles.
2111-M-2008. **$3.59. set**

10. SPACEMEN & ROBOTS CANDLE HOLDERS. Extraterrestrials to place beside Spaceship Topper Set. Silver-toned robots are 2-1/4 in. high; green spacemen are 2-1/8 in. high. (Candles not included.)
2111-M-2024. **$2.99 set**

11. SHINING CROSS. Lay flat or push into christening and religious occasion cakes. Embossed gold-tone finish with detachable pick. 3-3/4 in. high.
1105-M-7320. **S.99 each**

12. SNOW WHITE & DWARFS. Transform a cake into a fairy tale adventure. One 3 in. Snow White and 7 happy dwarfs. 1-1/2 to 2-1/2 in. high.
2113-M-2147. **$3.59 set**

13. COMMUNION ALTAR. Boy or girl at prayer will be a meaningful addition on the joyous event cake. Tulle veil on girl. Each 3 x 2-1/2 in. high.
Boy. 1105-M-7886. $1.99 each
Girl. 1105-M-7878. $1.99 each

14. CHURCH COMMUNION. Cathedral windows beautifully set off kneeling children on a lacy base. Heavenly touch on communion cakes. Tulle veil on girl. Each 6-1/2 x 4-7/8 in.
Boy. 111-M-2284. $6.99 each
Girl. 111-M-2276. $6.99 each

BIG TOP CAKE TRIMMERS TO HELP YOU MAKE THE GREATEST CAKE ON EARTH!

1. CAROUSEL SEPARATOR SET. *Place this perky parade of ponies between two cakes to create an enchanting merry cake-go-round. Set contains 2 brown and 2 white, snap-on 4-in. horse pillars, two 10 in. round plates — one clear acrylic, one plastic. Two 10 in. cardboard circles protect plates and add support.*
2103-M-1139. $9.99 set

2. ABC BLOCK SEPARATOR SET. *It's easy as ABC to create enchanting tiered party cakes for showers, children's birthdays, and more! Complete set includes acrylic and white plastic two 10 in. round plates; four snap-on 4 in. high block pillars and two 10 in. cardboard circles for plate support. Use plates alone to serve single cakes or treats.*
301-M-6016. $5.99 set

3. CAROUSEL CAKE TOP. *Place our 10 in. high merry-go-round with dancing clowns and flying flags on a 10 in. or larger birthday or celebration cake. Awning big top, 6 each of poles, horses, flags and clowns included.*
1305-M-9302. $4.99 set

4. CLOWN SEPARATOR SET. *Tricky twosome balances a 6 in. round cake on top plate over any size base cake. You can stand them up on either their hands or feet to hold your cake. Set includes two 7 in. scallop-edged separator plates and two snap-on clown supports. 4 in. high.*
301-M-909. $6.99 set

CIRCUS & TEEN CAKE TOPS

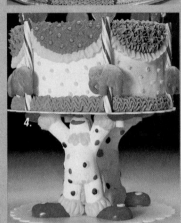

5. CIRCUS BALLOONS. *12 bright balloons in a bunch, 3 in. diam., 3 bunches per set.*
2113-M-2366. $1.99 set

6. CLOWN-IN-THE-BOX. *Zany pop-up. Extra cards included. 3-1/4 in. high.*
2113-M-2139. $1.29 each

7. POLKA DOT CLOWN. *He'll make sure the party's great. Hand-painted. 4-1/2 in. high.*
2113-M-2848. $2.59 each

8. JUGGLER CLOWN. *Turn your party cake into a 3-ring circus of fun. 4 in. high.*
2113-M-2252. $1.99 each

9. COMICAL CLOWNS. *Fun for all with a variety of faces. 2 in. to 2-1/2 in.*
2113-M-2635. $2.59 each

10. COUNTDOWN CLOWN. *Turn his face to any age from 1 to 6. Hand-painted. 4-1/2 in. high.*
2113-M-2341. $1.29 each

11. DERBY CLOWN. *A happy face for great cakes. On pick. 1-3/4 in.*
2113-M-2333. $1.99 pack of 4

12. SMALL DERBY CLOWN. *On pick. 3/4 in.*
2113-M-2759. $1.59 pack of 6

13. MARCHING MAJORETTE. *Hand-painted leader. 5 in. high.*
2113-M-2589. $1.99 each

14. TEEN SWINGERS. *Boy and girl dancers. 4 in. high.*
2113-M-2163. $1.99 set of 2

15. TELEPHONE TEENS. *Party line for fun. 3 girls/3 boys. 2 x 2-3/4 in. high.*
1301-M-706. $3.59 6 pc. set.

16. CAMPUS CHEERLEADER. *She'll pep up any party. 5-1/8 in. high.*
2113-M-2708. $1.59 each

Famous Character Cake Tops

1. NEW!

2. NEW!

3. NEW!

4. NEW!

1. NEW! BIG BIRD WITH AGE†††.
What a surprise when everyone's favorite feathered friend announces the birthday child's age. 3-9/16 in. high.
2113-M-1430. $1.99 each

††† © 1984 Children's Television Workshop. BIG BIRD, COOKIE MONSTER, OSCAR THE GROUCH, BERT and ERNIE © 1984 Muppets, Inc. All rights reserved.

2. NEW! SESAME STREET CANDLE SET†††. Let the lovable Sesame Street bunch burn brightly for the birthday boy or girl. 6 pc. set. 2 to 2-3/4 in. high.
2811-M-1004. $2.99 set

3. NEW! RAINBOW BRITE.™
She's the quickest, easiest way to add brightness and love to your celebration cakes. Lay flat on cake top or side. 3-1/2 in. high.
2113-M-4798. $1.59 each

© 1983, Hallmark Cards, Inc.

4. NEW! COOKIE MONSTER PICK†††.
No fooling around. He's a real friend when the decorating has to be fast. 3-1/8 in. high.
2113-M-3813. $1.59 each

†† © 1982 Children's Television Workshop. OSCAR THE GROUCH, BIG BIRD, COOKIE MONSTER © 1982 Muppets, Inc. All rights reserved.

5.

6.

7.

8.

9.

5. WONDER WOMAN†.
She'll turn birthday, Mom's Day, promotion and congratulations cakes into WONDERful treats.
3-3/8 in. high.
2113-M-2996. $1.99 each

† indicates Trademark of DC Comics, Inc.

6. BATMAN†. This dynamic uno will solve your decorating dilemmas in no time. He'll soon whip special-occasion cakes into shape. 3-1/2 in. high.
2113-M-2902. $1.99 each

7. SUPERMAN†. A powerhouse that transforms meek, mild cakes into blockbusters in no time.
3-3/8 in. high
2113-M-2945. $1.99 each

8. "BERRY" NICE STRAWBERRY SHORTCAKE. She'll be a standout at any celebration. Hand-painted. 3 in. high.
2113-M-4522. $2.59 each

9. STRAWBERRY SHORTCAKE. Lay flat on cake top or sides. Hand-painted. 3-1/2 in. long.
2113-M-4646. $1.29 each

© MCMLXXXIII American Greetings Corp.

10. BUGS BUNNY* & CARROT CANDLE HOLDERS. Six 2 in. high carrot candle holders, 6 in. high Bugs.
2113-M-2546. $3.59 set

11. LOONEY TUNES TOPPER SET. BUGS BUNNY* with SYLVESTER,* TWEETY,* PORKY PIG* and DAFFY DUCK.* 2-1/4 to 3-1/4 in. high.
2113-M-5006. $2.99 set

* indicates trademark of Warner Bros., Inc. © 1979

SESAME STREET CHARACTER CANDLES.
Include circle and age discs 1-6. 3-1/2 in. high.

12. OSCAR THE GROUCH.
2811-M-12. $1.09 each

13. BIG BIRD. 2811-M-39. $1.09 each

14. COOKIE MONSTER.
2811-M-47. $1.09 each

10.

11.

††CTW Trademark — Sesame Street and the Sesame Street sign are Trademarks and service marks of the Children's Television Workshop.

12. **13.** **14.**

1. **NEW!**

2. **NEW!**

3. **NEW!**

4.

NEW! BIG BIRD PICK†††. How easy it is to perk up the party cake or cupcakes with this mirthful bird. 3/8 in. high.
2113-M-3815. $1.59 each

2. NEW! RAGGEDY ANN & ANDY. Let America's favorite rag doll twins dance on your cake and watch little eyes dance with joy. Lay flat on cake top or sides. Set of Raggedy Ann and Andy. Each 3-7/8 in. high.
2113-M-2025. $1.99 set
© 1984 Bobbs-Merrill Company, Inc.

3. NEW! BIRTHDAY BEAR CARE BEAR.™ This cuddly optimist brings his special rainbow of birthday wishes to the party cake. Rainbow is age indicator, 1 to 6. 3-5/8 in. high.
2113-M-1475. $1.99 each
© MCMLXXXIV American Greetings Corp.

4. SESAME STREET SET††. BIG BIRD, OSCAR THE GROUCH, COOKIE MONSTER, BERT and ERNIE. 2 in. to 3-1/4 in. high
2113-M-1728. $2.99 set
†† © 1982 Children's Television Workshop. BIG BIRD, COOKIE MONSTER, OSCAR THE GROUCH, BERT and ERNIE © 1982 Muppets, Inc. All rights reserved

5. 6.

7.

8.

9.

5. GRIN 'N BEAR IT CATHY.™ This modern miss deserves the spotlight on party cakes. 3-3/4 in. high.
2113-M-4085. $2.59 each

6. CATHY™ SAYS. Lay flat on your cake top and add icing message. 3-1/2 in. high.
2113-M-2724. $1.29 each
© 1983 Universal Press Syndicate.

7. SYLVESTER* and TWEETY.* This famous cat and bird team will catch lots of attention on your cake. 6 in. high.
2113-M-2562. $2.59 set
* indicates trademark of Warner Bros., Inc. © 1979.

8. DARTH VADER™ & STORM TROOPER™ SET. They're a powerful combination to put on the party cake. Darth Vader, 4-1/2 in. high; Storm Trooper, 4-1/4 in. high. Handpainted.
2113-M-3641. $1.99 set

9. R2-D2™ & C-3PO™ SET. Friendly additions on cake top or sides. Hand-painted C-3PO, 4-1/2 in. high and R2-D2, 2-1/2 in. high.
2113-M-3607. $1.99 set
TM & © Lucasfilm Ltd. (LFL) 1983 All Rights Reserved.
Wilton Enterprises Authorized User

LOONEY TUNES* CHARACTER CANDLES. Each has circle insert and age discs 1-6. Each 3-1/2 in. high.

10. PORKY PIG.
2811-M-802. $1.09 each

11. BUGS BUNNY.
2811-M-888. $1.09 each

12. TWEETY.
2811-M-845. $1.09 each

STAR WARS™ CAKE CANDLES. Each has insertable age numbers, 1 thru 6 and messages. 3-1/2 in. high.

13. R2-D2™ CANDLE.
2811-M-608. $1.09 each

14. DARTH VADER™ CANDLE.
2811-M-624. $1.09 each

15. CHEWBACCA™ CANDLE.
2811-M-616. $1.09 each

PLEASE NOTE:
All prices, certain products & services reflect the U.S.A. domestic market and do not apply in Australia and Canada.

* indicates trademark of Warner Bros. Inc., © 1979

All plastic products made in Hong Kong.

137

USE THESE WINNING
CAKE TOPS AND
YOU'LL EASILY GET
THE DECORATOR OF
THE YEAR AWARD
FROM FAMILY AND
FRIENDS

1. NEW! IN-STEP JOGGER.
It's no sweat to decorate
with this. 3-3/4 in. high.
2113-M-4816. $1.99 each

2. NEW! TENNIS STAR. Set
her on the winner's congratulations or birthday cake. You'll be
loved for it. 4 in. high.
2113-M-2112. $1.99 each

3. NEW! GOLF PRO. Have this
determined lady tee off on a
celebration cake and you'll look
like a decorating pro. 4 in. high.
2113-M-1975. $1.99 each

**4. NEW! HOCKEY PLAYERS
SET.** You'll skate through the
decorating with these fast-moving
champions. (Available 9/1/84.)
2-pc. set. Each, 3-1/4 in. high.
2113-M-2474. $3.59 set

Sports Cake Tops

5. LITTLE LEAGUER.
All set for the game, he'll
be a big hit. 4-1/2 in. high
1306-M-7436.
$1.99 each

6. GLOVE 'N BALL PICKS.
Get your mitts on these and trim
your cakes super quick. 3/4 in.,
pack of 12.
1506-M-5056. $1.29 pack

7. BASKETBALL PLAYER.
Dashing dribbler is bound to star
on party cakes. Hand-painted.
3-3/4 in. high.
2113-M-9354. $1.59 each

**8. FEMALE BASKETBALL
TOPPER SET.** These gals will
be super scorers on your
special-event cakes. 5-1/4 &
4-1/8 in. high.
2113-M-4417. $2.59 each

9. JAUNTY JOGGER. You're sure
to win any cake decorating marathon
without huffing and puffing with this
little runner. Hand-painted. 4-1/4
in. high.
2113-M-2066. $2.59 each

**10. FRUSTRATED
FISHERMAN.** He's
all tied up trying to
bring the big catch
to the party. 4-1/2
in. high.
2113-M-2384.
$2.59 each

11. SHARP SHOOTER. He'll
fire up fun on birthdays or
Father's Day. Hand-painted.
6 in. high.
2113-M-2422. $2.59 each

12. FISHY SITUATION. A little
surprise sure to get smiles at the
party table. Hand-painted.
5 in. high.
2113-M-2074. $2.59 each

**13. GONE FISHIN'
SIGNBOARD.** Gets your message across on any cake. Pipe on
icing greeting. 4-1/2 in high.
Pack of 2.
1008-M-726. $1.29 pack

**14. END OF DOCK
FISHERMAN.** Good for a laugh.
Just ice cake, swirl with spatula
to resemble water and set on top.
5 in. high.
2113-M-4832. $2.59 each

15. BASEBALL SET. Your perfect
cake can't miss with this winning
team to top it. Includes batter,
catcher, pitcher and 3 basemen.
Hand-painted. Each 2 in. tall.
2113-M-2155. $2.59 set

16. BASEBALL TOPPER SET.
You're safe if you put this trio on your
athlete's cake. It's sure to steal the
show. Ump 2-3/4 in.; catcher, 2 in.;
player, 4-1/2 in. long.
2113-M-2473. $2.59 3-pc. set

1. SENSATIONAL SOCCER PLAYER. *Everyone will get a big kick out of this super sport atop your celebration cake. 5 in. high.* **2113-M-2627. $2.59 each**

2. SUPER SKATER GIRL. *Your roller derby queen will think you're a good skate when this speed demon rolls onto her cake. Hand-painted. 4-1/2 in. high.* **2113-M-4204. $1.59 each**

3. SUPER SKATER BOY. *They'll fall for this reckless racer. A timesaving decorating daredevil. Hand-painted. 4-3/4 in. long.* **2113-M-4247. $1.59 each**

4. GOOD SPORT COACH. *He looks sweet, but he's really a tiger. Have him highlight a winning team or coach's party cake. 4-1/2 in. high.* **2113-M-4140. $2.59 each**

5. BUMBLING BOWLER. *In spite of his defeat, his clumsy feat will turn your cake into a winner. 4-1/2 in. high.* **2113-M-2783. $2.59 each**

6. GYMNAST. *Lookin' good on birthday and celebration cakes. Hand-painted. 3-1/2 in. high.* **2113-M-4689. $1.99 each**

7. TENNIS RACKETS. *Court success and save decorating time with this whacking good pair. Lay on cake top or sides. 2-3/4 in. high.* **2113-M-3267. $.99 each**

8. COMICAL GOLFER. *Down on all fours, trying his hardest, he'll be good for a laugh. 2 in. high, 4-1/4 in. wide, 5-1/8 in. long.* **2113-M-2554. $1.99 each**

9. GOLF SET.* *A stroke of genius in easy decorating. Includes 4-1/2 in. high golfer, plus 3 each: 2-1/2 in. wide greens, 4 in. high flags, 5 in. clubs and golf balls.* **1306-M-7274. $1.99 set**

10. ARMCHAIR QUARTERBACK. *Most of us know this guy. Change screen to suit his taste. Man in chair. 3-3/8 in. high; T.V. 2-1/4 in. high.* **2113-M-1302. $2.59 set**

11. PRIZE CATCH FISHERMAN. *With his sole catch, he's perfect on Father's Day and birthday cakes. 7 in. high.* **2113-M-2228. $1.99 each**

12. FEMALE BOWLER. *She'll make your decorating roll right along. Perfect for birthday and banquet cakes. 5-1/4 in. high.* **2113-M-2503. $2.59 each**

13. MALE BOWLER. *The number one choice for your bowler's bash. 6-1/8 in. high.* **2113-M-2538. $2.59 each**

14. BOWLING PIN SET. *Set on cake top to resemble bowling alley and bowl them over. Ten 1-1/2 in. tall pins with four 1/2 in. balls. 14 pc. set.* **1306-M-4909. $1.59 set**

15. YOU'RE NUMBER 1! *Just push this big 1 into any good news and winning day cakes to tell them they're tops. Pack of 6.* **2113-M-4492. $1.29 pack**

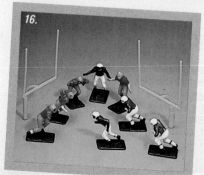

16. SUPER BOWL FOOTBALL SET. *Decorate a super cake in a hurry and win lots of fans! Great for birthdays as well as Super Sunday. Eight 2 in. high players and two 4-1/2 in. high goal posts included.* **2113-M-2236. $2.99 10 pc. set**

*CAUTION: Contains small parts. Not intended for use by children 3 years or under.
Plastic products made in Hong Kong.

PLEASE NOTE:
All prices, certain products and services reflect the U.S.A. domestic market and do not apply in Australia and Canada.

139

Adult Cake Tops

1. NEW! THE BIG 40

2. NEW!

3.

4.

5.

6.

7.

8.

4. BACKYARD GARDENER. *Plant this hoer atop birthday, Father's Day, special event cakes and more! He's got lots of get up and grow. 4-1/4 in. high.*
2113-M-1973. $1.99 each

5. ALL THUMBS. *Our handy-man special is a whimsical way to trim your favorite handyman's cake. 4-7/8 in. high.*
2113-M-2686. $1.99 each

6. PARTY GUY. *Your life-of-the-party will love this fellow sitting on his birthday, get well, bachelor's party cake and more. 3-1/8 in. high.*
2113-M-3739. $2.59 each

7. BIG BOSS. *He means business — funny business, that is! He'll take the work out of decorating your best boss's birthday, anniversary, retirement cake.*
2113-M-3798. $2.59 each

8. CARD SHARK. *He'll give you a winning hand decorating a favorite winner's cake. 4-1/2 in. high on 4 in. base.*
2113-M-2597. $2.59 each

9.

10.

13.

15.

16.

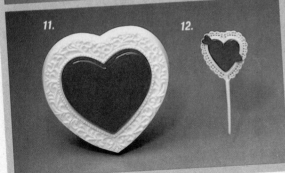

11.

12.

14.

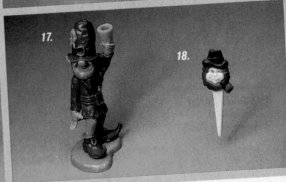

17.

18.

With this sign of luck your decorating can't run amuck. Emerald Shamrock, 3-1/4 in.; Pick, 1-1/4 in. on 1-7/8 in. pick.
9. EMERALD SHAMROCK. 2113-M-3313. $.99 each
10. SHAMROCK PICK. 2113-M-4387. $1.29 each

A show of love to place on special cakes!
11. HEART CHARM. *3-3/4 in. wide.*
2113-M-3518. $.99 each

12. VALENTINE PICKS. *1-1/2 in. heart on 1-1/2 in. pick.*
1502-M-1011. $1.29 pack of 12

13. LAZY BONES. *This snoozer is a super cake accent for Father's Day, and more. 2-1/2 in. high on 5-1/2 in. base.*
2113-M-2414. $2.59 each

14. ROYAL CROWN. *4-1/2 x 5-3/4 in.*
1310-M-7483. $4.59 each

Here's a simple way to make their day.
15. NUMBER 1 MOM. *Pink/white. 3-1/2 in. high.*
2113-M-3224. $.99 each
16. NUMBER 1 DAD. *Blue/white. 3-1/2 in. high.*
2113-M-3240. $.99 each
All eyes will smile when these fellows decorate your cake.

17. LUCKY LEPRECHAUN. *4-1/2 in. high.*
2113-M-1957. $2.59 each

18. LEPRECHAUN PICK. *1-3/8 in. on 1-3/4 in. pick.*
2113-M-4441. $1.29 pack of 6
All products made in Hong Kong.

1. **PILGRIM PALS.** Give thanks for a bountiful year with this symbolic Thanksgiving pair. Set includes 3-1/2 in. boy and 3-1/4 in. girl.
2113-M-3119. $1.59 set

2. **CORNUCOPIA.** Enjoy a fruitful holiday and year. Place this horn of plenty on any celebration cake. Perfect for Thanksgiving. 4-3/4 in.
2113-M-3003. $1.59 each

3. **LITTLE TRICKERS.** This trio is a treat on a Halloween cake. Pumpkin, 2-7/8 in. high; ghost, 2-1/2 in. high; monster, 3-1/4 in. high.
2113-M-3380. $2.99 set

4. **SANTA CLAUS.** Ho! Ho! Ho! He's a merry touch to add to a holiday confection. Hand-painted. 4-1/2 in. high.
2113-M-4506. $2.59 each

5. **STARS 'N STRIPES.** Display your patriotic pride atop or on the side of summer and holiday cakes. 3-1/4 in. high.
2113-M-4727. S.99 each

6. **BLACK POT.** Fun with Wacky Witch. Fill with candy. Cauldron is detachable. 4-1/2 in. high.
1207-M-5222. S.99 each

7. **WACKY WITCH.** She'll bewitch all with her charms on or beside the party cake. 5-1/4 in.
2113-M-6118. $1.99 each

8. **BOPPIN' BUNNY.** This happy hopper will bring glee to the Easter celebration. Fill detachable basket with candy 5-1/2 in. high.
2113-M-2465. $2.59 each

9. **EASTER BUNNY PICK.** 2 in. on 1-3/4 in. pick.
2113-M-4476. $1.29 pack of 6
10. **BUNNY FAMILY.*** 2-1/2 in. mom; three 1-1/2 in. high babies.
1305-M-7547. $1.59 set   *CAUTION. Contains small parts.
Not intended for use by children 3 years or under.

11. **HAPPY GHOST.** Ghostly fun! 4-3/8 in. high.
2113-M-3356. S.99 each
12. **SCARY GHOST.** Boo! He's 4-1/2 in high.
1316-M-400. $1.59 each
13. **BLACK CAT PICK.** 1-1/4 in. on 1-3/4 in. pick.
2113-M-4301. $1.29 pack of 6
14. **JACK-O-LANTERN PICK.** 1-5/8 in. on 1-3/4 in. pick.
2113-M-4328. $1.29 pack of 6

15. **HOLLY WREATH.** Boughs and berries. 3-1/2 in.
2113-M-4784. S.99 each

16. **JACK-O-LANTERNS.** 2 in. spooky pumpkins will get screams of glee.
2113-M-3135. $1.59 set of 4

17. **SNOWMAN PICK.** Jolly fellow. 1-5/8 in. on 1-3/4 in. pick.
2113-M-4360. $1.29 pack of 6
18. **CHRISTMAS TREE PICK.** 1-5/8 in. on 1-3/4 in. pick.
2113-M-4344. $1.29 pack of 6
19. **SANTA 'N TREE.** Santa, 2-5/8 in. tall, tree, 3-3/8 in. high.
2113-M-1647. $1.59 2-pc. set
20. **CHRISTMAS CAROLLERS.** A harmonious trio.
2113-M-2813. $2.59 each trio

Wilton
Wedding Cake Porcelains

1.

2.

NEW!

3.

The exquisite Wilton Wedding Cake Porcelains will add a lovely finishing touch to the wedding cake.

These gracious ornaments are not only a beautiful way to top off your wedding cake, but will also be a treasured keepsake to be handed down from one generation to the next. A wide assortment permits a choice that will tie in perfectly with the bridal party motif color. These carefully detailed porcelains make a very thoughtful bridal shower gift, too.

1-3. NEW! PROMISE. The lovely porcelain couple embrace tenderly in front of a clear crystal-look cut out heart accented with ribbon and delicate flowers. Transparent crystal-look base is especially beautiful atop a cake tiered with our crystal-look plates and pillars (see pages 158, 159). Promise is also featured on page 31.
(1) PINK. 117-M-311. *$24.99 each*
(2) BLUE. 117-M-309. *$24.99 each*
(3) LILAC. 117-M-307. *$24.99 each*

4.

5.

6.

4-5. CHERISH. *Porcelain couple graces a white porcelain base. Slot in base holds a porcelain wedding plate. Ornament 8-1/4 in. high, plate 7-1/8 in. diam.**
(4) LILAC. 117-M-173. *$34.99 each*
(5) PINK. 117-M-157. *$34.99 each*
YELLOW (Not shown). 117-M-190. *$34.99 each*

*Includes a gleaming brass nameplate to have engraved and then attach to the front of the base. It comes with top tier assembly tips for supporting added weight of ornament.

6. PORCELAIN PLATES. *How romantic for the bride and groom to serve their pieces of wedding cake on matching plates. And, they make a lovely bridesmaid gift, too.*

Porcelain Plates made in Japan. Couple, brass nameplate and flowers made in Korea. Plastic parts made in Hong Kong.

6A. FAITH. *Ribbons and rings in lilac tones.*
201-M-1660. $12.99 each
6B. HOPE. *Bells and flowers in pink tones.*
201-M-1635. $12.99 each
6C. JOY. *Wild flowers in yellow tones.*
201-M-1724. $12.99 each

Assembled in U.S.A.

Wilton
Wedding Cake Porcelains

NEW!

A beautiful cake creation deserves a truly beautiful cake ornament.

The Wilton Wedding Cake Porcelains are carefully crafted to be prized for their loveliness on your wedding day and for generations after. Each ornament captures forever the tenderness and love of the bridal couple. Whichever ornament you choose, you can count on it to lend dramatic impact to your wedding cake presentation.

1-3. NEW! RHAPSODY. *A porcelain bridal pair embrace tenderly under clear, crystal-look wedding bells and arch accented with blossoms and ribbon. Crystal-look base has a ridged, dimensional effect. 9-1/2 in. high.*

(1) PINK.	117-M-305.	*$24.99 each*
(2) LILAC.	117-M-303.	*$24.99 each*
(3) WHITE.	117-M-301.	*$24.99 each*

4-5. REFLECTION. *Stunning sophistication. A trio of lucite-like panels, tenderly touched with satin ribbons, rise dramatically behind the sleek white porcelain couple. Plastic base graced with cherry blossoms. 8-1/4 in. high.*

(4) PINK.	117-M-297.	*$24.99 each*
(5) BLUE.	117-M-130.	*$24.99 each*
LILAC *(Not shown).*	117-M-270.	*$24.99 each*

Assembled in U.S.A. PLEASE NOTE: All prices, certain products reflect the U.S.A. domestic market and do not apply in Australia or Canada.

6-7. CAPTIVATION. *Gentle gracefulness. White porcelain couple is romantically set beneath a traditional canopy. A sprinkling of baby roses and satiny streamers enhance the white plastic canopy and beveled-edged base. 10 in. high.*

(6) PINK.	117-M-238.	*$24.99 each*
(7) LILAC.	117-M-211.	*$24.99 each*
WHITE *(Not shown).*	117-M-254.	*$24.99 each*

ADD ROMANCE AND ENCHANTMENT TO YOUR BEAUTIFUL WEDDING TIERS.
These lovely hand-assembled creations will be treasured for years. All feature hand-painted couples, ornate plastic bases, floral sprays and fluffy tulle trims and bridal veils.

1. HEARTS TAKE WING. *Graceful white birds share a kiss before a glorious tulle-trimmed filigree heart. Handsome Baroque scroll base adds regal charm to tiered cake. 10-1/2 in. high.*
103-M-6218. $10.99 each

2. SPRING SONG. *A pair of songbirds perch gracefully on bough above fluffy tulle puff. Dainty flowers encircle lovebirds above filigree heart base. 9-1/2 in. high.*
111-M-2802. $12.99 each

3. CIRCLES OF LOVE. *A symbolic way to reflect love...two rings side by side, graceful doves and a filigree bell. All surrounded by flowers on delicate filigree heart base. 10 in. high.*
103-M-9004. $12.99 each

WEDDING ORNAMENTS

4-5. WEDDING ROSE. *Satiny rose highlights lacy heart duo. Splashed with tulle in your choice of 4 colors plus filigree bells and blooms. All on filigree heart base. 9 in. high.*

4-5. WEDDING ROSE.
(4) WHITE. 103-M-2328. $10.99 each
(5) MINT. 103-M-2281. $10.99 each
PINK *(not shown).* **103-M-2263. $10.99 each**
BLUE *(not shown).* **103-M-2301. $10.99 each**

6. WEDDING BELLS. *Dainty lace-covered bands encircle gala gathering of lovely filigree bells. Trimmed with roses and fluffy tulle. 10-1/2 in. high.*
103-M-1356. $12.99 each

Plastic parts made in Hong Kong. Flowers made in Korea.
All ornaments are hand-assembled in U.S.A.

HIGHLIGHT LAVISH CAKE TIERS WITH FRILLY ROMANTICS BEDECKED WITH BELLS, TULLE AND LACE! *Choose one of these Wilton ornaments for the top of that special wedding cake. Designed to complement both contemporary and traditional themes, these ornaments are sure to add a glorious touch.*

1-2. PERT 'N PRETTY. *Openwork bell, lacy heart and filigree heart base are accented with pastel tulle, coordinating satiny bows and tiny silk-like flowers. 9 in. high.*

(1) BLUE. 103-M-2220. **$10.99 each**
(2) WHITE. 103-M-2204. **$10.99 each**
YELLOW *(not shown).* 103-M-2247.
$10.99 each

3. BRIDAL BELLS. *Lustrous blending of satin-covered bells and delicate flowers. Tulle fluff accents large openwork bead heart atop lacy filigree heart base. 9 in. high.*

YELLOW BELLS. 103-M-1798. **$12.99 each**
WHITE BELLS. 103-M-1755. **$12.99 each**
PINK BELLS. 103-M-1763. **$12.99 each**

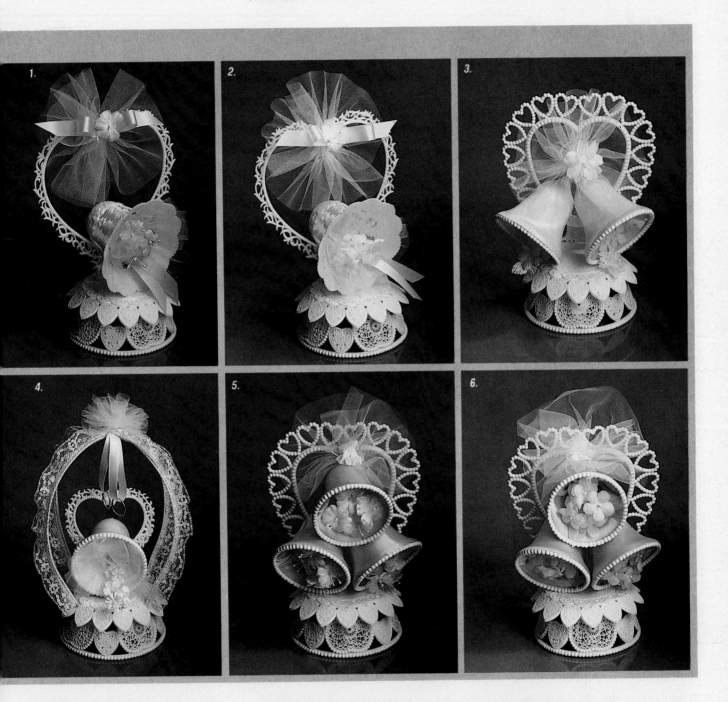

4. EVERLASTING LOVE. *Wedding bands suspended from satin ribbons add impact to lace ruffled arches surrounding satin-covered bell and openwork heart. Daintily floral spray and tulle puff add softness. 10 in. high.*
103-M-236. $12.99 each

5-6. SOPHISTICATED. *A touch of tulle and openwork bead heart are an enchanting backdrop for the lush flower-filled trio of satin-covered plastic bells. Flower and tulle shades are designed to coordinate in your choice of soft pastels or white. 9 in. high.*

5-6. SOPHISTICATED.
(5) PINK. 103-M-1887. **$14.99 each**
(6) BLUE. 103-M-1879. **$14.99 each**
WHITE *(not shown).*
103-M-1852. **$14.99 each**

PLEASE NOTE: All prices, certain products and services reflect the U.S.A. domestic market and do not apply in Australia or Canada.

MAKE DREAMS COME TRUE WITH AN ENCHANTING ORNAMENT!
These fabulous eye-catchers feature handmade fabric flowers, beautifully detailed plastic trims, satiny ribbons, fluffy tulle and lacy ruffles. Charming couples are hand-painted plastic.

1. RELUCTANT GROOM ORNAMENT. *Fabric flowers and pretty bell frame our whimsical couple on fancy heart base. A fun-loving, light-hearted fantasy all will enjoy. 10 in. high.*
110-M-1003. $15.99 each

2. LOVE DUET. *Doves alight on symbolic double rings with a lovely gathering of fabric flowers springing up from base — all in front of charming movable openwork gate. 8 in. high.*
103-M-43903. $8.99 each

3. MORNING ROSEBUD. *The happy couple stands before movable openwork gate while pair of doves look down. Embossed base is trimmed with fabric roses. Groom's coat available in white or black. 8 in. high.*
BLACK COAT. 101-M-44013. $8.99 each
WHITE COAT. 101-M-44020. $8.99 each

Wedding Ornaments

4. SWEET CEREMONY. *Large bead heart forms backdrop for elegant ornament featuring openwork chapel bell. Top is accented by tulle puff and dainty flowers. Bridal couple stands in center on openwork filigree heart base. 10 in. high.*
BLACK COAT. 101-M-22011. $10.99 each
WHITE COAT. 101-M-22028. $10.99 each

5. ROSEBUD BRILLIANCE. *Lovebirds and rosebuds accent the gazebo of love. Perfect setting for the adoring couple. 8-1/2 in. high.*
BLACK COAT. 101-M-44315. $8.99 each
WHITE COAT. 101-M-44323. $8.99 each

6. CIRCLES OF LACE. *Blisssful pair stands together in a lace-covered three-ring dome trimmed with tulle puff and filigree bell. 12 in. high.*
BLACK COAT. 114-M-8014. $12.99 each
WHITE COAT. 114-M-8022. $12.99 each

Plastic parts made in Hong Kong. Flowers made in Korea. All ornaments are hand-assembled in the U.S.A.

REFLECT THE LOVE THEY SHARE WITH A LASTING MEMENTO!
Top their once-in-a-lifetime cake with hearts and flowers, wedding bells and lovebirds, lacy trims and delicate tulle. Each adds a graceful crowning touch.

1. SPELLBOUND. *Entranced bridal couple stands inside of a romantic gazebo. Picturesque garden setting is highlighted by delicate floral trim and peaceful doves perched on the roof. 9 in. high.*
YELLOW FLOWERS. 110-M-406. $10.99 each
PINK FLOWERS. 110-M-422. $10.99 each

2. TENDERNESS. *The child-like couple stands atop openwork filigree heart base. Heart-shaped frame is trimmed with magnificent satin-like roses, lily of the valley and a dramatic spray of tulle. 10-1/2 in. high.*
110-M-112. $12.99 each

3. HEART-TO-HEART. *Sweet bridal couple is surrounded by two elaborate hearts...front heart is open, back is filigreed; both are trimmed with lace. Center flower highlights filigree heart base. 9 in. high.*
110-M-376. $14.99 each

4. LOVE TOKEN. *Adorable bridal couple stands under symbolic chapel bell. Three-ringed dome is lace-covered and trimmed with an elegant tulle puff. 11 in. high.*
110-M-538. $12.99 each

PLEASE NOTE: All prices, certain products and services reflect the U.S.A. domestic market and do not apply in Australia or Canada.

5. MOONLIT SNOW. *Loving couple stands under sparkling bell and floral sprays. Choose white or black couple; black, white or tan suits. 9-1/2 in. high.*

Couple	Coat	Stock No.	Price
WHITE.	BLACK.	114-M-62418.	$14.99
WHITE.	WHITE.	114-M-62426.	$14.99
WHITE.	TAN.	114-M-62434.	$14.99
BLACK.	BLACK.	116-M-62417.	$14.99
BLACK.	WHITE.	116-M-62429.	$14.99
BLACK.	TAN.	116-M-62433.	$14.99

6. ENCHANTMENT. *An archway of white orchids and baby blooms entwines around an old-fashioned arched trellis; picket fence gate envelops the newlyweds. On filigree heart base. 10 in. high.*

BLACK COAT. 114-M-9002. $14.99 each
WHITE COAT. 114-M-9023. $14.99 each

ADORN YOUR WEDDING TIERS WITH A ROMANTIC ORNAMENT.

Each ornament features a beautiful bridal couple in a romantic setting enhanced with handmade fabric flowers, satiny ribbon and lovely tulle.

1-2. NEW! TENDER HEART. A beautifully detailed wedding cake ornament. The charming bisque porcelain couple are posed in front of a lace-edged heart with filigree border. Flower puffs encircle the couple. Choose a groom with either black or white coat. (White coat not shown.)

	Coat	Flowers	Cat. No.	Price
(1)	Black	Pink	112-M-200	$19.99 each
	Black	Blue	112-M-300	$19.99 each
	Black	White	112-M-100	$19.99 each
(2)	White	Pink	112-M-500	$19.99 each
	White	Blue	112-M-400	$19.99 each
	White	White	112-M-600	$19.99 each

3. ROSE CASCADE The lovely bride and handsome groom are encircled with flowers, leaves and tulle.
Black coat. 114-M-13816. $12.99 each
White coat. 114-M-13824. $12.99 each

4. NEW! VERSION OF ROSE CASCADE with charming bisque porcelain couple that's sure to become a keepsake for the bridal couple.
White Coat. 112-M-9000. $17.99 each
Black Coat. 112-M-8000. $17.99 each

WEDDING ORNAMENTS

1. NEW!

2. NEW!

3.

4. NEW!

5.

6. NEW!

7.

8.

5. MOONBEAM'S EMBRACE. The glowing couple is posed under a double archway of delicate star flowers and white cascading blossoms. White filigree plastic base. Black Coat only.
114-M-144. 10-1/2 in. high.
$14.99 each

6. NEW VERSION! MOONBEAM'S EMBRACE with bisque porcelain couple to be cherished as a keepsake and passed from one generation to the next. 10-1/2 in. high.

White Coat.
112-M-1000. $19.99 each
Black Coat.
112-M-2000. $19.99 each

7. ORCHIDS FOREVER. Dainty doves and glittering bell top a sparkling glass brandy snifter filled with dreamy white and yellow flowers and classic couple. 10-1/2 in. high.
Black Coat.
114-M-73614. $21.99 each
White Coat.
114-M-73622. $21.99 each

8. MANTILLA. Meaningful moments are reflected in the attitude of the lovely bridal couple. Delicate fabric flowers frame a cathedral window graced with a golden cross. Heart-shaped petals encircle the filigree plastic base. 11 in. high.
Black Coat.
114-M-45416. $14.99 each
White Coat.
114-M-45424. $14.99 each

CONGRATULATE THE HAPPY COUPLE ON YEARS OF SHARING AND CARING

Numeral wreaths or hand-painted couples are adorned with handmade floral sprays or festive bows.

1-2. PETITE ANNIVERSARY. Doves alight at the base of the 25th silver or 50th golden anniversary wreath. 6-3/4 in. high.
(1.) 50th. 105-M-4273. $4.99 each
(2.) 25th. 105-M-4265. $4.99 each

3. ANNIVERSARY WREATH. Traditional numeral wreath is glorified with matching bow and two white doves on filigree heart base. 9 in. high.
25th Anniversary Silver
102-M-1513. $6.99 each
50th Anniversary Gold
102-M-1520. $6.99 each

4. DOUBLE RING DEVOTION. For silver or golden anniversary cakes... shining symbolic rings of gold or silver encircle anniversary couple. Lady's gown coordinates with wedding bands. 5-1/2 inches high.
25th Anniversary Silver
105-M-4613. $6.99 each
50th Anniversary Gold
105-M-4605. $6.99 each

ANNIVERSARY ORNAMENTS

5. ANNIVERSARY YEARS. Filigree heart base holds anniversary wreath with snap-out numbers — 5,10,15,20,40. Trim with tinted icing flowers or ribbons in coordinating cake colors. 5-3/4 inches high.
105-M-4257. $4.99 each

6. ANNIVERSARY WALTZ. Choose handsome couple standing in front of bow trimmed 25th or 50th year emblem wreath. Wreath and gown coordinate. 9 inches high.
25th Anniversary Silver
102-M-5519. $8.99 each
50th Anniversary Gold
102-M-5527. $8.99 each

7. SILVER SENTIMENTS. 25 years together deserve a tribute as special as this silvery beauty. A sparkling wreath is lavished with bursts of tulle and two symbolic wedding rings. It's all sitting pretty on a crystal-look base. 7-1/2 inches high.
102-M-1084. $6.99 each

8. 50 YEARS OF HAPPINESS. A glorious occasion is celebrated with a special tribute for the loving couple. Gleaming gold-finish anniversary wreath is festooned with blossoms and golden leaves. The numeral 50 is gold-finish also. It's a fitting way to mark a beautiful event. It's all presented on a white plastic filigree heart base. 10 inches high.
102-M-223. $14.99 each

25 YEARS OF HAPPINESS
(not shown)
102-M-207. $14.99 each

149

DELICATE PETITES ENHANCE DAINTY WEDDING TIERS.

Beauty in a smaller size. Perfectly sized for smaller cakes, these ornaments feature handsome hand-painted couples, ornate plastic trims, hand-made fabric flowers, tulle puffs and delicate touches of lace.

1-2. NEW! HAPPY HEARTS with beautiful bisque procelain bride and groom. The bridal couple is posed before a cut-out heart that's tied with a satiny bow; a spray of delicate blossoms trails the heart.

	COAT	COLOR	CAT. NO.	PRICE
(1)	WHITE.	PINK.	108-M-219.	$13.99
	WHITE.	BLUE.	108-M-211.	$13.99
	WHITE.	LILAC.	108-M-215.	$13.99
(2)	BLACK.	LILAC.	108-M-213.	$13.99
	BLACK.	BLUE.	108-M-209.	$13.99
	BLACK.	PINK.	108-M-217.	$13.99

3-4. PETITE FLORAL FANTASY. The choice of many brides…a swirl of star and yellow-centered flowers create a lovely archway for the bride and groom to march through. 6-1/2 inches high.

(3) BLACK COUPLE.
BLACK COAT. 113-M-22519. $8.99 each
WHITE COAT. 113-M-22527. $8.99 each

(4) WHITE COUPLE.
BLACK COAT. 104-M-22511. $8.99 each
WHITE COAT. 104-M-22528. $8.99 each

P E T I T E   O R N A M E N T S

5. PETITE SPRING SONG. Lovebirds cooing on a branch just for wooing. Surrounded by flower arch and puff of tulle. 7 inches high.
106-M-159. $8.99 each

6. PETITE DOUBLE RING COUPLE. A duet of lovebirds and wedding bands accent the handsome pair. 5-1/2 inches high.
BLACK COAT. 104-M-42413. $6.99 each
WHITE COAT. 104-M-42420. $6.99 each

7. PETITE WHITE BIRDS. Lovebirds wooing and cooing under pristine white ruffled arches. They're a charming twosome that will add a graceful elegance to your wedding cake. A burst of pink tulle enhances their delicate beauty. A glittering bell adds a charming note, suspended from the center of the arches. The white plastic base is so romantic with delicate scrollwork hearts. 6 inches high.
111-M-133. $6.99 each

8. LOVERS IN LACE. A classic couple is posed under a graceful arch that is beguilingly ruffled with lace and topped with a puff of tulle. The white plastic base is encircled with romantic, scroll-work hearts. The handsome groom wears a white coat or a black coat; the choice is yours.
BLACK COAT. 104-M-818. $8.99 each
WHITE COAT. 104-M-826. $8.99 each

**DAINTY ORNAMENTS ADD A
BEAUTIFUL FINISHING TOUCH.**

These delicate ornaments are intricately
designed to enhance the smaller wedding cake and
to become a memento to be cherished by the
bridal couple.

1. PETITE DAINTY CHARM. Traditional
twosome enhanced with fan of tulle and delicate
floral spray. Black coat only. 5-1/2 inches high.
WHITE.	104-M-32310.	$8.99 each
LILAC.	104-M-1172.	$8.99 each
PINK.	104-M-1156.	$8.99 each
YELLOW.	104-M-1123.	$8.99 each

2. PETITE BELLS OF JOY. A cluster of filigree
bells dotted with a rose, are encircled with lace-
covered bands and topped with tulle. 6-1/2" high.
106-M-2658. $8.99 each

3-4. NATURAL BEAUTY. Graceful lovebirds
perched in front of a delicate open heart with a
lovely intricate border. It's lavished with dainty
floral sprays and a matching satiny bow. A white
filigree base is the perfect ending. 6 inches high.
(3) WHITE. 106-M-1163. $6.99 each
(4) PINK. 106-M-1120. $6.99 each

Not Shown
LILAC. 106-M-1147. $6.99 each
PEACH. 106-M-1104. $6.99 each

PETITE ORNAMENTS

5. LA BELLE PETITE. Engaging blossoms spill
from a delicate, openwork chapel bell of filigree
plastic. Framing the graceful bell is an airy heart
of dainty filigree plastic. The puff of cloud-like tulle
is the perfect accent. It's poised on a white
plastic base of romantic scroll-like hearts.
5-1/2 inches high.
106-M-248. $6.99 each

6. PETITE TRIPLE BELLS. Church bells will
be ringing on your special day and these bells
will be the perfect ornament for your wedding
cake. The glittering trio is crafted of white
filigree plastic for an airy, openwork look. They're
topped with a rose and a fluff of delicate tulle.
The white filigree plastic base has a romantic
heart design. 5-1/2 inches.
106-M-4250. $6.99 each

7. PETITE DOUBLE RING. Fluttering doves and
bands of love on filigree heart base are a classic
choice. A burst of tulle sprays from center.
5-1/2 inches high.
106-M-4316. $4.99 each

8. PETITE HEAVENLY BELLS. A medley of
filigree bells at the feet of an angelic cherub. He
holds graceful doves fluttering aloft. 7 inches high.
111-M-3000. $6.99 each

Plastic parts and trims made in Hong Kong.
Flowers and Bisque Couple made in Korea.
Assembled in U.S.A.
PLEASE NOTE: All prices, certain products and services
reflect the U.S.A. domestic market and do not apply in
Australia or Canada.

1. PETITE GARDEN HOUSE. 7 pcs.
205-M-8298. (5 x 9 in.) $3.99 each

2. PICKET ARCHWAY. Swinging gate and trellis.
205-M-343. (5-1/2 x 5-1/4 in.) 2.59 each

3. ARCH CANOPY TRELLIS. Basketweave.
205-M-6015. (3-1/2 x 6-3/4 in.) $2.59 each

4. WISHING WELL.
Handle turns removable bucket.
205-M-327. (3 x 4-3/4 in.) $3.59 each

5. FILIGREE HEARTS. Lace-edged open heart.
White plastic.
7 in. 205-M-1500. $1.98 for 3
4 in. 205-M-1528. $2.16 for 6

6. SEED PEARL HEART.
Beaded heart in white plastic.
205-M-1005. (7 x 6-1/2 in.) $2.64 for 3

7. CURVED GOTHIC WINDOW. White plastic. 2 pcs.
205-M-3059. (5 x 9 in.) $3.59 each

8. HEART BASE. White. Two sizes. 2 pcs.
201-M-7331. (4-1/4 x 2 in.) $2.59 each
201-M-7846. (3-1/4 x 1-1/2 in.) $1.99 each

9. GARDEN GAZEBO. With heart base. 4 pcs.
205-M-4100. (4-1/4 x 8-1/2 in.) $3.99 each

10. PETITE GOTHIC WINDOW.
For every blessed event. 2 pcs.
205-M-2672. (5 x 7-1/4 in.) $2.59 each

11. FLORAL SCROLL BASE. Baroque design. 2 pcs.
201-M-303. (4-1/2 x 2-1/2 in.) $2.59 each

12. ITALIAN FILIGREE ARCHWAY.
White openwork. 2 pcs.
205-M-8115. (4-1/2 x 7 in.) $3.99 each

13. GATETOP ARCH.
Gates open on heart base. 2 pcs.
205-M-3482. (8 in. high.) $2.59 each

14. SWIRLS. 1-1/4 x 2-1/2 in. White.
1004-M-2100. $2.29 pack of 12

15. LACY HEART. 3-3/4 x 3-1/2 in. White.
1004-M-2305. 12 for $2.04

WEDDING TRIMS

16. SCROLLS. 2-3/4 x 1-1/4 in. White.
1004-M-2800. 24 for $1.92

17. CURVED TRIANGLE. 3 x 3-1/4 in. White.
1004-M-3001. $2.29 pack of 12

18. CONTOUR. 3-3/4 x 2-3/4 in. White.
1004-M-2003. $2.29 pack of 12

19. ARTIFICIAL LEAVES.
Green or white cloth, gold or silver foil.
Order 1005-M-number

	1-7/8 In.	1-1/4 In.
Gold.	6518. $1.99	6712. $1.79
Silver.	6526. $1.99	6720. $1.79
Green.	4655. $1.99	4670. $1.79
White.	6501. $1.99	

20. LARGE DOUBLE WEDDING RINGS.
3-3/8 in. diam.
Gold.	201-M-3007.	$1.59 each
Silver.	201-M-3147.	$1.59 each
Pearl.	201-M-1007.	$1.29 each

21. FLOWER SPIKES.
Fill spike with water, insert in cake, add fresh flowers.
1008-M-408. (3 in.) $2.29 pack of 12

22. ROSE CASCADE ARCH. Roses, lily of the valley.
204-M-13807. (19 in. long.) $4.99 each

23. LILAC BOUQUET. Spray of delicate white blooms.
204-M-1681. (8 in. long.) $3.30 each

24. STAR FLOWER SPRAY.
Star flowers with pearl stamens.
204-M-62409. (20 in. long.) $4.99 each

25. ORCHID SPRAY. Full-bloom orchids.
204-M-10700. (19 in. long.) $4.99 each

26. BLOSSOMING SPRAY. Star flowers and blossoms.
204-M-2252. (14 in. long.) $3.30 each

1. ADORATION. *Dainty dancing cherubs.*
111-M-141. *(4-1/2 in. high.)* **$5.99 each**

2. CHERUB CARD HOLDER. *Charming place markers.*
(card not incl.)
1001-M-9373. *(1-5/8 x 3-3/8 in.)* **$2.80 for 4**

3. ANGEL FOUNTAIN. *Decorate the fountain area.*
1001-M-406. *(3-3/4 in. high.)* **$1.99 each**

4. ANGEL WITH HARP. *Four heavenly winged angels.*
1001-M-7028. *(3-1/2 in. high.)* **$3.32 for 4**

5. MEDITERRANEAN CUPID. *Ideal for small tiers.*
1001-M-601. *(4 in. high.)* **$1.99 each**

6. MUSICAL TRIO.
Cherub band for cakes, centerpieces.
1001-M-368. *(3-1/2 in. high.)* **$1.99 set**

7. CLASSIQUE VASE.
1008-M-7364. *(8 in. high.)* **$3.59 each**

8. FROLICKING CHERUB. *White.*
1001-M-244. *(5 in. high.)* **$2.59 each**

9. WINGED ANGELS. *Two angels per package. White.*
1001-M-457. *(2-1/2 x 2 in.)* **$2.40 for 3 packs**

10. KISSING LOVE BIRDS. *Use on top or between tiers.*
1002-M-206. *(5-1/2 in. high.)* **$3.79 each**

11. ANGELINOS.
1001-M-503. *(2 x 3 in.)* **6 for $2.88**

12. KNEELING CHERUB FOUNTAIN.
Fill the fountain with icing flowers.
1001-M-9380. *(4 in. high.)* **$1.59 each**

13. IRIDESCENT DOVES.
1002-M-508. *(2 x 1-1/2 in.)* **6 for $2.64**

14. IRIDESCENT GRAPES.
1099-M-200. *(3 in. long.)* **$3.79 pack of 4**

15. LARGE FLUTTERING DOVES.
1002-M-1806. *(4 x 2-3/4 in.)* **$2.29 pack of 2**

16. SMALL DOVES. *White.*
1002-M-1709. *(2 x 1-1/2 in.)* **2 for $1.20**

GLITTERED SMALL DOVES. *Non-edible glitter coated.*
1006-M-166. *(Not shown.)* **$1.59 pack of 12**

17. FILIGREE BELLS.

CAT. NO.	IN. HIGH	PRICE
1001-M-9446.	1 IN.	12/$1.44
1001-M-9421.	2 IN.	6/$1.56
1001-M-9438.	2-3/4 IN.	6/$1.56
1001-M-9403.	3 IN.	3/$1.50
1001-M-9410.	4-1/4 IN.	3/$1.89

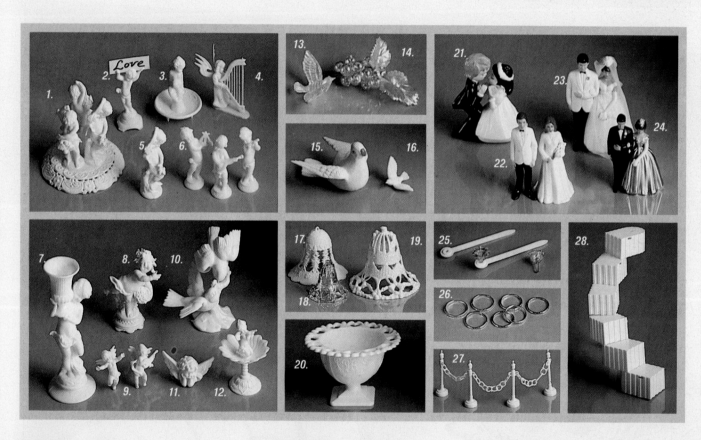

18. IRIDESCENT BELLS.

CAT. NO.	IN. HIGH	PRICE
1001-M-8016.	1-1/2 IN.	Pk. of 12/$2.59
1001-M-8024.	1-3/4 IN.	6/$2.16
1001-M-8032.	2 IN.	6/$2.46
1001-M-8040.	3 IN.	3/$3.39

19. GLITTERED BELLS.

CAT. NO.	IN. HIGH	PRICE
1007-M-9060.	1-1/4 IN.	12/$1.20
2110-M-9075.	1-3/4 IN.	Pk. of 6/$1.09
1007-M-9087.	2 IN.	6/$1.50
2110-M-9090.	3 IN.	Pk. of 6/$2.19
1007-M-9109.	5 IN.	3/$3.09

20. HEART BOWL VASE. *Heart embossed design.*
1008-M-9685. *(3-1/4 in. high.)* **$1.99 each**

21. KISSING COUPLE. *Tender twosome.*
202-M-171. *(4 in. high.)* **$3.99 each**

22. WEDDING COUPLE. *Use on filigree bridge, stairs.*
WHITE COAT. 214-M-237. **$2.99 set**
BLACK COAT. 214-M-253. **$2.99 set**

23. BRIDAL COUPLE. *Tulle veil and skirt overlay.*
REGULAR COUPLE 4-1/2 In. Tall.
WHITE COAT. 202-M-8121. **$3.99 each**
BLACK COAT. 202-M-8110. **$3.99 each**
PETITE COUPLE. 3-1/2 In. Tall.
BLACK COAT. 2102-M-820. **$3.59 each**
WHITE COAT. 203-M-8220. **$3.59 each**

24. ANNIVERSARY COUPLE. *25th or 50th anniversary.*
25th SILVER. 203-M-2827. **$3.59 each**
50th GOLDEN. 203-M-1820. **$3.59 each**

25. PUSH-IN CANDLE HOLDERS. *Pegs and holders.*
1107-M-8131. **$1.59 set**

26. SMALL WEDDING RINGS. *With slit for interlocking.*
SILVER. 1002-M-1016. **$1.39 pack of 24**
GOLD. 1002-M-1008. **$1.39 pack of 24**

27. OLD-FASHIONED FENCE. *12 ea. posts and pegs, 144 snap-together links.*
1107-M-8326. **$2.29 set**

28. STAIRSTEPS. *24 stairs, inserts and holders.*
1107-M-8180. **$5.29 set**

Unassembled. Includes instructions. Plastic modeling glue required.

Plastic parts and trims made in Hong Kong. Flowers made in Korea. Assembled in U.S.A.

PLEASE NOTE: All prices, certain products and services reflect the U.S.A. domestic market and do not apply in Australia or Canada.

SERVE AND SUPPORT YOUR CAKES STYLISHLY AND SECURELY. Wilton has the best selection of paper products, cake boards, boxes and cake stands — all designed to add that professional touch!

1. RECTANGLE DOILY. Larger 10 x 14 in. size makes this fancy openwork doily ideal for large sheet cakes and hors d'oeuvres. Use as placemats, too! Pack of 6.
2104-M-1605. $1.99 pack

2. ROUND PARCHMENT DOILIES.
Attractive Normandy lace-look pattern.
8-IN. 2104-M-1397. $1.99 pack of 10
10-IN. 2104-M-1532. $1.99 pack of 8
12-IN. 2104-M-1591. $1.99 pack of 6

3. CAKE BOXES. Easy way to store, transport and give your cakes! Sturdy white cardboard boxes (like bakeries use) lie flat for easy storage; fold easily into shape. Pack of 12.

10-IN. SQUARE (4 in. deep). 1912-M-2061. $5.00 pack
12-IN. SQUARE (5 in. deep). 1912-M-2045. $6.00 pack

14-IN. SQUARE (5 in. deep). 1912-M-2029. $7.00 pack
19 x 13-IN. RECTANGLE (3-1/2 in. deep). 1912-M-2002. $10.00 pack

4. TUK-N-RUFFLE.
Trim your cake with grease-resistant lacy plastic ruffle with tulle overlay. Offset sewn to ruffle best. Attach to serving tray or board with royal icing or tape. Order 60-ft. bolt or by the foot!

COLOR	PER FOOT		60 FT. BOLT	
Green	801-M-1501	$.35	802-M-1504	$11.99
Yellow	801-M-1100	$.35	802-M-1105	$11.99
Pink	801-M-708	$.35	802-M-702	$11.99
Blue	801-M-200	$.35	802-M-206	$11.99
White	801-M-1003	$.35	802-M-1008	$11.99
Silver	801-M-90	$.40	802-M-95	$18.99
Gold	801-M-147	$.40	802-M-44	$18.99

DOILIES, RUFFLES, BOXES & CAKE BOARDS

5. RECTANGLE CAKE BOARDS. Large 13 x 19 in. corrugated cardboard sheets are extra versatile — cut to fit most any size cake! Particularly handy for shaped cakes or cakes surrounded by fancy settings. Cover with Fanci-Foil for an attractive serving plate.
2104-M-552. $3.99 pack of 6

Plastic products made in Hong Kong. Aluminum cake stand made in Korea.

6. ROUND CAKE CIRCLES.
Sturdy corrugated cardboard sheets are perfect for tier cakes to protect your separator plates! Cover with foil (sold on facing page) for the prettiest look.

6-IN. 2104-M-64. $1.99 pack of 10
8-IN. 2104-M-80. $2.99 pack of 12
10-IN. 2104-M-102. $3.59 pack of 12
12-IN. 2104-M-129. $3.59 pack of 8
14-IN. 2104-M-145. $3.59 pack of 6
16-IN. 2104-M-160. $4.79 pack of 6

PLEASE NOTE: All prices, certain products and services reflect the U.S.A. domestic market and do not apply in Australia or Canada.

SHOW 'N SERVE CAKE BOARDS, FOIL & STANDS

1. SHOW 'N SERVE CAKE SERVING BOARDS. Cardboard cake boards provide support and add a decorative touch with scalloped edge and printed lace pattern. Available in 6 sizes, all protected with grease-resistant coating. Use with tiered cakes to protect your separator plates, add a lacy look, too.

8-IN. 2104-M-1125. $2.99 pack of 10
10-IN. 2104-M-1168. $3.59 pack of 10

12-IN. 2104-M-1176. $3.99 pack of 8
14-IN. 2104-M-1184. $3.99 pack of 6

16-IN. 2104-M-1192. $5.59 pack of 6
14 x 20-IN. RECTANGLE.
2104-M-1230. $5.59 pack of 6

2. FANCI-FOIL WRAP. Cover cake boards to create inexpensive cake or canape servers. Serving side has a non-toxic grease-resistant surface, safe for food. Continuous roll: 20 in. x 15 ft.
ROSE. 804-M-124. $4.99 each
GOLD. 804-M-183. $4.99 each
SILVER. 804-M-167. $4.99 each
BLUE. 804-M-140. $4.99 each

3. ROUND ROTATING CAKE STAND. Sleek 12-in. turntable accommodates cakes up to 10 inches in diameter. Fashioned in sturdy white molded plastic, cake stand is extra strong with a well-balanced base (can be used with Sheet Plate, see #4). Turn as you work for easier decorating, more attractive results.
307-M-817. $13.99 each

5. TRIM 'N TURN CAKE STAND. Hidden ball bearings allow plate to turn smoothly as you decorate. Fluted edges add beauty. Compact and easy to store, white molded plastic stand holds up to 100 pounds. Versatile 12-in diameter.
2103-M-2518. $7.99 each

4. SHEET ROTATING CAKE STAND. Large 13 x 9-in. rectangular surface for decorating any shaped, novelty or sheet cake. White molded plastic cake stand has strong base (interchangeable with round turntable).
307-M-833. $17.99 each

SHEET PLATE ONLY (fits onto Round Rotating Cake Stand #3).
307-M-850. $12.99 each

6. PROFESSIONAL CAKE STAND. A wise investment! This heavy-duty metal stand is 4-5/8 in. high. Convenient rotating 12 in. diameter decorating platform can hold large cakes and tiered wedding cakes. Long-lasting aluminum (6 lbs. 12 oz.).
307-M-2501. $34.99 each

TIERED CAKE STANDS & SETS

1. CRYSTAL-CLEAR CAKE DIVIDER SET.* White plastic separator plates are held by 1/2 in. diameter, clear plastic twist legs which penetrate cake and rest right on plate (dowel rods not needed). Includes one each: 6 in., 8 in., 10 in., 12 in., 14 in. and 16 in. plates. 24 clear plastic twist legs, each 7-1/2 in. high.
Order individually or save 25% on set.
301-M-9450. $45.99 set

PLATES	NUMBER	PRICE
6 IN.	302-M-9730	$2.99 each
8 IN.	302-M-9749	$3.99 each
10 IN.	302-M-9757	$4.99 each
12 IN.	302-M-9765	$6.99 each
14 IN.	302-M-9773	$8.99 each
16 IN.	302-M-9780	$10.99 each

7-1/2 IN. TWIST LEGS. 303-M-9794. $3.99 pack of 4

NEW! 9 IN. TWIST LEGS. Add extra height and space between your tiers!
303-M-977. $3.99 pack of 4

2. TALL TIER STAND SET.* Holds up to six impressive tiers! Includes: five twist-apart columns 6-1/2 in. high with 1 bottom and 1 top bolt; 18 in. footed base plate; 16 in., 14 in., 12 in., 10 in., and 8 in. separator plates (interchangeable, except footed base plate). White plastic. **Buy individually or save 25% on set.**
304-M-7915. $45.99 set

*Assemble at reception hall.

PLATES FOR TALL TIER STAND.

SIZE	NUMBER	PRICE
8 IN.	302-M-7894	$3.99 each
10 IN.	302-M-7908	$4.99 each
12 IN.	302-M-7924	$5.99 each
14 IN.	302-M-7940	$8.99 each
16 IN.	302-M-7967	$11.99 each
18 IN.	302-M-7983	$14.99 each

COLUMNS

6-1/2 IN.	303-M-7910	$1.59 each
7-3/4 IN.	304-M-5009	$2.59 each
13-1/2 IN.	303-M-703	$4.29 each

TOP COLUMN CAP NUT. 304-M-7923. $.79 each
GLUE-ON PLATE LEGS. 304-M-7930. $.59 each
BOTTOM COLUMN BOLT. 304-M-7941. $.99 each

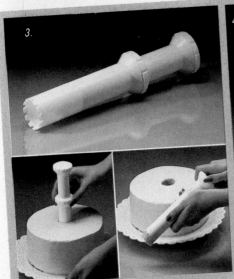

3. CAKE CORER TUBE. Prepare your tiers quickly and neatly for the Tall Tier Stand column. Serrated edge removes cake center with one push. Ice cake before using. Plastic 7 in. long solid center fits into 6-1/2 in. long hollow corer to eject cake bits. Cleans easily in soapy water.
156 **304-M-8172. $1.99 each**

4. SUPER STRONG CAKE STAND. Molded embossed base holds up to 185 pounds of cake! High-impact polystyrene material and underweb of ribbing make this stand super strong. 2-3/4 in. high with arched sides. Full 18 in. diameter accommodates larger cake bases.
307-M-1200. $12.99 each

5. 4-ARM BASE STAND. Replace Tall Tier Base Plate (shown in #2) with this support then add separator plates (sold in #2) up to 12 in. diameter. For proper balance, add up to 3 graduated tiers to center column. Heavy-duty white plastic. Base bolt included.
304-M-8245. $11.99 each
BASE BOLT ONLY.
304-M-8253. $.59 each

FOUNTAIN & TIER ACCESSORIES

1. FLOWER HOLDER RING. White plastic holder is perfect for fresh or silk flower arrangements. Position at base of the Kolor-Flo Fountain. 12-1/4 in. diameter, 2 in. high.
305-M-435. $4.99 each

2. FILIGREE FOUNTAIN FRAME. The perfect finishing touch around the Kolor-Flo Fountain. Eight lacy, white plastic scallops snap together easily. 9 in. diameter, 3-1/2 in. high.
205-M-1285. $2.99 each

3. ROUND SEPARATOR PLATES. Dainty scalloped edge accents cakes beautifully. Includes eight 4-in. plastic legs.

14 IN. ROUND PLATE. 302-M-148. $5.29 each
16 IN. ROUND PLATE. 302-M-946. $7.29 each

4. LACY-LOOK PILLARS. Elegant white plastic pillars add a pretty touch. Insert fabric to coordinate with bride's color scheme for an original accent. 12 in. high.
303-M-8976. $2.99 each

5. ROMAN COLUMNS. Handsome 10-1/4 in. classicly styled pillar may be used with Kolor-Flo Fountain (remove one fountain tier). Clean lines make white plastic pillars so elegant!
303-M-8135. $2.59 each

PLEASE NOTE: All prices, certain products and services reflect the U.S.A. domestic market and do not apply in Australia or Canada.

6. THE KOLOR-FLO FOUNTAIN. The ultimate cake highlight. Cascading waterfall lit with sparkling lights is the perfect way to enhance elegant formal tiers. Add liquid icing color to tint the water a delicate coordinating pastel shade. Add fresh flowers to create a lovely table centerpiece. See photo.

Water pours from three levels. Top levels can be removed for smaller fountain arrangement. Lit by intricate lighting system with two bulbs for extra brilliance. Plastic fountain bowl is 9-3/4 in. diameter. 110-124 v. A.C. motor with 65 in. cord. Pumps water electrically. Directions and replacement part information included.
306-M-2599. $79.99 each

All plastic products made in Hong Kong.
Kolor-Flo Fountain made in Germany.

NEW!

TIERED CAKE STANDS & SETS

1. NEW! CRYSTAL-LOOK TIER SET. This dynamic plate and pillar combination features an elegant cut-glass look. Pillars have many faceted cuts that catch the light. The transparent round plates are edged with the same diamond-look cuts and have been strengthened to support the largest cake. Set includes two 17 in. plates and four 13-3/4 in. pillars. Combine with our crystal-look wedding ornaments (142-153) and Kolor-Flo fountain for a romantic look. Plastic.
301-M-1387. $39.99 set
17 INCH CRYSTAL LOOK PLATE. 302-M-1810. $12.99 each
13-3/4 INCH CRYSTAL LOOK PILLARS. 303-M-2242. $3.99 each

2. FILIGREE BRIDGE AND STAIRWAY SET. Connect your decorated cakes with this impressive pair of stairs for an exciting formal presentation. Position ornament on the center of the graceful filigree platform. Stairs 16-3/4 long, platform 4-3/4 in. by 5 in. White plastic.
205-M-2109. $9.99 set
STAIRS ONLY. 205-M-1218. $4.99 each
FILIGREE BRIDGE ONLY. 205-M-1234. $3.99 each

3. FIVE-COLUMN TIER SET. Glorify your formal creation with five 13-3/4 in. Roman columns and two 18 in. round scallop-edged separator plates. A beautiful choice to use with Wilton wedding ornaments and the Kolor-Flo fountain. White plastic.
301-M-1980. $29.99 set
13-3/4 INCH ROMAN PILLARS. 303-M-2129. $2.99 each
18 INCH ROUND SEPARATOR PLATE. 302-M-1225. $8.99 each

4. ARCHED TIER SET. Impressive way to support tiers over the Kolor-Flo Fountain (page 157). Set includes: Six 13 inch arched columns, two 18 inch scroll-edged round separator plates and six angelic cherubs to attach to columns with icing or glue.
301-M-9752. $44.99 set
18 INCH PLATE. 302-M-504. $12.99 each
13 INCH PILLARS. 303-M-9719. $3.99 each
13 INCH PILLARS. Save on pack of 6. 301-M-9809. $18.99 pack

When you shop Wilton for quality you also get a money-back guarantee, if not satisfied!
Count on quick delivery — your order arrives within 10 days after we receive it.

1. CRYSTAL-LOOK PLATES with cut-glass look edge. Designed for use with your our crystal-look pillars on p. 160. Four sizes; 4 in. plastic pegs included.

7 In. 302-M-2013. **$1.99 each**
9 In. 302-M-2035. **$2.99 each**
11 In. 302-M-2051. **$3.99 each**
13 In. 302-M-2078. **$4.99 each**

Crystal-Look Feet fit all separator plates.
305-M-613. **$1.29 set of 4**

Crystal-Look Bowl adds a gracious touch.
205-M-1404. **$1.99 each**

2-3. ROUND SEPARATOR PLATES. Scallop-edged plates in standard and hard-to-find odd sizes. Strongly constructed to last for years. Use with Round Performance Pans™ pages 166, 167. Each includes 4 inch plastic pegs.

2. ROUND SEPARATOR PLATES.
Standard sizes.
6 In. 302-M-67. **$1.79 each**
8 In. 302-M-83. **$2.29 each**
10 In. 302-M-105. **$3.29 each**
12 In. 302-M-120. **$4.29 each**
14 In. 302-M-148. **$5.29 each**
16 In. 302-M-946. **$7.29 each**

3. ROUND SEPARATOR PLATES.
Odd sizes.
7 In. 302-M-1306. **$1.99 each**
9 In. 302-M-1322. **$2.79 each**
11 In. 302-M-1349. **$3.79 each**
13 In. 302-M-1365. **$4.79 each**
15 In. 302-M-1403. **$6.29 each**

SEPARATOR SETS

4. SQUARE SEPARATOR PLATES. Pair up with Square Performance Pans™ p. 168. Edges are gracefully scalloped. 4 in. plastic pegs included.

7 In. 302-M-1004. **$2.99 each**
9 In. 302-M-1020. **$3.99 each**
11 In. 302-M-1047. **$4.99 each**
13 In. 302-M-1063. **$5.99 each**

7. SEPARATOR PLATE FEET.
Elegant Queen Anne-look feet with scrollwork design are a perfect finishing touch. They'll fit all separator plates.
301-M-1247. **$1.29 set of 4**

5. HEART SEPARATOR PLATES. Match up with heart pans, p. 182. 4 in. plastic pegs included. Select from four versatile sizes.
6 In. 302-M-709. **$1.79 each**
9 In. 302-M-717. **$2.29 each**
12 In. 302-M-1144. **$3.99 each**
15 In. 302-M-1194. **$5.99 each**

8. DOWEL RODS. 12 in. long, 1/4 in. wide wooden rods. Essential for supporting stacked cakes and tiers. Cut and sharpen with strong shears and knife. See page 86 for tiered cake assembly technique.
399-M-1009. **$1.44 for set of 12**

6. HEXAGON SEPARATOR PLATES. Delicate scallop-edged plates to combine with square, round and hexagon pans, page 168. With plastic pegs.
7 In. 302-M-1705. **$2.99 each**
10 In. 302-M-1748. **$3.99 each**
13 In. 302-M-1764. **$5.99 each**
16 In. 302-M-1799. **$6.99 each**

9. PLASTIC PEGS. Order extras! 4 in. pegs fit any Wilton separator plate. Keep tier cake layers in position and securely hold plate in place. Dowel rods must be inserted in cake for support. (See page 86 for how to use.)
399-M-762. **$1.44 for set of 12**

All plastic products made in Hong Kong.

1. CRYSTAL-LOOK PILLARS. Transparent cut glass look. Designed for use with our crystal look plates on p. 159.
3 IN. 303-M-2171. $1.99 pack of 4
5 IN. 303-M-2196. $2.99 pack of 4

2. EXPANDABLE PILLARS. Sleek six piece column adjusts from 3" to 10" just by moving sections. A versatile must for busy decorators. Pack of 4.
303-M-1777. $8.99 each pack

3. GRECIAN PILLARS. Regal pillars with classic scrolls. Add snap-on trims. Pack of 4.
3 IN. 303-M-3605. $2.00 pack
5 IN. 303-M-3702. $3.00 pack

4. CORINTHIAN PILLARS. Resemble authentic Greek columns. An impressive addition. Pack of 4.
5 IN. 303-M-819. $3.59 pack
7-1/2 IN. 303-M-800. $4.59 pack

5. ARCHED PILLARS. Grecian pillars with arched support structure. Embossed leaf design. Pack of 4.
4-1/2 IN. 303-M-452. $2.99 pack
6-1/2 IN. 303-M-657. $4.99 pack

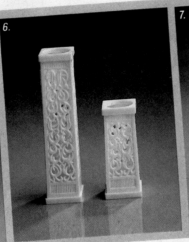

6. SQUARE FILIGREE PILLARS. Airy openwork design. Add a hint of color by placing pastel tulle inside pillar. Pack of 4.
3 IN. 303-M-8070. $2.00 pack
5 IN. 303-M-7716. $3.00 pack

7. IRIDESCENT GRECIAN PILLARS. Lustrous styrene plastic columns shimmer and glisten. 5 in. high.
303-M-3257. $4.99 pack of 4

8. SWAN PILLARS. Classic pillars with graceful swans are an enchanting combination and an exciting way to hold cake tiers. 4 in. high. Pack of 4.
303-M-7724. $3.00 pack

9. PLASTIC STUD PLATES. Create separator plates. Glue these studs onto back-to-back cardboard cake circles. Fit Wilton pillars.
301-M-119. $1.79 pack of 8

10. DANCING CUPID PILLARS. Charming cherubs are a captivating way to hold cake tiers. 5-1/2 in. Pack of 4.
303-M-1210. $7.99 pack

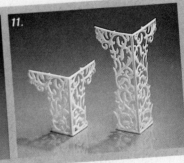

11. SNAP-ON FILIGREE. Add a lacy look to Grecian pillars in a snap.
Fits 3" PILLARS.
305-M-389. $1.60 pack of 4
Fits 5" PILLARS.
305-M-397. $2.00 pack of 4

12. SNAP-ON-CHERUBS. Accent Corinthian and Grecian pillars with heavenly angels. (Pillars not included.) 3-1/2 in. high.
305-M-4104. $1.29 pack of 4

1. CLASSIC SEPARATOR PLATE SETS. Grecian pillars and scalloped edged plate sets in 8 plate diameters and 2 pillar heights. Set includes 2 plates, 2 pillars and 4 pegs.

6 IN. PLATE SET WITH 3 IN. PILLARS.
2103-M-639. $4.99 set
7 IN. PLATE SET WITH 3 IN. PILLARS.
2103-M-925. $5.99 set
8 IN. PLATE SET WITH 5 IN. PILLARS.
2103-M-256. $6.99 set

9 IN. PLATE SET WITH 5 IN. PILLARS.
2103-M-912. $7.99 set
10 IN. PLATE SET WITH 5 IN. PILLARS.
2103-M-108. $8.99 set
11 IN. PLATE SET WITH 5 IN. PILLARS.
2103-M-939. $9.99 set
12 IN. PLATE SET WITH 5 IN. PILLARS.
2103-M-124. $10.99 set
13 IN. PLATE SET WITH 5 IN. PILLARS.
2103-M-955. $11.99 set

2. ANGELIC SERENADE. Cherub quartet will add just the right note of harmony to your medley of cake and icing. The plates have delicately scalloped edges to add to the charm and grace of your presentation. 8 in. high with 8 in. diameter plates.
301-M-607. $8.99 each

SEPARATOR PLATES

3. HARVEST CHERUB SEPARATOR SET. A heavenly four-some adds a touch of enchantment to tiered cakes the year around. Includes four 7 in. Harvest Cherub pillars, two 9 in. separator plates (lower plate has 12 in. overall diameter).
301-M-3517. $9.99 set

ADD IMPACT AND DRAMA TO YOUR DECORATED CAKES!
You'll be pleased with any set you choose. They're all in white plastic and designed to add a formal elegance to your cake presentation. To protect the surfaces of your plates be sure to use Wilton Cake circles sold on page 154.

4. 30-PC. SQUARE TIER SET. Includes scalloped-edge square plates with 5 inch Grecian Pillars. Also includes 2 each: 7 in.. 9 in.. 11 in. plates. 12 classic pillars and 12 pegs.
301-M-1158. $24.99 set

5. 54-PC. GRECIAN PILLAR AND PLATE SET. Deluxe collection provides you with round scalloped-edge separator plates and 5 inch pillars. Includes 2 each: 6, 8, 10, 12 and 14 inch plates. with 20 fluted pillars, and 24 pegs.
301-M-8380. $35.99 set

Plastic products made in Hong Kong

Wilton KITCHEN COLLECTION
PRODUCTS FOR EASIER FOOD PREPARATION.

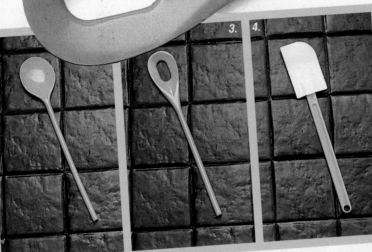

1. 2. 3. 4.

NEW WILTON PRODUCTS FOR EASIER FOOD PREPARATION

1-3. MELAMINE SET. *Dishwasher-safe; won't absorb stains or odors. Unique and practical shapes, 11 in. long. Set includes: 1. Corner Spoon, 2. Cook's Spoon and 3. Blender Scraper. (U.S.A.)* **415-M-716. $4.99 set**

4. ALL-PURPOSE SPATULA. *Stain-resistant flexible blade, plastic handle, 11-1/2 in. long. (Hong Kong.)* **415-M-822. $1.49 each**

KITCHEN COLLECTION

5. 6. 7. 8. 9.

5-6. WIRE WHISKS. *For smooth sauces, quick beaten egg whites, more! Stainless steel wires are sealed in handle with epoxy for heavy duty performance, long life. (Taiwan.)*

5. WIRE BALLOON WHISK. *12-1/4 in. long.* **415-M-816. $5.99 each**

6. ALL-PURPOSE WHISK. *11 in.* **415-M-814. $5.99 each**

7. ALL-PURPOSE SCRAPER. *Dishwasher-safe, stain-resistant plastic. 4 x 6 in. (Hong Kong.)* **415-M-826. $1.29 each**

8. PASTRY BRUSH. *Non-shed synthetic bristles, plastic handle. 8-1/2 in. long. (Taiwan.)* **415-M-812. $3.99 each**

9. PASTRY & BASTING BRUSH. *Synthetic bristles, plastic handle. Won't shed. 12-1/2 in. long. (Taiwan.)* **415-M-810. $3.99 each**

10. HAND-HELD SIFTER. *Trigger action handle, 3 mesh screens with 3 agitators for finer sifting. Stainless steel; rust-proof. 5 cup capacity. (Japan.)* **415-M-617. $7.99 each**

11. 4-PC. MEASURING CUP SET. *Stainless steel can even be used on stove (great for melting butter!). 1/4, 1/3, 1/2 and 1 cup sizes. (Taiwan.)* **415-M-559. $4.99 set**

3-PC. MEASURING CUP SET *(not shown). Clear plastic with standard and metric measurements. 1, 2 and 4 cup sizes. (Hong Kong.)* **415-M-555. $5.99 set**

12. CAKE TESTER. *Tests inside of cake to make sure it's done. Stainless steel with easy-to-hold plastic head. 6 in. long. (Taiwan.)* **415-M-625. $.69 each**

13. PIZZA CUTTER. *Serrated 2-5/8 in. diameter stainless steel wheel, plastic handle. See "Pizza Recipes" book, page 103. (Japan.)* **415-M-1250. $3.99 each**

14. 4-PC. MEASURING SPOON SET. *Stainless steel spoons on convenient ring. 1/4, 1/2 and 1 tsp. plus Tbsp. Dishwasher-safe. (Taiwan.)* **415-M-557. $1.99 set**

15. SHAKER. *All-purpose plastic shaker has easy-fill twist-off cap. Use for flour, sugar, much more! Dishwasher-safe. (Hong Kong.)* **415-M-679. $1.99 each**

10. 11. 13. 15. 12. 14.

PLEASE NOTE: All prices, certain products and services reflect the U.S.A. domestic market and do not apply in Australia or Canada.

16.

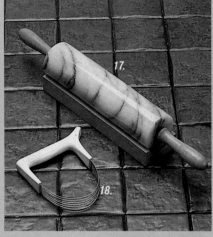

17.

18.

19.

20.

21.

22.

23.

16. 6-PC. STAINLESS STEEL MIXING BOWL SET.
Long-lasting and dishwasher-safe; non-skid base. Three convenient sizes (1-1/2, 3 and 5-qt.), each with its own plastic lid for airtight storage. (Korea.)
415-M-225. $21.99 set

17. MARBLE ROLLING PIN.
A favorite of great cooks. Keeps pastry cooler for lighter crusts; extra weight requires less "elbow grease". Standard 10 in. long barrel with wooden handles; wooden resting cradle included. (Taiwan.)
415-M-658. $10.99 each

18. PASTRY BLENDER.
Smooth non-rust stainless steel wires with comfortable plastic handle. (Taiwan.)
415-M-820. $2.99 each

19. PIE CRUST LATTICE CUTTER.
Durable plastic 10 in. grid is dishwasher-safe. (Hong Kong.)
415-M-181. $3.99 each

20. PASTRY CLOTH/ ROLLING PIN COVER SET.
Machine washable heavy cotton; cloth is 20 x 24 in. (U.S.A.)
415-M-818. $3.99 set

21-23. COOLING RACKS.
For proper cooling of cakes, pies, cookies! Chrome-plated steel. (Taiwan.)

21. 13 x 19-IN. RACK.
(33cm x 48cm). Sheet-cake perfect!
415-M-175. $4.99 each

22. 10 x 14-IN. SET.
(25cm x 36cm). Set of 2 layer-cake perfect racks.
415-M-200. $4.99 each

23. 10-IN. ROUND SET.
(25cm). Set of 2 pie-perfect racks.
415-M-125. $3.99 set

24. GRATER.
Four sides give you four textures. Stainless steel with plastic grip. 9 in. high. (Hong Kong.)
415-M-824. $4.99 each

25. PASTRY BAG.
Professional quality 16-in. (40cm) polyester bag is strong and reusable; stays soft and flexible washing after washing. (Japan.)
404-M-1201. $5.99 each

26. TARTLET MOLD SET.
Six fluted aluminum molds make individual treats 3-1/4 x 2 x 3/4 in. deep. (Korea.)
2105-M-3794. $3.99 each

24.

25.

26.

1. NEW!

2. NEW!

1. NEW! COOKIE HOLLY WREATH KIT. The cookie boughs of this edible evergreen will disappear leaf by leaf. You could easily make more with this convenient kit. Beautiful design for fall also given. Includes 5 plastic cookie cutters (4 are double-edged for a choice of patterns and sizes), 1 plastic decorating tip, 4 packets of liquid icing color, 3 disposable bags and illustrated step-by-step baking and decorating instructions.
2104-M-3664. $4.99 kit

2. NEW! GREAT EGGS™ KIT. Make an array of gorgeous sugar or confectionery coating eggs and designs. This kit comes complete with 2 plastic egg molds, 2 plastic sheet molds, vinyl decorating bag, 1 plastic coupler, 2 plastic decorating tips and a decorator's brush, plus complete instructions for 8 fun designs.
2104-M-3616. $6.99 kit

CENTERPIECE SETS

3. NEW! SWEETHEART COOKIE GREETING CARD KIT. Show someone you care in a very personal way. Bake and decorate a unique cookie greeting. Kit includes 4 easy-to-do designs, 4 greeting card boxes and liners, 2 plastic decorating tips, 1 plastic heart cookie cutter, 1 liquid color packet, 2 disposable decorating bags, cookie and icing recipes and complete baking and decorating instructions.
2104-M-4310. $4.99 kit

COOKIE GIFT CARD BOXES
1912-M-2696. $1.99 4 boxes

4. SANTA COOKIE SLEIGH KIT.
This 3-dimensional flight of fantasy centerpiece is as much fun to make as it is to look at. Kit includes directions for 3 different sleighs, 4 durable, plastic cutters that are double-edged for quick pattern reversal, decorating tips, icing colors and disposable decorating bags.
2105-M-2690. $4.99 kit

5. GINGERBREAD HOUSE KIT.
Sturdy punch-out pattern pieces make it easy to create a magical house. Has complete making and decorating instructions and recipes.
2104-M-2946. $3.99 kit

6. CHRISTMAS COOKIE TREE KIT. Ten plastic cutters and complete illustrated instructions let you create a beautiful, edible holiday table centerpiece.
2105-M-3424. $4.99 kit

Plastic parts made in Hong Kong.
Decorating bags made in Japan.

All prices, certain products and services reflect the U.S.A. domestic market and do not apply in Australia and Canada.

3. NEW!

4.

5.

6.

Excelle™ is the extra special, extra thick aluminum bakeware that will last a lifetime. Excelle bakeware is deeper than most other bakeware; this generous depth reduces the chance of overflow, and the unique, extended, easy-grip rims make handling the pans in and out of the oven easy, even with hot mitts.

1. ROUND PANS (2-1/4 IN. DEEP). The perfect shape for a beautiful cake every time. Ideal for single or multi-layer cakes.
12 IN. ROUND. 2105-M-8736. $11.99 each
10 IN. ROUND. 2105-M-8710. $8.99 each
8 IN. ROUND. 2105-M-8680. $7.50 each

2. SQUARE PANS (2-1/4 IN. DEEP). A classic shape that's a must in every kitchen. Ideal for coffee cakes, fruit-topped cakes, decorated cakes and more!
12 IN. SQUARE. 2105-M-8922. $14.99 each
10 IN. SQUARE. 2105-M-8906. $11.99 each
8 IN. SQUARE. 2105-M-8779. $8.99 each

3. SHEET PANS (2-1/4 IN. DEEP). Bake delicious desserts or mouth-watering main dishes — again and again. Sizes to meet every baking occasion — from small family dinners to party buffets.
11 x 15 IN. SHEET. 2105-M-8647. $14.99 each
12 x 18 IN. SHEET. 2105-M-8663. $16.99 each
9 x 13 IN. SHEET. 2105-M-8604. $10.99 each
7 x 11 IN. SHEET. 2105-M-8620. $8.99 each

4. LOAF PAN (3-1/6 IN. DEEP). The best pan for meat loaf, quick breads, pound cake and fruit bread.
9 x 5 IN. LOAF. 2105-M-8949. $8.99 each

EXCELLE™ PREMIUM BAKEWARE

All pans made in Korea.

PLEASE NOTE:
All prices, certain products and services reflect the U.S.A. domestic market and do not apply in Australia and Canada.

PERFORMANCE PANS® BAKEWARE

WILTON ROUNDS...THE BAKING CLASSICS!

- 2 inches deep
- Professional, quality aluminum
- Durable and dishwasher safe
- Complete batter and icing amounts
- Decorator Icing Recipe on label

A. 10 IN. ROUND. 2105-M-2207.
$6.50 each

B. 8 IN. ROUND. 2105-M-2193.
$5.50 each

C. 6 IN. ROUND. 2105-M-2185.
$4.99 each

A.

B.

C.

D. 16 IN. ROUND. (Measure oven size before ordering.) 2105-M-3963.
$13.50 each

E. 14 IN. ROUND. 2105-M-3947.
$10.50 each

F. 12 IN. ROUND. 2105-M-2215.
$8.50 each

When you shop Wilton for quality you also get...a money-back guarantee and quick delivery. Your order will arrive within 10 working days after we receive it! And you can charge your order... VISA and MasterCard are welcome!

D.

E.

F.

Wilton
Performance PANS®
PREMIUM BAKEWARE

To decorate this exciting round cake see page 20.

Did you see the NEW Wilton Icing Mix?
It's a cake decorator's dream because it offers everything the best home-made buttercream icing does with the convenience of a mix. For icing mix variations see p. 81. For complete details see p. 131.

Discover how to decorate this elegant cake on page 41.

3 IN. DEEP ROUND PANS— VERSATILE BASICS!
• Bakes cakes 2-layers high
• Professional, quality aluminum
• Durable and dishwasher safe
• Ideal for tortes, fruit and pound cakes
• Excellent for cakes to be covered with fondant icing
• Decorator's Icing Recipe on back of label

A. 10 IN. DIAM. 2105-M-9945. $8.50 each

B. 8 IN. DIAM. 2105-M-9104. $6.50 each

C. 14 IN. DIAM. 2105-M-9988. $11.50 each

D. 12 IN. DIAM. 2105-M-9961. $9.50 each

The Wilton Home Study Course shows you how to make an ordinary cake extraordinary! You'll go at your own pace right at home. Lessons include quality Wilton products and expert instruction. For complete details turn to page 129.

All pans made in Korea.
PLEASE NOTE: All prices, certain products and services, reflect the U.S.A. domestic market and do not apply in Australia and Canada.

PERFORMANCE PANS®

SQUARES & HEXAGONS... THE COLLECTIBLE BAKING GREATS!
- 2 inches deep
- Professional, heavy gauge aluminum insures even baking
- Complete batter and icing amounts included
- Decorator's Icing Recipe on label

SQUARE PANS. Attractive layer and tier cakes are in the baking. Select from a wide range of sizes. See pages 7, 31, 44, 55, 65 and 67 for some sensationally decorated square cakes.

8 IN. SQUARE.
2105-M-8191. $6.50 each

10 IN. SQUARE.
2105-M-8205. $8.50 each

12 IN. SQUARE.
2105-M-8213. $10.50 each

14. IN. SQUARE.
2105-M-8220. $13.50 each

16 IN. SQUARE. (Check oven size when ordering.)
2105-M-8231. $15.99 each

HEXAGON PANS: Bake handsome cakes for all occasions. See pages 8, 21, 27, 38 and 79 in the idea portion for some dynamic ways to decorate.

12 IN. HEXAGON.
2105-M-5133. $7.99 each

9 IN. HEXAGON.
2105-M-5125. $5.99 each

NOT SHOWN:
NEW! 6 IN. HEXAGON.
2105-M-5122. $3.99 each
NEW! 15 IN. HEXAGON.
2105-M-5136. $9.99 each

This with-it square will highlight the celebration, see it on page 54.

Wilton®
Performance PANS®
PREMIUM BAKEWARE

**SHEET & PETALS BAKE IT ALL
...FROM BASIC TO BREATH-
TAKING!** Select from a wide range
of sizes, all 2 inches deep. Each is
an ideal choice for wedding showers,
birthdays, gifts or just to perk up your
own spirits! Quality you can count on
for all your baking needs.

BAKE-IT-ALL SHEET PANS. Create
crowd-pleasing cakes and main
course dishes. Ideal for brownies and
bar cookies. See some creative ways
to decorate on pages 4, 22, 33, 38,
52 and 61.

7 x 11 IN. SHEET.
2105-M-2304. $5.50 each

9 x 13 IN. SHEET.
2105-M-1308. $6.99 each

11 x 15 IN. SHEET.
2105-M-158. $9.50 each

12 x 18 IN. SHEET.
2105-M-182. $11.50 each

It's fast and easy to create a party
sheet cake that's just right for the
occasion. Just ice your cake, add
easy icing trims and complete it with
a Wilton Cake Top. There's one for
every occasion—humorous or
serious. See the wonderful collection
on pages 132-141. You'll find at least
one that's exactly what you want.

BAKE-IT-PRETTY PETAL PANS.
Cakes with graceful rounded edges
look so elegant to begin with, so very
little decorating is needed to make
them look totally outstanding. On
pages 28 and 33 are two more petal
cakes you're sure to love!

9 IN. PETAL.
2105-M-5109. $5.99 each

12 IN. PETAL.
2105-M-5117. $7.99 each

NOT SHOWN:
NEW! 6 IN. PETAL.
2105-M-4346. $3.99 each

NEW! 15 IN. PETAL.
2105-M-4344. $9.99 each

All pans made in Korea.

PLEASE NOTE:
**All prices, certain products and services,
reflect the U.S.A. domestic market and do
not apply in Australia and Canada.**

PERFORMANCE PANS®

1. NEW!

2. NEW!

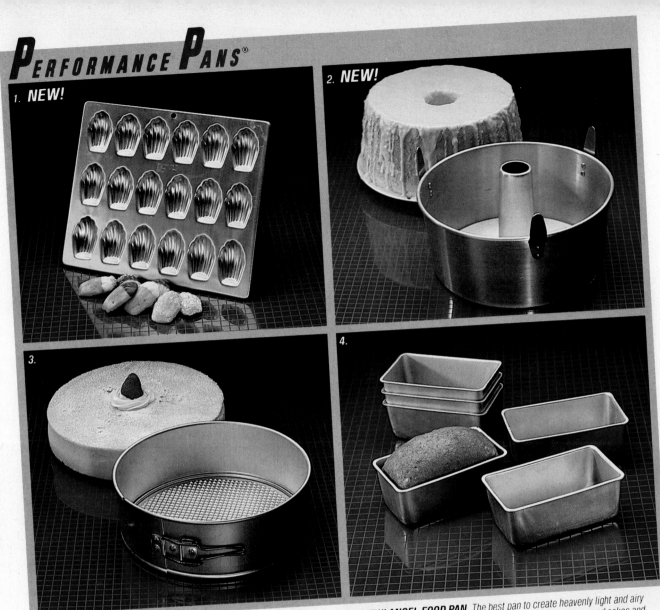

3.

4.

1. NEW! MADELEINE PAN. A European favorite. Delicate little cakes perfect for luncheons, buffets or impressive dinners. Recipes included. Serve alone or with ice cream or fruit. 7-3/4 x 9-1/2 in.
2105-M-2266. $5.99 each

3. SPRINGFORM PAN. The essential pan for cheesecake. Textured bottom for best baking results. 9 in. diameter. 3 in. deep.
2105-M-5354. $8.99 each

2. NEW! ANGEL FOOD PAN. The best pan to create heavenly light and airy angel cake; great for down-to-earth chiffon cakes, fruit cakes, pound cakes and more! Generous-length cooling legs attached. 10 in. diameter, 4-1/4 in. deep.
2105-M-2525. $10.99 each

4. LITTLE LOAFERS. Bake individual cakes or loaves of bread for parties and gifts. Great for molding ice cream and gelatin, too. Set of six, each 4-3/8 x 2-3/8 x 1-1/2 in. deep. Each takes 1/2 cup batter.
512-M-1089. $5.99 set

Wilton. Performance PANS®
PREMIUM BAKEWARE

A versatile selection of traditional and specialty pans to help you create superb international recipes or your family favorites with equal elegance.

5.

5. PIE PANS. Quality pans for all types of pies — fruit, custard, or no bake, one or two crust. A size for every occasion. All are 1-1/4 in. deep.
NEW! 8 IN. PIE PAN. 2105-M-1267.
$3.99 each
9 IN. PIE PAN. 2105-M-4030.
$4.99 each
NEW! 10 IN. PIE PAN. 2105-M-1266.
$5.99 each

1. *NEW!*

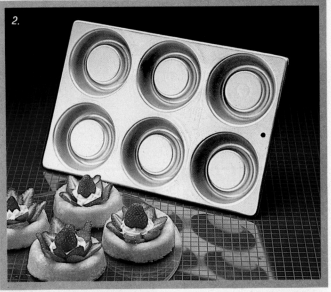

2.

1. NEW! MINI MUFFIN PAN. *Make a dozen dainty muffins, miniature fruit cakes, mini cupcakes and more! Perfect for holiday treats, too! 7-3/4 x 10 x 3/4 in. deep. Takes 2" diam. paper cupcake liners.*
2105-M-2125. $5.99 each

2. SHORTCAKES 'N TREATS PAN. *Six individual servings of shortcakes, brownies, ice cream, gelatin and more are a breeze to make with this unique pan. 8 x 12-1/2 x 1 in. deep.*
2105-M-5966. $6.50 each

3. *NEW!*

4.

5.

6.

3. NEW! TWELVE-CUP MUFFIN PAN. *Company for breakfast? Bake a dozen muffins, cupcakes or rolls. Create an original molded party dessert with fruit, ice cream or gelatin, too. 10-1/2 x 13-1/2 x 1 in. deep.*
2105-M-2375. $8.99 each

4. SIX CUP MUFFIN PAN. *Bake breakfast muffins or rolls for the family. Perfect for party cupcakes or single-serving molded desserts, also. 7-3/8 x 10-3/4 x 1 in. deep.*
2105-M-5338. $6.50 each

PLEASE NOTE: All prices, certain products and service reflect the U.S.A. domestic market and do not apply in Australia and Canada.

5. LONG LOAF PAN. *Perfect for party size sandwich loaf and meat loaf, or to create an elegant birthday, anniversary or other party cake. Takes 9 cups batter. Cooling legs attached. 16 x 4 x 4-1/4 in.*
2105-M-1588. $8.99 each

6. LOAF PAN. *Bake a pound cake, fruit cake, quick yeast or nut bread. Ideal for main dishes, like meatloaf, too. 8-3/4 x 4-1/2 x 2-3/4 in. deep.*
2105-M-3688. $4.99 each

All pans made in Korea.

1. NEW!

1. NEW! TART PANS. Hearty lunch or dinner quiches, custard desserts and luscious fruit-topped cakes work equally well in these pans. Lift-out bottoms for convenient removal of food to serving trays. Three popular sizes.

8 IN. TART PAN.
2105-M-3877. **$4.50 each**
9 IN. TART PAN.
2105-M-3613. **$4.99 each**
10 IN. TART PAN.
2105-M-3267. **$5.50 each**

Wilton.
Performance PANS®
PREMIUM BAKEWARE

2. NEW!

3. NEW!

2. NEW! POPOVER PAN. Treat your family and guests to light, golden popovers. Great with butter and jelly for breakfast, ice cream and fruit for dessert. Quality pan for perfect popovers. Recipe included on label. 6-cup. 9 x 16 in.
2105-M-4992. **$12.99 each**

3. NEW! TWIN FRENCH BREAD PAN. Bakes two long loaves of crusty, crisp, tender French bread. So handy, you'll use it often. 18'' long.
2105-M-1268. **$5.99 each**

4. NEW!

5.

4. NEW! CHARLOTTE MOLD/PAN. The ideal mold/pan for fabulous desserts, including the famous charlotte cake. Great for fruit cakes, molded gelatins and ice cream—steamed puddings, too!
2105-M-1270. **$5.99 each**

5. 14-IN. PIZZA PAN. Its waffle-textured surface bakes crispier crusts. Ideal size for family pizza. Pizza crust recipe and tasty dessert ideas on back of label.
2105-M-3912. **$6.99 each**

1. NEW! JELLY ROLL PAN. *Make a delicious jelly roll or ice cream cake roll with this pan. It's the perfect size. Popular jelly roll recipe and baking hints included on back of label. Great for cookies, brownies, biscuits, fancy pastries, too! 10-1/2 x 15-1/2 x 1 in. deep.*
2105-M-1269. $7.50 each

See the complete line of Cookie Maker products, including pastry bags and tips on pages 104-111.

2. NEW! FANCY RING MOLD/PAN. *Make beautiful decorated cakes, fancy gelatins and unusual ice cream desserts. The fluted shape is just perfect for parties. Mold cold salads, too. This quality aluminum pan is 10 in. in diameter and 3 in. deep. Delicious recipe on back of label. See page 72 for another delightful party cake idea!*
2105-M-5008. $7.99 each

3. COOKIE PAN. *You can bake cookies, bar cookies, brownies, biscuits and fancy pastries with this versatile pan. Super size to bake more at one time. 12 x 18 x 1 in. deep.*
2105-M-4854. $8.50 each

PLEASE NOTE:
All prices, certain products and services reflect the U.S.A. domestic market and do not apply in Australia and Canada.

4. RING MOLDS/PANS. *Bake or mold cakes, ice cream, gelatins, salads in these multipurpose pans. Two convenient sizes. Both 3 in. deep.*
NEW! 8 IN. RING.
2105-M-190. $5.99 each

10-1/2 IN. RING.
2105-M-4013. $7.99 each

5. COOKIE SHEETS. *Perfect for all pressed, sliced, rolled and drop cookies. No sides for easy slide off. Long grip for easier handling. Two sizes.*
NEW! 10 x 15 COOKIE SHEET.
2105-M-1265. $5.50 each

12-1/2 x 16-1/2 COOKIE SHEET.
2105-M-2975. $6.50 each

To make elegant pastries that are sure to impress family and friends, get the new Fancy Cookie Making and Pastry Kit. It includes delicious continental pastry recipes plus quality tools such as the pastry bag, tips and instructions. See page 109 for more about this unique kit.

All pans made in Korea.

PERFORMANCE PANS® TIER SETS

FOR YOUR LAVISH TIER CREATIONS COLLECT COMPLETE TIER PAN SETS & SAVE!

1. 4-PC. HEXAGON PAN SET. See how impressive a hexagon wedding masterpiece can be on page 27. Set includes 6, 9, 12 and 15 inch pans, each 2 inches deep. Retail value if purchased separately, $27.96.
2105-M-3572. $24.99 set

2. 4-PC. PETAL PAN SET. Gala and graceful whether a few or many tiers high. See Petal Perfection on page 28. Set includes a 6, 9, 12 and 15 inch diameter pans, 2 inches deep. Retail value if purchased separately, $27.87.
2105-M-2134. $24.99 set

3. 5-PC. SQUARE PAN SET. This basic baking collection consists of 8, 10, 12, 14 and 16 inch pans, 2 inches deep. Retail value if purchased separately, $54.99.
505-M-104. $45.99 each

4. 5-PC. ROUND PAN SET. Create tiered treasures sure to get a round of applause. See Grand Tribute on p. 26 (16 in. round sold on p. 166) — an elaborate wedding wonder no one will forget! Set includes 6, 8, 10, 12 and 14 inch diameters, 2 in. deep. Retail value if purchased separately, $35.99.
504-M-118. $29.99 each

5. 3-INCH DEEP ROUND PAN SET. Ideal choice for fondant and marzipan covered wedding cakes. Set includes 8, 10, 12 and 14 inch diameter pans. Retail value if purchased separately, $35.99.
2105-M-2932. $29.99 set

1. HEART MINI-TIER SET. Bakes 5, 7-1/2 and 9 in. one-layer cakes with just one cake mix. Set includes three quality aluminum pans, two scallop-edged separator plates, six clear plastic twist legs, complete decorating instructions.
2105-M-409. $10.99 set

HEART MINI-TIER PLATE SET ONLY.
301-M-9728. $2.99 set

2. ROUND MINI-TIER SET. The ideal size tiered cake for small, special gatherings. Includes 5, 6-1/2 and 8 in., diameter pans, 1-1/2 in. deep. With 5-1/2, 7 in. separator plates and 8 clear plastic twist legs. Takes one cake mix. Decorating instructions show you how.
2105-M-98042. $10.99 set

ROUND MINI-TIER PLATE SET ONLY.
301-M-9817. $2.99 set

3. BEVEL PAN SET. Bakes slanted cake edges that can be positioned on top or beneath your cake layers. See pages 29 and 41 for two impressive examples. Ideal for elegant Lambeth Method decorating. Set includes 8, 10, 12 in. tops and 14 and 16 in. bases. Use with coordinating 2 or 3 in. deep pans.
517-M-1200. $25.99 set

TIER SETS

4. HEART PAN SET. Bakes the most romantic cakes for showers, birthdays, weddings and more. Set includes 6, 9, 12 and 15 in. diameter aluminum pans. Retail value if purchased separately, $27.96.
504-M-207. $24.99 set

6 IN. HEART. 2105-M-4781. $3.99 each	**12 IN. HEART.** 2105-M-5168. $7.99 each
9 IN. HEART. 2105-M-5176. $5.99 each	**15 IN. HEART.** 2105-M-4609. $9.99 each

5. CLASSIC ROUND PAN SET. Create handsome graduated tiers for formal parties and weddings. Set includes 6, 8, 10 and 12 in. pans. (Round pans sold separately on pages 165, 166, 167, 176 and 177.) Retail value if purchased separately, $25.49.
2105-M-2101. $17.99 set

All pans made in Korea.

PLEASE NOTE: All prices, certain products and services, reflect the U.S.A. domestic market and do not apply in Australia and Canada.

175

AN INVESTMENT IN EXCEPTIONAL

3 IN. DEEP ROUND PANS

A.   B.   C.   D.

Wilton Cake Pans For The Professional
OVENCRAFT™

SHEET PANS

A.   B.   C.   D.

---

3 IN. DEEP ROUND PANS.
Bake cakes to 2-layer height. Excellent choice for busy bakers.
A. *14 x 3 IN. 2105-M-5610. $11.50 each*
B. *12 x 3 IN. 2105-M-5609. $10.50 each*
C. *10 x 3 IN. 2105-M-5608. $8.50 each*
D. *8 x 3 IN. 2105-M-5607. $6.50 each*

SHEET PANS.
Bake 2 in. high cakes. Indispensable for crowd-pleasing celebration cakes.
A. *12 x 18 IN. 2105-M-5618. $14.50 each*
B. *11 x 15 IN. 2105-M-5617. $11.99 each*
C. *9 x 13 IN. 2105-M-5616. $9.99 each*
D. *7 x 11 IN. 2105-M-5615. $6.99 each*

QUALITY!

Now, available, bakeware comparable to the kind professional bakers use. Expertly crafted to satisfy the most devoted decorator and those who value the very best!
- Specially designed to bake perfect straight-sided cakes.
- Smooth anodized finish aids in cake release.
- Durable, extra-heavy gauge aluminum provides even heating for best baking results.
- Icing recipe, baking hints and cake cutting guide on back of labels.

2 IN. DEEP ROUND PANS

Featuring These Unique Advantages...

ANODIZING

TIGHT RADIUS

SQUARE CORNERS

EXTRA-HEAVY GAUGE

SQUARE PANS

2 IN. ROUND PANS.
Bake 2 in. high cakes. A wide choice of sizes — all essential for tiered cakes.
A. 16 IN. 2105-M-5606. $13.50 each
B. 14 IN. 2105-M-5605. $10.50 each
C. 12 IN. 2105-M-5604. $8.50 each
D. 10 IN. 2105-M-5603. $6.50 each
E. 8 IN. 2105-M-5602. $5.50 each
F. 6 IN. 2105-M-5601. $4.99 each

SQUARE PANS.
Bake 2 in. high cakes. Essential for lavish creations bound to impress!
A. 14 IN. 2105-M-5614. $13.99 each
B. 12 IN. 2105-M-5613. $11.50 each
C. 10 IN. 2105-M-5612. $8.99 each
D. 8 IN. 2105-M-5611. $7.50 each

All pans made in Korea.
PLEASE NOTE: All prices, certain products and services, reflect the U.S.A. domestic market and do not apply in Australia and Canada.

177

FAVORITE SHAPED PANS

1. NEW!

1. NEW! MINI FOOTBALL HELMET PAN. Bakes six winning little cakes that will have a big impact on fans and players alike. Perfect for Super Bowl, tailgate parties, birthdays, Dad's Day and more! Decorate in your favorite team's colors — alternate decorating ideas and instructions on label. Each well takes 1/2 cup of batter. Aluminum pan is 13 x 8-3/4 x 1-1/8 in.
2105-M-4308. $6.99 each

2. MINI PUMPKIN PAN. Bakes six individual pumpkin cakes. Perfect party treats, so easy to decorate. Mold ice cream and gelatin surprises, too! Alternate ways to decorate and instructions on label. Each well takes 1/2 cup of batter. Aluminum pan is 12-1/4 x 8 x 1-3/8 in.
2105-M-1499. $6.99 each

3. JACK-O-LANTERN PAN. Thrill kids of all ages with a smiling or scary pumpkin face. See the mystery pumpkin on page 67. It's easy and fun to decorate. Directions include a harvest pumpkin cake, too. One-mix aluminum pan is 12-1/4 x 11-5/8 x 2 in.
2105-M-3068. $5.99 each

4. CLASSIC HOUSE PAN. A cake that's in the right place anytime of the year. It can be a spooky Halloween house, a welcoming Christmas open house (see page 76) and lots more. Instructions tell how to make six clever house cakes! One-mix pan is 13-1/2 x 10-1/4 x 2 in.
2105-M-5370. $7.99 each

5. HAPPY BIRTHDAY PAN. Bakes the big birthday message right into the cake. It couldn't be simpler to decorate — just outline and cover with stars (try the Triple-Star Tip, p. 115, for super fast results). 10 in. diameter, 1-1/2 in. deep aluminum pan takes one cake mix.
2105-M-1073. $7.99 each

All pans made in Korea.
PLEASE NOTE: All prices, certain products and services, reflect the U.S.A. domestic market and do not apply in Australia and Canada.

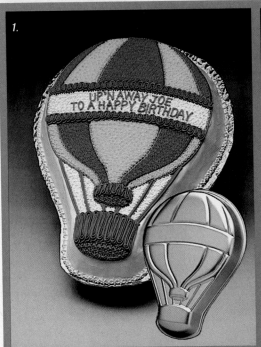

1. UP 'N AWAY BALLOON PAN.
The sky's the limit when it comes to decorating a cake for your favorite adventurer or dreamer. More decorating ideas included. One-mix aluminum pan is 14-1/2 x 10-1/2 x 1-7/8 in.
2105-M-1898. $7.99 each

2. TURKEY PAN.
You'll give thanks that this fine feathered friend is so easy to decorate! One-mix aluminum pan is 17 x 19-1/2 x 2 in.
2105-M-3114. $5.99 each

3. 1-PC. BOOK PAN.
With this pan you've got any occasion covered. A best seller for birthdays, graduation, holidays and more! It's a great greeting card, too. 5 decorating ideas included! One-mix aluminum pan is 13 x 9-1/2 x 2 in. deep.
2105-M-972. $7.99 each

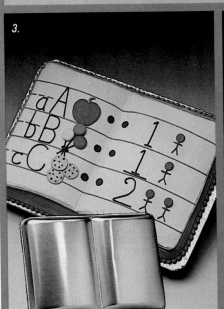

4. CIRCUS CLOWN PAN.
All will cheer when this happy faced fellow arrives. Add your special message to his balloons. With instructions for three more lovable clowns. One mix aluminum pan is 15-1/4 x 11-3/4 x 1-7/8 in.
2105-M-3823. $7.99 each

5. OVAL PAN SET.
Creates a classic, pretty shape for birthdays, holidays and more! Each aluminum pan is 9 x 6-3/4 x 1-3/4 in. deep. Takes one cake mix to fill both pans. Birthday and Easter decorating ideas included.
2105-M-1553. $5.99 set

6. NEW! MINI CLOWN PAN.
You're headed for fun with this exciting new pan. Bakes six individual cakes to decorate with wonderful funny faces. Complete instructions and alternate decorating ideas on label. Each pan well takes 1/2 cup of batter. Aluminum pan is 12 x 9-1/2 x 1-1 4 in.
2105-M-5621. $6.99 each

6. NEW!

1. SANTA'S LIST PAN. *Little faces will be all aglow at the sight of this famous face. Decorating directions show you how to turn his wish list into a stocking, candy cane or gift. One-mix aluminum pan is 12-1/4 x 11-1/2 x 1-7/8 in.* **2105-M-1995. $5.99 each**

2. CANDLELIT TREE PAN SET. *Bakes a beautiful stand-up tree cake centerpiece. Our 2-piece aluminum pan takes 6 cups of firm-textured batter. Add easy icing trims and candles. See the delightful way to decorate on p. 23. Set comes with 6 baking clips, heat conducting core and white plastic base/server (candles shown not included). Check oven height, pan is 11 in. high.* **2105-M-719. $12.99 set**

3. GINGERBREAD HOUSE KIT. *Create a magical dream! Sturdy punch-out pattern pieces make it easy. Complete instructions and recipes for making four unique fantasy confections. See the dramatic holiday masterpiece on p. 73.* **2104-M-2946. $3.99 kit**

CHRISTMAS PANS

4. NEW! STAND-UP SNOWMAN PAN KIT. *This pan offers you the option of making a one-mix snowman cake that lies flat or bake two cakes and position together for a 3-dimensional cake sensation! Kit also comes with decorating tools, icing colors and instructions. Aluminum pan is 11-1/2 x 6-1/2 x 2-3/4 in. high.* **2105-M-1394. $7.99 kit**

5. NEW! COOKIE HOLLY WREATH KIT. *Bake and decorate a fun-to-eat centerpiece wreath. You get the plastic cookie cutters, decorating tools, icing color, recipes and instructions you need to make a festive holiday or a warm, harvest fall wreath. This symbol of love is a treat to make the year 'round...use your ingenuity!* **2104-M-3664. $4.99 kit**

6. NEW! MINI CHRISTMAS TREE PAN. *Bakes a forest of individual holiday tree cakes. So easy to decorate — just add easy icing trims. Label shows you clever alternate decorating idea. Aluminum pan is 13 x 10-1/2 x 1-1/4 in.* **2105-M-1779. $6.99 each**

1. MINI SANTA PAN. Bakes six individual serving cakes in the shape of everyone's favorite rosy cheeked fellow. Alternate ways to decorate and instructions on pan label. One 2-layer cake mix yields 12-18 cakes. Aluminum pan is 10-1/2 x 10 x 1-1/8 in.
2105-M-4692. $6.99 each

2. NEW!

2. NEW! SANTA'S SLEIGH PAN. This merry gent in old-fashioned sleigh is the perfect cake to present during the holidays. 5 ways to decorate — holiday and year round. Aluminum pan is 13 x 10-7/8 x 2 in.
2105-M-3235. $5.99 each

3. TREELITEFUL PAN. It's a trim-the-tree party cake. Spruce up with easy icing trims. See p. 78 for a clever decorating idea. One-mix aluminum pan is 15 x 11 x 11-1/2 in.
2105-M-425. $5.99 each

4. HOLIDAY HOUSE KIT. Make a welcoming cake centerpiece. Decorate with icing trims and candy. Kit includes icing colors, decorating tools and instructions. See pages 25. 36 and 69 for more clever ways to decorate. One-mix aluminum pan is 8-5/8 x 9 x 3 in.
2105-M-2282. $7.99 kit

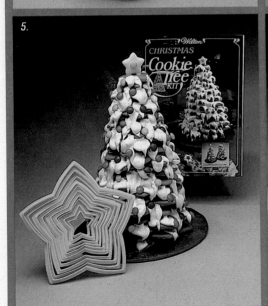

5. CHRISTMAS COOKIE TREE KIT. Set of 10 sturdy plastic cookie cutters cut out star shapes that you ice. stack together and trim to create an impressive. fun-to-eat holiday confection. Complete illustrated instructions. cookie and icing recipes.
2105-M-3424. $4.99 kit

6. SANTA COOKIE SLEIGH KIT. This magical flight of fantasy is fun to make and a joy to behold. Kit comes with plastic cookie cutters that are double-edged for quick pattern reversal. decorating tools. icing colors. instructions. cookie and icing recipes.
2105-M-2690. $4.99 kit

All pans made in Korea
Plastic parts made in Hong Kong
Decorating bags made in Japan.

1. NEW!

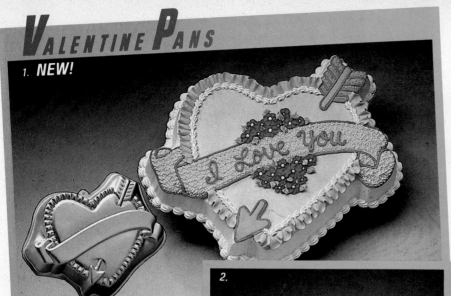

1. NEW! CUPID'S HEART PAN. It will get your message of love across not just on Valentine's Day but on Mother's Day, birthdays, anniversaries and wedding showers. Instructions included for decorating pretty and amusing delights sure to win hearts. One-mix aluminum pan is 13-3/4 x 10 x 2 in.
2105-M-4911. $5.99 each

2. BE MINE PAN. This straight from the heart request is sure to have takers. A loving attention-getter so easy to decorate. One-mix aluminum pan, 12 x 12 x 2 in., includes alternate decorating ideas.
2105-M-4331. $5.99 each

3. HAPPINESS HEART PAN SET. Bakes a show of your affection on any happy occasion. This versatile pan set takes one cake mix. Each aluminum pan is 9 x 1-1/2 in. deep.
2105-M-956. $5.99 set

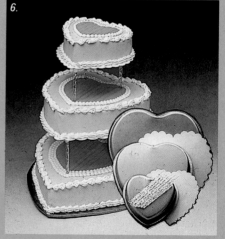

4. HEART MINICAKE PAN. Bake cakes or mold Candy Melts™ brand confectionery coating (p. 120). gelatin and ice cream into charming, single-size serving desserts. Six-hearted aluminum pan is 8 x 12-1/8 in. Each heart is 3-1/2 x 1-1/4 in. deep. 1-1/2 cups of batter makes 6 cakes.
2105-M-11044. $6.99 each

5. DOUBLE TIER HEART PAN. Bakes a classic heart with a tiered effect. The simplest decorating will look impressive on this elegant cake. Directions give you 4 ways to decorate. One-mix aluminum pan is 11-1/2 x 11 x 2-1/4 in.
2105-M-1699. $7.99 each

6. HEART MINI-TIER SET. Perfect tiers for small happy gatherings. With one cake mix you can bake 5. 7-1/2 and 9 in. one-layer cakes to position on two scallop-edged separator plates and six clear plastic legs.
2105-M-409. $10.99 set
HEART MINI-TIER PLATE SET ONLY.
301-M-9728. $2.99 set

All pans made in Korea. Plastic trims. doll picks. separator plates. legs and topper made in Hong Kong.

1. PIANO KIT. A grand cake idea for every music lover. Pans take one mix. Kit includes two 1-1/2 in. deep aluminum pans (6-3/4 x 7-3/4 in. and 9-1/2 x 7 in.). With plastic top, base, 4 snap-on legs, prop stick. 2 candelabras, pedals, bench, music board and keyboard. With instructions.
501-M-8093. $11.99 kit

PIANO ACCESSORY KIT ONLY.
503-M-8084. $6.99 set

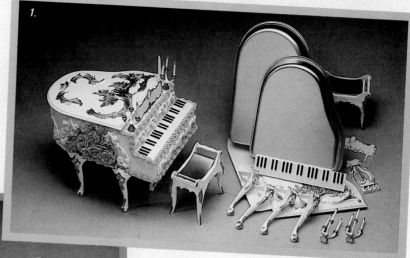

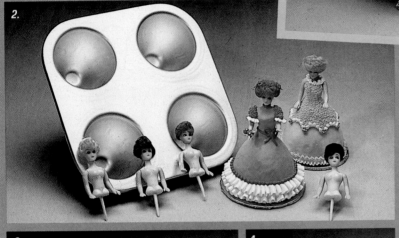

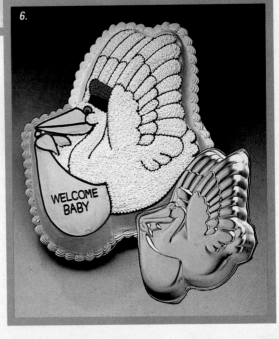

2. PETITE DOLL PAN SET. All dolled up and ready to celebrate a birthday. wedding shower and more. Set includes aluminum pan with four 3-1/2 in. diam.. 3 in. deep wells and four 4-1/2 in. doll picks.
2105-M-3408. $12.99 each

PETITE DOLL PAN ONLY.
508-M-302. $7.99 each

SMALL DOLL PICKS. 4-1/2 in. on pick.
1511-M-1019. $4.99 pack of 4

3. WONDER MOLD KIT. A living cake doll perfect for birthdays. bridal showers and more. Aluminum pan (8-1/2 in. diam.. 5-1/2 in. deep). with heat-conducting rod to assure even baking, takes 5-1/2-6 cups of firm-textured batter. Kit contains pan, rod, stand. 7 in. doll pick and instructions.
2105-M-565. $10.99 each

WONDER MOLD PAN ONLY (without doll pick).
502-M-682. $8.99 each

TEEN DOLL PICK. 7 in. tall. same as in kit.
2815-M-101. $2.59 each

4. FRECKLE-FACED LITTLE GIRL. For a little girl's cake, choose this cute sweetie. See how adorable she looks on p. 8. 6-1/2 in. tall.
2113-M-2317. $2.59 each

5. HUGGABLE TEDDY BEAR PAN. This best buddy cake will be adored by all. Easy to decorate for birthdays. baby showers. school treats and more. Aluminum pan is 13-1/2 x 12-1/4 x 1-7/8 in.
2105-M-4943. $7.99 each

6. GOOD NEWS STORK. The expectant mom will beam when this special delivery cake arrives. Alternate decorating ideas for birthdays and travel. too. One-mix aluminum pan is 13 x 11-3/4 x 2 in.
2105-M-4587. $7.99 each

Shaped Pans

1. NEW!

2. NEW!

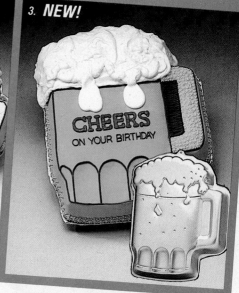

3. NEW!

1. NEW! MINI SHAMROCK PAN. *Irish eyes will be smilin' when they're looking over festive clover-shaped cakes. This one-mix aluminum pan bakes six individual holiday cakes. Alternate decorating ideas on label make it very versatile. Measures 13-1/4 x 9-3/4 x 1-1/4 in.* **2105-M-3459. $6.99 each**

2. NEW! TRAIL RIDER PAN. *Bake and decorate a cake with lots of get up and go! You'll get a lot of mileage out of this aluminum pan... perfect for birthdays, Dad's Day, going away and more. Pan is 15-3/4 x 8-1/2 x 2 in.* **2105-M-5583. $7.99 each**

3. NEW! GOOD CHEER MUG PAN. *Brimming with happy wishes...it's a cake toast to good times. Several clever decorating ideas included make it a year 'round delight. See more ideas on pages 16 and 66. One-mix aluminum pan is 13 x 10-1/2 x 2 in.* **2105-M-5496. $7.99 each**

4.

5.

6.

4. HORSESHOE PAN. *It's a lucky guess that you'll bake lots of super celebration cakes with this one-mix aluminum pan. A real winner for birthdays, graduations, promotions and more. 12 x 1-3/4 in.* **2105-M-3254. $7.99 each**

5. BALL PAN. *Round out your decorating talents with this unique pan and have a ball. Make firm textured cakes to stand alone or use half or whole ball cakes atop larger cakes (see pages 7, 17, 22, 52 and 65 for clever ideas). Set includes two 6 in. diameter half ball pans and two metal baking stands. Each pan section takes 2-1/4 cups batter.* **502-M-3002. $7.99 set**

BALL PAN BAKE STANDS ONLY. **503-M-881. $.99 each**

6. ROCKIN' JUKE BOX PAN. *It's no song and dance...this cake will be a big hit at birthdays, parties, any day there's something to sing about. Alternate decorating ideas, too. One-mix pan is 14 x 10-1/4 x 2 in.* **2105-M-5311. $7.99 each**

All pans made in Korea. Plastic parts made in Hong Kong.

PLEASE NOTE: All prices, certain products and services reflect the U.S.A. domestic market and do not apply in Australia and Canada.

1. NEW! SAILBOAT PAN. You'll breeze through decorating this free-spirited cake. It's a sunsational idea for birthdays, Dad's Day, just for fun and more! Instructions include several alternate cake ideas. One-mix aluminum pan is 12-5/8 x 10-3/8 x 2 in.
2105-M-5532. $7.99 each

2. T-SHIRT PAN. Design your own signature shirt that fits someone to a "T." Directions tell how to decorate for Dad's Day, tennis event, christening, birthdays and more. One-mix aluminum pan is 13-1/4 x 12-1/2 x 2 in.
2105-M-2347. $6.99 each

3. FREE-WHEELIN' TRUCK PAN. You'll zoom through the decorating and drive 'em wild with this super cake idea. Instructions for three different models included. One-mix aluminum pan is 16-1/4 x 8 x 1-7/8 in.
2105-M-1197. $7.99 each

4. GUITAR PAN SET. This cake will be instrumental in striking just the right note of party fun. Fun to decorate, too. Just ice, place plastic trims and add simple icing touches. Plastic neck, bride and pick guard included. Add strings for a realistic effect. One-mix aluminum pan is 17-3/4 x 8-1/2 x 2 in.
501-M-904. $8.99 set
PLASTIC GUITAR TRIM ONLY.
503-M-938. $1.59 each

5. BOWLING PIN PAN. Create lots of striking cakes with this 2-part aluminum pan. Make a stand-up cake or lay half cakes atop or along sheet cake (see pages 22 and 33). Set includes two 14 in. pans and two baking racks. Takes one cake mix.
502-M-4424. $8.99 set
BOWLING PIN BAKE RACKS ONLY.
503-M-989. $1.99 each

1. NEW!

1. NEW! GREAT EGGS™ KIT. Create dazzling sugar and candy egg surprises that are bound to impress. Kit includes 2 plastic egg molds, decorating bag, tips, coupler, brush and 2 candy mold sheets. Illustrated instructions and recipe book included. **2104-M-3616. $6.99 each**

2. HAPPY EASTER EGG PAN. This happy holiday message bakes right into your egg-shaped cake. Just outline message and cover with stars —it's so easy! Change message for other events. One-mix pan is 13 x 9-1/4 x 1-7/8 in. **2105-M-3749. $5.99 each**

3. EGG PAN SET. Create an egg-ceptional delight…get some clever ideas on pages 49 and 50. Two-piece aluminum pan takes just one cake mix. Each half is 8-3/4 x 5-3/8 in. and has ring base for level baking. **2105-M-700. $9.99 each**
EGG PAN RING ONLY.
503-M-954. $.99 each

4. EASTER BUNNY PAN. Bakes a happy holiday friend that you'll decorate quick as a bunny. Alternate decorating ideas included. One-mix pan is 17 x 10-7/8 x 1-3/4 in. **2105-M-2495. $5.99 each**

5. EGG MINICAKE PAN. Bake up eight party-size cakes. Great for molding ice cream, gelatin and Candy Melts™ brand confectionery coating, too. Half oval wells are 3-1/4 x 2-3/8 in. One cake mix yields about 24 cakes. Decorating guide on label. **2105-M-2118. $6.99 each**

6. CROSS PAN. Perfect for so many meaningful events. Many cake ideas included. One-mix aluminum pan is 14-1/2 x 11-1/8 x 2 in. **2105-M-2509. $5.99 each**

1. FROG PAN. Everyone will leap at the chance to get a piece of this perky party cake. A hoppy treat, so easy to decorate. One-mix aluminum pan is 13-7/8 x 13-1/4 x 2 in.; instructions included. **2105-M-2452. $6.99 each**

2. BUNNY PAN. Bakes a cottontail cutie that's so easy to decorate. Pan takes 6 cups of firm-textured cake batter. Two-part, snap-together aluminum pan is 8-3/4 x 10-1/4 in.; instructions included. **2105-M-2223. $9.99 each**

3. LITTLE LAMB PAN. Creates a lovable 3-D delight for Easter, baby showers and more. Use firm-textured cake batter (6 cups) 2-pc. aluminum pan is 10 x 7 in. tall. With instructions. **2105-M-2010. $8.99 each**

4. PANDA PAN. An adorable cake for birthdays, baby showers, holidays and more. Two-part aluminum pan takes 6-1/2 cups firm-textured cake batter. Includes 6 clips, heat-conducting core and instructions. Pan is 9-1/2 x 8-5/8 in. tall. **2105-M-603. $12.99 each**

PETS 'N PALS PANS

5. NEW! HOLIDAY BUNNY PAN. This egg-traordinary bunny cake is a honey! The perfect hare for your Easter fare. More fun ideas on pages 6, 37, 51. Two-part aluminum pan is 12 in. high and takes 6-1/2 cups of firm-textured batter. With instructions. **2105-M-5885. $9.99 each**

All pans made in Korea. Plastic tips, molds, coupler made in Hong Kong. Decorating bags made in Japan.

PLEASE NOTE: All prices, certain products and services, reflect the U.S.A. domestic market and do not apply in Australia and Canada.

187

1. LITTLE LOCOMOTIVE PAN.
This old-fashioned steam engine is engineered to make fun on birthdays, Father's Day, vacations and more. One-mix aluminum pan is 11 x 14-1/4 x 2 in. With instructions.
2105-M-4498. $7.99 each

2. SPORTSCAR PAN. Bake up a sleek car cake, then shift into high gear and zoom through the speedy decorating techniques. One-mix aluminum pan is 17 x 8-7/8 x 1-3/4 in. Instructions included.
2105-M-2428. $7.99 each

3. CHOO CHOO TRAIN PAN. You'll be on the right track for birthdays, Father's Day, club meetings and more when you make this streamlined stand-out. Two-part aluminum pan snaps together. Pan sides are each 10 x 6 x 2 in. Takes 6 cups of firm-textured batter. Instructions included.
2105-M-2861. $8.99 each

4. NUMBER ONE PAN. One way to tell someone they're great! Includes baby's first birthday and other winning cake ideas. One-mix aluminum pan is 14 x 10-1/8 x 2 in.
2105-M-7918. $6.99 each

ALL-OCCASION PANS

5. NEW! WIZARD PAN. Conjure up this magical cake on birthdays, Halloween, promotions, holidays and more. Alternate decorating ideas turn this man of mystery into a princess, Santa and Cowboy. One-mix aluminum pan is 14-1/2 x 11 x 2 in.
2105-M-2633. $7.99 each

6. NEW! MYSTICAL DRAGON PAN. This blast from the past is fired up for fun on birthdays, Halloween, get well and more. Alternate decorating ideas include a turtle, kangaroo and more! One-mix aluminum pan is 11-3/4 x 12-3/4 x 2 in.
2105-M-1750. $7.99 each

1. NEW! MICKEY MOUSE PAN. Hey there, hi there, ho there, he's as welcomed as can be! Just "write" for birthdays, holidays and more. Instructions show you how to change his pencil into flowers, an art brush and decorating bag. One-mix aluminum pan is 15-1/8 x 11-1/2 x 2 in.
2105-M-4358. $8.99 each

1. NEW!

2.

3.

2. DONALD DUCK PAN. Wow! What a decorated delight. Can't you feel his excitement and imagine the joy he will bring! Change his cake into a drum, gift and more — easy directions tell how. One-mix aluminum pan is 12 x 14-1/4 x 1-7/8 in.
2105-M-4556. $8.99 each

Walt Disney's Mickey Mouse. Donald Duck © Walt Disney Productions.

3. STRAWBERRY SHORTCAKE™ PAN. She's an adorable sight, sure to delight. Turn her strawberry into a heart. cupcake or gift for any special day. One-mix aluminum pan is 13 x 12-3/4 x 2 in.
2105-M-4458. $8.99 each

© MCMLXXXII American Greetings Corp.

4.

5.

4. SMURF™ PAN. This adorable little guy will be the apple of everyone's eye. Four more smurfing great ways to decorate. He'll make any day special. One-mix aluminum pan is 15-3/4 x 12 x 1-7/8 in.
2105-M-5435. $8.99 each

5. SMURFETTE™ PAN. Golly, what a dolly! Personalize her big balloon or change it into a candy cane, heart or tennis racket — instructions tell you how. One-mix aluminum pan is 16 x 11 x 1-7/8 in.
2105-M-5419. $8.99 each

© 1983 Peyo
Licensed by Wallace Berrie & Co. Inc.
Van Nuys. CA

Pans made in Korea.

1. **NEW!**

1. NEW! RAINBOW BRITE™ PAN. Invite this lovable, adorable little girl to brighten birthdays, holidays, school gatherings and more with her colorful personality! She'll make you a decorating star! Five delightful ways to decorate included. One-mix aluminum pan is 15 x 11 x 2 in.
2105-M-4798. $8.99 each

© 1983 Hallmark Cards. Inc.

PLEASE NOTE: All prices, certain products and services, reflect the U.S.A. domestic market and do not apply in Australia and Canada.

2. BIG BIRD CAKE PAN. What a great big bundle of fun! Decorate him with a balloon, clock, umbrella, sunshine or ice cream cone — decorating instructions tell you how. One-mix aluminum pan is 13-1/2 x 10-3/4 x 1-7/8 in.
2105-M-3653. $8.99 each

3. ERNIE CAKE PAN. This gifted guy stops by to give the birthday boy or girl a big surprise. Turn his gift into 3 other things — instructions included. One-mix aluminum pan is 14-1/2 x 10 x 1-7/8 in.
2105-M-3173. $8.99 each

CTW Trademark © 1983 Children's Television Workshop. BIG BIRD. ERNIE. COOKIE MONSTER
© Muppets. Inc. All rights reserved. CTW Trademark — Sesame Street and the Sesame Street sign are trademarks and service marks of the Children's Television Workshop.

4. RAGGEDY ANN™ PAN. Every girl, little or grown, adores this moppy-haired doll. She'll make 'em jump for joy and you will, too...she's easy to decorate. One-mix aluminum pan is 16-3/4 x 9-1/8 x 1-7/8 in.
2105-M-4986. $8.99 each

© 1981 The Bobbs-Merrill Company Inc.

5. COOKIE MONSTER CAKE PAN. He takes the cake! This lovable Sesame Street friend should be on hand for birthdays, holidays and more. Fun and easy to do! One-mix aluminum pan is 14-1/2 x 11-1/2 x 1-7/8 in.
2105-M-4927. $8.99 each

CTW Trademark © 1983 Children's Television Workshop.

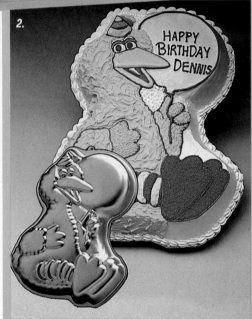

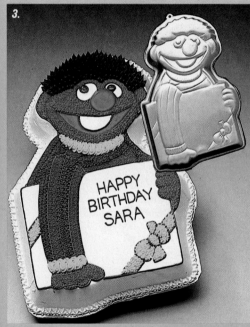

1. NEW! PORKY PIG†. It's "plane" to see, pilot Porky will get the party off the ground! Alternate decorating ideas include a rocket and car, too. One-mix aluminum pan is 12 x 12-1/2 x 2 in. T-h-a-t-'s all folks!
2105-M-2371. $8.99 each

Pans made in Hong Kong.
Plastic parts and trims made in Hong Kong.

1. NEW!

2. SUPER HEROES PAN.** Call on this versatile pan to get you out of any cake making dilemma. These two favorite guys will come to the rescue on birthdays, Dad's Day, promotions and lots more. Set contains sculptured 13 x 13 x 2 in. one-mix aluminum pan, plastic face masks and chest emblems for both SUPER-MAN* and BATMAN.*
2105-M-8507. $8.99 each

3. C-3PO™ PAN. They'll think you're a genius when this brilliant protocol droid cake joins the party. This one-mix aluminum pan measures 13-1/8 x 13 x 1-7/8 in.
2105-M-1464. $8.99 each

4. BUGS BUNNY PAN†. They'll get a big bang out of this unbeatable drummer. Instructions show how to turn his drum into a clock, horn and basket for birthdays and holidays. One-mix aluminum pan is 11 x 16 x 2 in.
2105-M-3351. $8.99 each

5. CATHY™ PAN. Here's a liberated lady that knows how to cope with birthdays, holidays, just about anything! Just change what she's holding so it relates to the situation. One-mix aluminum pan is 10 x 14-1/2 x 1-7/8 in.
2105-M-4641. $8.99 each

DECORATOR'S INDEX

PAN INDEX